PSYCHOTHERAPY: AN EROTIC RELATIONSHIP

Psychotherapy: An Erotic Relationship explores the most intimate elements of the psychoanalytic relationship: the erotic feelings and fantasies that patients and therapists often experience towards one another. David Mann challenges the classical psychoanalytic view that the erotic transference and countertransference are forms of resistance that threaten the therapeutic process, and argues that they are potentially a powerful source of creative transformation.

The author proposes that the erotic is seldom absent from the relationship between therapist and patient. Making use of extensive clinical material, theoretical insights and recent research on infants, he suggests that the development of the erotic derives from interactions between parent and child. Similarly, the erotic nature of the unconscious of both the therapist and the patient have an interactive effect on each other and on the therapeutic process. The author shows that, while the erotic always contains elements of past relationships, it also expresses hope for a different outcome in the present and future. In this hope lies the potential for transformation.

Individual chapters focus on the function of the erotic within the unconscious; erotic pre-Oedipal and Oedipal material; the importance of homoerotic functions in therapy; sexual intercourse as a metaphor for psychological change; the significance of the primal scene and the difficulties of working with perversions.

Psychotherapy: An Erotic Relationship offers psychotherapists and psychoanalysts a deeper understanding of the interaction between the erotic transference and countertransference, and shows how these aspects of therapy can be used to enhance the therapeutic process.

David Mann is a practising psychoanalytic psychotherapist. He works in private practice and primary care and is a member of the Association of Psychoanalytic Psychotherapists and the United Kingdom Council for Psychotherapists. He teaches on several psychotherapy training programmes and runs workshops on erotic transference and countertransference throughout the UK and Europe. He has extensively published in leading national and international psychotherapy journals.

PSYCHOTHERAPY: AN EROTIC RELATIONSHIP

Transference and countertransference passions

David Mann

London and New York

First published 1997
by Routledge
11 New Fetter Lane, London EC4P 4EE

Simultaneously published in the USA and Canada
by Routledge
29 West 35th Street, New York, NY 10001

Routledge is an imprint of the Taylor & Francis Group

Reprinted 1999

© 1997 David Mann

Typeset in Times by Routledge
Printed and bound in Great Britain by Clays Ltd, St. Ives PLC

British Library Cataloguing in Publication Data
A catalogue record for this book is available from the British Library

Library of Congress Cataloging in Publication Data
Mann, David, 1954–
Psychotherapy, an erotic relationship : transference and
countertransference passions / David Mann.
Includes bibliographical references and index.
1. Psychotherapists–Sexual behaviour. 2. Psychotherapy patients–Sexual
behaviour. 3. Psychotherapist and patient. I. Title.
RC480.8.M36 1997
616.89′14′023–dc20   96–27225
                                                                              CIP

ISBN 0–415–14851–0 (hbk)
ISBN 0–415–14852–9 (pbk)

For Michelle, with whom I learned just how transformational love and the erotic can be, and our son Mark, who was conceived from our love.

CONTENTS

Acknowledgements   viii

INTRODUCTION   1

1 THE EROTIC TRANSFERENCE   4

2 OF CUPID'S BLINDFOLD AND ARROWS: EROTIC
   TRANSFERENCE, REAL OR UNAUTHENTIC?   27

3 THE PSYCHOTHERAPIST'S EROTIC SUBJECTIVITY   55

4 VARIETIES OF EROTIC COUNTERTRANSFERENCE   68

5 THE HOMOEROTIC TRANSFERENCE–
   COUNTERTRANSFERENCE MATRIX   101

6 TRANSFERENCE AS SYMBOLIC SEXUAL INTERCOURSE   120

7 TRANSFERENCE AS SYMBOLIC PRIMAL SCENE   138

8 TRANSFERENCE PERVERSIONS   162

9 THE TEMPTATION OF TRANSGRESSION   180

Notes   196
References   198
Index   209

ACKNOWLEDGEMENTS

First and foremost, I would like to thank Michelle MacGrath for her help at every stage of writing this book, from discussion of the main ideas right down to correcting my punctuation. Without her this book would have felt an impossible task.

The responsibility for the ideas in this book are mine. However, I extend my thanks to three friends and close colleagues whose critical appreciation, encouragement and patience helped shape earlier drafts of these chapters: Gillian Bowden, Brede Carr and Vivian Marshall.

Various people made contributions that influenced the development of my ideas in this book. I would like to thank: Eleanore Armstrong-Perlman, Paul Atkinson, Bob Hinshelwood, David Kay, Elizabeth Nicholson, Peter Phillips, Sheila Powell, Andrew Samuels and Chrysoula Worrall.

During the last seven months of writing this book, I was fortunate enough to be asked to facilitate a post-qualification seminar group at the Institute of Psychotherapy and Counselling (WPF) on 'Transference and Countertransference Perspectives'. This put many stimulating ideas in my direction. I would like to thank Celia Harding for the invitation and opportunity to run this group and, particularly, the members of my seminar group for their contributions during the discussions.

I received much encouragement and support from the staff at the Crown Dale Medical Centre. In particular, I would like to thank Suzanne Rackham, Sandra Hales and doctors Maria Elliot, Patrick White, Caroline Taylor, Mark Chamley and Colin Gatwood.

I also received helpful advice from Routledge, especially from my editor, Edwina Welham, and the three anonymous readers of the early version of this book.

I must also acknowledge the influence of my patients, supervisees and participants on my workshops 'Working with the erotic transference and countertransference'. I feel a deep sense of gratitude as they have taught me so much.

Eight of these chapters were written especially for this book. Chapter 3 is a slightly revised version of an article which first appeared in the *British Journal of Psychotherapy* (1994a) 10 (3).

Thanks are due to Jonathan Cape for permission to quote Salman Rushdie on page 138.

INTRODUCTION

This book is about how the erotic affects the transference and countertransference. This is not an exposition on the nature of the erotic or love. It is, rather, about how the erotic has significance in the analytical relationship between patient and therapist. To summarize this whole book in a single sentence: I consider that the erotic pervades most if not all psychoanalytic encounters and is largely a positive and transformational influence.

My understanding of the erotic transference and countertransference is drawn mostly from my clinical practice and teaching experience. I work primarily with the ideas of the British Object Relations tradition, drawing heavily on the ideas of Winnicott, Fairbairn and Klein. It is, though, a critical appreciation of this tradition. Work with patients made it necessary for me to think afresh about much of the material they presented. This is also true of my teaching. For the last five years, I have been running workshops on 'Working with the erotic transference and countertransference' in the UK and Europe. The needs of the participants on these courses required that I think my ideas through; they also produced much interesting material of their own.

In addition to my clinical and teaching experience, I also draw on several other sources. Obviously the existing psychoanalytic literature on the erotic transference and countertransference needs to be considered. This is not an onerous task as so little has been written on the subject. It is an aspect of my own personality that I am interested in those areas that do not stimulate general curiosity. I like to ask 'Why not?' especially if this relates to a subject like the erotic. As the reader will find, I agree with some authors and not others. I see my own offering as one of standing on the shoulders of those who have gone before me rather than one of discarding the past.

This book also makes use of two other sources of information. The first is the recent upsurge in infant observation data that is giving psychoanalysis a much clearer understanding of the infant's mind. The second is that of mythology. This is a source of interest partly because myths are well-told tales, but mostly because I consider they represent the deep psychological preoccupations of humanity throughout recorded history. In that sense, they

1

help broaden the findings from the clinical setting into wider, more significant areas of human experience. Earlier drafts of some chapters also included anthropological evidence for the same purpose, though shortage of space meant this was later deleted.

Each chapter is intended to stand on its own, although the book was written with the whole very much in mind. Chapter 1 outlines my main proposals about the erotic transference. It is considered as a transformational opportunity, partly because it deals with the deepest layers of the psyche, but also because it destabilizes both the patient's and the therapist's equilibrium, thereby offering major therapeutic opportunities for growth to develop. The erotic is explored from the point of view of two lovers, each seeking transformation through erotic and love experiences. This model is applied in its symbolic manifestation to the therapeutic encounter: the erotic transference signifying that the patient, like a lover, is seeking to change him or herself at the deepest levels. The erotic is located and described, therefore, as emerging from an interactional context.

Chapter 2 is the only chapter that does not include my own clinical material. This chapter is primarily a review of the psychoanalytic literature on the erotic transference. I am largely critical of the psychoanalytic tenets that regard the erotic as a resistance and as something merely created by the analytic situation, and therefore not genuine. I am careful to describe in their own words those I disagree with. I would hope that those who disagree (or agree) with me will show the same consideration.

Chapter 3 attempts to place the psychotherapist's own erotic experience into the therapeutic process. What the therapist feels is not only the result of what the patient puts there or stimulates. Since psychotherapists have their own erotic unconscious and erotic agendas we might as well consider how this affects the clinical work.

Chapter 4 is a more refined focus on the variety of erotic countertransference that a therapist may experience. This is considered particularly from the point of view of relating to the stage of development of the patient. The erotic countertransference is therefore described from the parent's point of view in relation to the stage of the infant. I delineate four positions: the erotic pre-Oedipal mother, the erotic Oedipal mother, the erotic pre-Oedipal father and the erotic Oedipal father.

Chapter 5 deals with the homoerotic transference and countertransference. The homoerotic seems to cause the greatest anxieties to patient and analyst alike. This chapter attempts to place the homoerotic within a developmental context. Consequently, the homoerotic can have a positive role within the transformational erotic transference and countertransference. This chapter is biased towards the male therapist working with the male patient. For obvious reasons, I felt a detailed account of a woman therapist with a woman patient was outside my personal experience, though I hope some of the ideas I draw out are applicable to the female analytic dyad.

Chapters 6 and 7 were originally written as one piece. In fact, the rest of the book arose out of the issues these chapters produced. Chapter 6 locates the origins of the individual's erotic experience in the infant's relationship with the mother. This is reproduced in the adult's experience with sexual partners and is played out in the transference during therapy.

Chapter 7 takes this idea further to the significance of the primal scene, which is a crystallization of the Oedipal situation. The good enough phantasy of the primal scene is described as essential for a creative experience. Clinical material is presented to demonstrate both how a non-good primal scene phantasy encapsulates psychological defensiveness and how the patient's image of the primal scene is played out in the transference.

Chapter 8 looks at the effects of perversions on the transference and countertransference. Perverse states of mind are described as potentially highly destructive on the transference and countertransference matrix where the therapeutic dyad can degenerate into a perverse couple.

Chapter 9 deals with the necessity of crossing boundaries, as this is integral to a healthy curiosity. The patient and therapist are described as needing to find themselves in a place where neither has been before, in order to locate a new experience that will offer transformation.

I do not presume that this book will solve all difficulties in working with the erotic transference and countertransference which, in my experience, is often the most problematic part of the therapy. However, I have found these ideas of use in clinical practice, and I would hope that, at the very least, this book might help therapists to think afresh about how the erotic can be considered in the clinical, analytical situation.

David Mann
Cornwall and London
April 1996

1

THE EROTIC TRANSFERENCE

> She's all States, and all Princes I,
> Nothing else is.
> (John Donne *The Sun Rising*)

The erotic is at the heart of unconscious fantasy life. The infant, born from the erotic encounter of the parents, will find his or her[1] earliest experiences are enveloped in the pre-Oedipal eroticism of mother and child. As the field of erotic experiences widens, the individual will encounter both wonder and tragedy. Satisfaction of the erotic becomes the most treasured and the most painful of human experiences. By its very nature it is psychically binding.

The erotic is usually understood as sexual desire. However, in early Greek Orphic mythology, Eros is associated with more than sexual arousal: he is described as being the first of the gods; without him none of the rest could have been born. He is hatched from an egg and sets the universe in motion. In some traditions, he is equated with the sun. Eros created life on earth, piercing the barren world with his life-giving arrows and where the earth was pierced luxuriant greenery appeared. He breathed into the nostrils of clay forms of men and women giving them the spirit of life. Eros, the erotic, is thus about creativity. In later versions of the myth, Eros is depicted as the son of Aphrodite. It is not until another son is born, Anteros the god of passion, that Eros can grow up. He flies about on golden wings shooting his arrows at random, setting hearts on fire. In even later versions of the myth, he falls in love with Psyche, who became the personification of the soul. Eros was never considered sufficiently responsible to rank among the ruling Olympian family of gods.

The erotic is the very creative stuff of life and is inextricably linked to passion. It is a maverick, capable of the unexpected, and is the therapeutic momentum in analysis. The issue is one of passion, an intensity of feeling with no easy resolution; but out of the heat of passion old links are weakened and new links can be forged. Passion of all kinds dominate the analytic setting: hate, anger, aggression, envy – and hardly less so, love and the erotic. However, the erotic transference, like Eros himself, has been left to the mar-

4

gins of analysis, never quite making it to the acceptable family of ideas in psychoanalytic theory and practice.

THE EROTIC AND METAPHOR

Before proceeding further, some clarification of terms needs to be attempted. The subject matter under discussion, the erotic, is such an emotive and passionate area of human life, I doubt that a clear, watertight and agreeable definition of the term is possible, nor will one be attempted here. This is true in ordinary life. How much more difficult the task becomes in the analytic setting and in psychoanalytic writing which attempts to be objective. Having immersed myself in the analytic literature, I have discovered that one obvious theme emerges: there are no reliable, objective reports on this important subject. What we have are subjective experiences out of which various investigators try to make sense – this book being no exception. It is, I consider, an extremely positive process so long as we do not lose sight of the subjective nature of our thinking.

Therefore, I do not propose a tight definition of 'erotic'. Quite the contrary, I will keep my terms loose, even unclear, to allow a wide range of material to be considered in the clinical transference and countertransference. I do not believe that a term like 'erotic' or 'love' can be precisely defined; nor do I think any single definition will produce a unified agreement.

There is no detached stance to the erotic, since it permeates psychological activity and is a basic human quality. Thus the individual cannot stand beyond it to gain an objective perspective on what it really is. The only perspective is one that works its way through the erotic. This very procedure is in itself an expression of the erotic bond towards others. Since there is no cool detachment, there is only passion, sometimes hot or cold or all the degrees in between. This should not pose a problem so long as we keep in our minds the contribution made by passion when we begin discourse. Even the most ardent rationalist is making a passionate statement about conviction.

I would propose that the erotic is primarily psychological and not physical, although it is usually considered in terms of sexual excitement. Animals have sex but, to the best of our knowledge, they do not bring a psychological component, an underlying erotic fantasy, to it. Humans, on the other hand, do, whether consciously or unconsciously. That is to say, the erotic is a psychological experience independent of sexual reproduction and the desire for children. As Bataille (1957: 29) succinctly describes it:

> Eroticism is one aspect of the inner life of man. We fail to realise this because man is everlastingly in search of an object *outside* himself but this object answers the *innerness* of the desire [author's italics].

I am not, therefore, limiting the erotic solely to genital arousal. The erotic may include fascination, disgust, or incestuous desire, which we may consider in Kumin's (1985) term as 'erotic horror'. (This will be discussed further in Chapter 3.)

Without Eros, there would be nothing to modify aggressive or hateful feelings in the context of relationships with others. The erotic tends towards individualization, promoting autonomy and radical evaluations of one's life. It binds the individual to seek further and more advanced forms of development. Love and sexuality are processes of growth.

Let me define my use of the word passion. The *Collins English Dictionary* defines it as follows: 'from the Latin, *pati* to suffer. Any strongly felt emotion, ardent love or affection; intense sexual love; a strong enthusiasm for an object, concept, etc.'. I do not advocate unbridled passion. Passion brings us close to the meaning of 'love' which derives from the Old English, '*lufu*' and the Indo-European '*leubh*'. Both have the same etymological root as Sanskrit '*lubh*', meaning 'to desire'. Love often accounts for many of the intense moments in most lives. It is this intensity that has placed it at a high premium for over three thousand years of recorded human literature.

I will mostly be using the term erotic. I prefer this to the 'sexual' or 'love transference'. The erotic implies both of these and more, unifying the different implications we attribute to love and sex. Clearly love and sex are not the same thing, though with adults they are often inextricably linked. I bring both the idea of love and sex into the unifying concept of Eros. The erotic includes all sexual and sensual feelings or fantasies a person may have. It should not be identified solely with attraction or sexual arousal as it may also include anxiety or the excitement generated by the revolting. In my use of the term, it will imply an emphasis on fantasy rather than actual sexual activity: there is no sexual activity devoid of an underlying fantasy; on the other hand, fantasies do not always lead to activity.

There is an additional reason why I prefer to define the discussion in terms of the erotic rather than by that of love. Anthropology, while giving full accounts of the sex life of other societies, makes few references to love which is not necessarily a prerequisite for marriage or non-marital sexual contact. Endleman (1988) concludes:

> Erich Fromm postulates in *The Art of Loving* that love, defined as 'the overcoming of human separateness . . . the fulfilment of the longings for union', is a universal need of all human beings. The data on the various societies considered here should lead us to question whether this is universal, unless we include in it *attachment* (my italics) to *any* (author's italics) other human being, or any succession of a number of different other human beings.

> (1956: 47)

Love may not be a prerequisite for all societies at all times but all societies possess an erotic fantasy life.

I would also see the erotic at the heart of psychoanalytic metaphor. As I have suggested elsewhere (Mann 1991a), it is often through metaphor that we can detect the latent meaning of ideas. In the British Object Relations School there are two deeply significant metaphors for therapy: (1) the analytic couple is seen in terms of the mother and infant dyad; (2) psychological development between this pair is the 'analytic child'. Let us hold these two images to the light and explore their relationship. The analytic couple, therapist and patient, have an analytic baby, the psychological growth of the analysand (and often of the therapist, too). The metaphor is pregnant with meaning: the mother and infant produce a baby together. The metaphor is one of incest: the oldest (historically) and the most primitive (in phantasy) of all incest, that between mother and child. The use of metaphor is not accidental, but unconsciously determined. Yet how dangerous and how appropriate! The metaphors place the incestuous encounter at the heart of the analytic experience; prohibited erotic desire that finds expression and restraint in the Oedipal scenario is the site of both the greatest dangers and, simultaneously, of the release of the greatest creative potential.

LOVE AND THE EROTIC

In the course of this book I will outline why it is important to keep the double edge of the erotic – the positive and the negative – held in balance during the psychotherapeutic process. It can be highly tempting to fall too much one way or the other and forget that both sides need to be kept in perspective. I stress this because it is my impression that the positive side of the erotic is often neglected in psychoanalytic theory. This is most overtly seen in the dominant trend to view the erotic or, as it is sometimes called, the love transference and countertransference as negative, as aspects of the patient's resistances.

First let us consider love and the erotic in general. That they are multifaceted is no surprise. Surveying the literature in his introduction to a book on three thousand years of love poetry, the poet Jon Stallworthy writes:

> Even if one sets aside poems about the love of Country, poems about the love of Nature, poems about the love of God, one is left with a mountain of poems about the Beloved, beside which the poems on any other single subject seem but a mole hill.

> (1973: 19)

Even allowing for a degree of exaggeration by Stallworthy in the name of artistic licence, I would nevertheless think that this suggests the erotic is also at the heart of conscious as well as unconscious fantasy life. Such a fundamental preoccupation for all nations at all periods of recorded history indicates nothing less than a universal phenomenon.

I suggest that one of the most important, if not the most important reason why the erotic is such a preoccupation in psychic life is that it offers an opportunity for self-transformation. In the lines that preface this chapter, the poet John Donne describes the enrichment of love in his eulogy to the erotic, *The Sun Rising*. The erotic transforms Donne and his lover into something greater than either might have been without it, in this instance (with considerable poetic licence) into powerful nations and monarchy. Through the erotic both grow and are enriched. Of course, in this particular instance, Donne's transformation is idealistic and omnipotent, full of the joys of the erotic. It can, however, also be unsatisfactory and painful, though that may be no less full of transformational opportunities.

This transformational quality of the erotic is at the heart of love. When in love, the lover is seeking the most intimate experience one can find with another. Lovers wish to know the details of the other's emotional life: they exchange secrets, share night-time and day-time dreams; they probe each other physically and psychologically to explore their own depth and the depth of the other. In this way they reach new heights and lows. When in love, people wish to be completely known and understood by the beloved. They wish to transform themselves into somebody even more lovable, to improve their faults and change bad habits or anything dislikeable about themselves. This applies as much to the mother and baby as it does to adult lovers and, of course, the therapeutic relationship.

Erotic fantasy life and desire are a confluence of the past, present and future. The erotic component of the unconscious psyche is structured by the gains and losses experienced as human sexuality develops. McDougall notes that:

> The oedipal crisis obliges children to come to terms with the impossible wish to incarnate both sexes and to possess both parents. Concomitantly, in accepting their ineluctable monosexuality, humankind's young must compensate in other ways for the renunciation of their bisexual longings.

> (1996: x)

The erotic thus takes its place at the centre of the human psyche. Love is a mixture of past and future as it converges in the present. The regressive element impels us to seek and rediscover something from the past. In this sense, love is an attempt to restore a lost unity. The wounds to the infant's narcissistic omnipotence provide for a certain degree of repetition of past experience. It is this side of the erotic that is highlighted when the erotic transference is considered in terms of resistance to the therapeutic process.

Erotic fantasy and desire are not, therefore, only about repetition. The infant that grows to be an adult is not simply transferring incestuous desires on to a non-family member when he or she seeks an adult sexual relationship. The erotic also pulls us in the opposite direction: to greater differentiation and individuation; thus the erotic is drawn to greater complexity and more diverse and complex structures. It also seeks a transformation, to heal the disappointments and failures of the past unfulfilled erotic desire. This is true even of those patients who are addicted to destructive relationships driven by severe repetition compulsion.

In particular, by healing past disappointments the individual is hoping for and seeking, a different, more satisfying outcome to erotic desire than was encountered in the family. In looking for something different, erotic fantasy seeks to heal old wounds and transform the individual into something better, stronger, more healthy, more alive, more complete, more mature and more developed. Through the erotic, the psyche seeks growth. It provides the mechanism and the impetus to transform our unconscious life.

The erotic, then, is a mixture of past experience as it meets the hopes for the future. This mixture of past and future, experience and hopes, converge in the present in the desire that will be both the same as the past (a rediscovery of satisfaction with the parent), but also different and new, which will heal or transform the past traumas into something new, something enhanced and more developed.

PSYCHOTHERAPY: AN EROTIC RELATIONSHIP

What I have said so far about the transformational qualities of the erotic between the mother and infant or between lovers, also applies to the therapist and patient. The reason why I am stressing the transformational side of the erotic is to counterbalance the common idea amongst psychoanalytic practitioners that the emergence of love or the erotic in therapy is a form of resistance in the patient. Now, given that the erotic is generally considered positive by humanity at large for three thousand years and that erotic experience (fantasy as well as activity) has such a high premium in an individual's life, we must then pose the question: Why is the erotic considered a negative form of resistance in psychoanalysis?

Some of the explanation for this is to be found in the historical development of psychoanalysis which has created basic assumptions in our theory and practice. I also consider that there have, in addition, been clinical exigencies that have encouraged the psychoanalytic practitioner to see the erotic transference as something undesirable, even disreputable, thus keeping it at a distance.

Consider this: it is my proposition that the emergence of the erotic transference signifies the patient's deepest wish for growth. Like those in love, patients wish to be known and understood, to change what they do not like about themselves, to alter what makes them unlovable. Through the erotic, light is shone on the deepest recesses of the psyche. The fundamental nature of the erotic is that it is psychically binding and connects individuals at the most intimate and deepest of levels. The erotic transference, therefore, is potentially the most powerful and positive quality in the therapeutic process. The development of the erotic transference is a major transitional stage in which the repetitive and transformational desire of the patient's unconscious meet at a passionate junction. The heart of the unconscious is visible in all its 'elemental passion', and in so opening allows for the prospect of transformation and psychic growth.

To elaborate this idea further I also make use of two psychoanalytical concepts, Bollas's (1987) idea of the 'transformational object' and Baker's (1993) notion of the 'psychoanalyst as a new object'. For Bollas, a transformational object, such as a mother, 'is experientially identified by the infant with the processes that alter self experience' (1987: 14). In this respect, the mother is less significant as an object than as processes identified with internal and external transformation.

Bollas notes that, as adults, transformational objects may be sought in a change of job, relationship, religious faith or aesthetic experience. It is an object-seeking that recurrently enacts a pre-verbal memory. Bollas continues his idea to say that, in therapy, the patient needs the therapist's interpretation to match his or her internal mood, feelings or thoughts which leads the former to 're-experience the transformational object relations' (1987: 23). In my view, it is not always an attempt to seek out an idealized pre-verbal past. There is also a need for a transformational object to offer a genuinely new experience, either to heal the wounds of a less than 'good enough' pre-verbal experience, or simply to find something new, sufficiently different from previous experience, that encourages growth and development. This latter aspect of the transformational object may utilize the idea developed by Baker (1993). Citing Strachey (1934) and Loewald (1960) as precedents, he describes the analyst as making him or herself available as a new kind of object relationship between the analyst and patient. This is done by slowly eliminating the impediments represented by the transference.

Now, both Bollas and Baker are thinking mostly in terms of the mother and baby couple and their symbolic equivalents, the analyst and analysand. It seems to me, however, that the 'transformational object' and 'new object' are aspects of what are sought in intimate adult relationships, especially in significant (not casual) sexual relationships: spouses, partners, lovers. The erotic transference can be said to signify the emergence of the desire to find a 'new transformational object' that will facilitate intrapsychic changes.

The capacity to love or form erotic attachments is not a goal, but a process. There is no position outside the erotic. Any attempt to understand the erotic is itself an act of erotic development: an act of love and intimacy at the deepest levels. The erotic is an active process.

Lear (1990: 15) makes the observation that:

Love has become almost taboo within psychoanalysis. Analysts talk of sex and aggression with ease, but as soon as anyone starts to talk of love, from somewhere there instantly comes the response: But what about aggression? This would be reason enough for love to command our attention.

This is my view entirely.

I am in full agreement with the American analyst Bach (1994: 22) when he writes: 'I see the goal of analysis as *opening pathways to object love*' (author's italics). There can be only one way to love and that is through love. Writing to Jung, Freud says much the same in a letter dated 6 December 1906:

> *Essentially, one might say, the cure is effected by love.* And actually transference provides the most cogent, indeed, the only unassailable proof that neuroses are determined by the individual's love life [my italics].
>
> (cited in McGuire 1974 (letter 8F): 10)

In other words, analysis requires both the analysand's emotional engagement with the analyst and the analyst's empathy and love towards the patient. Through this process, analysis facilitates individuation. As Lear (1990: 28) remarks: 'In that sense, psychoanalysis is itself a manifestation of love'. What is particularly striking in Freud's letter is that it does not rest very easily with his expressed views that transference love – which he uses synonymously with the erotic – is a form of resistance. I will explore Freud's views about this more thoroughly in the next chapter.

In my view, it becomes difficult to maintain the classical psychoanalytic position that the emergence of the erotic transference primarily represents a form of resistance to the therapeutic process. I acknowledge that sometimes this may be the case, though I am inclined to think that more often it is not. If there is a resistance present, I consider it more likely to be located in the therapist's anxiety about the erotic heating to boiling point and dangerously overflowing.

I am also of the view that the erotic transference is not solely a construction of the analytic situation. In my opinion the erotic transference, in particular the love components, are as real as love experienced outside the analytic setting. That is to say, transference love is real love. Attempts to see this transference as unreal or unauthentic, deprive the transference of its vitality and transformational opportunities. (This issue will be explored in depth in Chapter 2.) It is because the erotic is real and not a facsimile that something dynamic can be made from it. Psychic growth emerges from authentic, and not unauthentic, experience.

In my opinion, because the erotic is at the heart of unconscious fantasy life it is, therefore, necessarily at the heart of the therapeutic process.

In this sense, psychotherapy is an erotic relationship between the analyst and patient: a transaction between two psyches that have the erotic at their centre.

To explore this further it is necessary to look at the origins of psycho-analysis which introduce the erotic into the therapeutic encounter.

IN THE BEGINNING WAS THE EROTIC

The widely held view that the erotic transference and countertransference are destructive and a form of resistance is inextricably linked to the erotic origins of psychoanalysis itself. Unfortunately for the protagonists at the time, neither seemed to understand the meaning of the experience. The two joint discoverers, or perhaps we might say, the primal couple – the Adam and Eve of psychoanalysis – were Joseph Breuer and Anna O. It is worth spending some time on this case as it sets the scene for the next one hundred years of psychoanalysis.

Breuer was Freud's early mentor. He was treating his patient Anna O with the cathartic method. Anna O was a very intelligent, hysterical, 21-year-old woman. She was also very attractive. Anna christened their work together 'chimney sweeping' and the 'talking cure'. The sexual nature of such imagery is indicative of their relationship. Breuer treated her twice daily for one and a half years, the treatment suddenly coming to an end in circum-stances which are not made clear in *Studies on Hysteria* (Freud and Breuer 1895). In later years, Freud gave a fuller version of why this treatment was suddenly terminated. Breuer had developed what we would now call a strong erotic countertransference towards his interesting patient and would talk about her endlessly with his wife, who became increasingly jealous, morose and unhappy. Finally recognizing his wife's state of mind, he brought the treatment to an end on the pretext that Anna was very much better. That same evening, he was summoned back to her household to find her as ill as ever. She appeared to be in the throes of a hysterical childbirth, the logical consequence of the phantom pregnancy that had been invisibly developing in response to Breuer's ministrations. Though shocked by this, Breuer calmed her down using hypnotism, fled the house in a cold sweat and, on the following day, went with his wife on a second honeymoon. It is probably true to say that Breuer was the first recorded casualty of unacknowledged erotic countertransference and Anna O the first casualty of unrecognized erotic transference.

This treatment made a great impression on Freud. Jones (1953) tells us that when Freud told this story to his wife Martha, she is reported to have identified herself with Breuer's wife and feared the same might happen to her. Freud reproved her vanity in supposing that other women would fall in love with him and denied the possibility saying, 'For that to happen one has to be a Breuer'. Martha seemed to understand the problem better than

Freud at that time. It took him a while to see that Anna O's reaction was not the exception, but the rule.

There are two significant features from the case of Anna O that I would wish to highlight, since they set the tone for investigation into the erotic transference and countertransference in psychoanalysis for a hundred years. First, is that the erotic transference is mostly seen as problematic; it is considered to represent a form of resistance and is largely viewed as an aspect of the negative transference. What is true for the erotic transference is even more so for the erotic countertransference, which has widely been held to signify difficulties in the analyst.

There are exceptions to both these views within psychoanalysis. I shall be looking in more depth shortly at the arguments for and against the erotic transference as a resistance. For now, I will merely state my opinion: I believe psychoanalysis has been mistaken in its view that the erotic transference and countertransference are an aspect of the negative transference. It is important to acknowledge that the erotic transference may worry both the therapist and the patient. However, that said, I wish to turn the prevailing view on its head and state that the erotic transference and countertransference are potentially the most useful and constructive aspects of any analysis.

This brings me to the second significant feature of the Anna O case: that the erotic transference in therapy is generally considered dangerous. With this I agree – up to a point. It harmed Anna O, Breuer and his wife, as it has harmed a good many other patients, therapists and their families since. However, if we have some trust in the psychoanalytic programme itself, we might reach new conclusions. When Freud first encountered the transference, he considered it the greatest resistance to the therapeutic cure. In time, and with courageous brilliance, it dawned on him that what he had perceived as an obstacle was potentially the greatest therapeutic aid. Contradictions in Freud's thinking regarding the erotic are dealt with in Chapter 2. I wish to propose in true Freudian style that, if we regard the erotic as the most dangerous part of most therapeutic encounters, then it would also follow that the greatest potential advantages also lie in precisely that area; it is up to the therapist to turn the dangers into therapeutic gain.

I wish to be careful here and not overstate my case or over-simplify the situation within psychoanalysis. For some time there have been voices running counter to the prevailing view, and these days the erotic component of the therapeutic encounter is gradually becoming easier to think and speak about clearly. For several years now, I have been running workshops for psychotherapists and counsellors around Britain and Europe on 'Working with the erotic transference and countertransference'. Numerous observations emerge from many of the participants in these workshops. One which confirms my long-held belief is that the erotic is pervasive in psychotherapy. Nearly all the psychotherapists, analysts and counsellors on these courses are able to give at least a few instances of both the erotic transference and countertransference. Another pattern to emerge in these workshops is the widespread uncertainty about how to work with either. The picture to materialize from this is that, though the erotic transference is pervasive in the therapeutic setting, there has been a lack of discussion about what it means and what to do about it, both at the level of training and in the literature. The principal contexts are supervision, which is often problematic, and informal discussion with professional peers. Most often it is not discussed at all.

In a curious way the erotic had for many years been almost distilled out of psychoanalytic discourse. I do not mean that the erotic had disappeared, rather that it was not thought about. The French analyst Andre Green (1995) has posed the question: 'Has sexuality anything to do with psycho-analysis?' noting that direct discussion of sexuality has become marginalized in psychoanalytic thinking. He notes that the contemporary and fashionable focus on object relations, pre-genital fixations, borderline pathology and the-ories of technique drawn from observations of children has obscured the meaning and importance of sexuality in psychoanalytic theory and practice. I agree with this up to a point. My own view is that, with the possible excep-tion of borderline states, object relations, pre-genital fixations and infant observations not only contain erotic elements but the erotic is fundamental to their understanding. In saying this, I would stress two points: that the erotic is determined by unconscious fantasy and is thus not merely related to genital excitement, and that the relationship between mothers and babies is extremely erotic.

Green notes that the object relations model raised the breast to the supreme position taking precedence over the genital stage. In its metaphoric usage, the penis was now seen as a giving, feeding organ, a kind of breast. Implicit in such metaphor is that fellatio was the nearest approximation of a fully satisfying relationship. To continue in Green's own words:

> the role of a sexual relationship is not to feed and nurture but to reach ecstasy in mutual enjoyment.
>
> It is difficult for me to think that the capacity for a woman to enjoy sex is drawn from the unconscious memories of 'having loved and cherished and safely enjoyed the nipple in active sucking' (Hoffer 1991: 696). If this is considered to be the only condition I can foresee frigid-ity in the background.
>
> (Green 1995: 877)

To a certain extent I agree with Green that the penis (and I would add the vagina) has become de-erotized in the use of analytic metaphor. My point of departure with Green is that the erotic is not only a function of genital excitement. Along with the object-relations theorists (Green cites Fairbairn and Klein in particular), he, too, has de-erotized the breast to a position of mere nurturance. It is as though the only function of the breast is to feed, thereby neglecting the fact that it is also an erotic organ. A more detailed discussion of the erotic experiences of the mother–baby dyad will be undertaken in Chapter 6.

The struggle to get the erotic transference and countertransference on to a respectable footing is partly due to a general reluctance to see the erotic dimension of maternity. Such a reluctance is found in society at large. I would expect that the de-erotization of the mother is related to the anxiety generated by the erotic mother–infant dyad. In that respect, I would extend an observation made by Searles (1979) who considers that what the therapist resists are the bad mother components of his or her own identity. I would add that it is also the erotic mother (and father) components which are equally resisted in the therapist's identity. In the Oedipus myth we see this dramatically expressed. Oedipus commits incest and patricide and for punishment is blinded and exiled. Jocasta, on the other hand, commits only incest, but her punishment is suicide. Naiman (1992) questions why her punishment is so severe for the lesser crime? We may conclude that the son's crimes are less taboo than those of the mother. Psychically, the son's desire for the mother is less taboo than hers for him. Her transgression is, therefore, greater. I suggest this partly explains the difficulty of the therapist's task in coming to terms with the erotic countertransference including identification with the erotic pre-Oedipal and Oedipal mother.

TECHNICAL INNOVATIONS AND THE EROTIC

When I say that the origins of psychoanalysis are in the erotic, I do not simply mean Freud's discovery of the universality of sexual desire in the human psyche, though this is clearly relevant to my case. In addition to this, the development of psychoanalysis and, indeed, its very origins are based on the clinical encounter with the erotic transference and the physician's attempt to minimize its influence on him or herself.

The difficulties that Freud encountered in dealing with his erotic countertransference have been well noted before by other writers, for example, Stone (1961), Anzieu (1986), Glenn (1986) and Moi (1990). Schachter (1994) wonders whether the sexual abuse that Freud received from his nursemaid Resi up to the age of two and a half contributed to his sense of guilt in sexual matters. Freud had recalled to Fliess that Resi 'was my teacher in sexual matters . . . who gave me a high opinion of my own capabilities'. Her sudden departure and imprisonment for stealing from the Freud household may have been felt by the young Freud to be a draconian punishment for their illicit sexual activity. Schachter admits that no matter how plausible this explanation is, it is still speculation.

I am of the view that, just because technical changes and theoretical formulations had their origins in Freud's difficulties primarily with the erotic, this does not invalidate their use by later generations of therapists. After all, any theorizing must inevitably be a product of the thinker's personality and in that sense is autobiographical. The issue of the procedures stemming from Freud's own struggles merely raises the obligation for practitioners always to remain willing to question the basic assumptions of what we do in clinical practice.

Freud, therefore, struggled to evolve a technique which would not sexually excite the patient and enable him to avoid his own 'troublesome erotic countertransference' (Schachter 1994). The procedures he evolved are inherited by today's psychoanalytic practitioners: his abandonment of touching the patient's head, or any form of physical contact, as he thought this too sexually arousing; moving the chair behind the couch to reduce the patient's opportunity to embrace him (this will be discussed in greater depth when we consider the primal scene in Chapter 7); and, of course, the importance of the therapist's neutrality in staying emotionally detached from the patient, and his or her commitment not to consider the love transference as resulting from his or her own personal charms. Freud usually adopted a technical device for personal reasons and only later formulated its theoretical basis.

Many of the major innovations of psychoanalytic technique can thus be said to be an attempt by the analyst to step outside the universality and inevitability of the erotic nature of analysis. In effect, Freud attempted the impossible: psychoanalysis established the universal nature of erotic desire, or sexual drive, in the mind while at the same time attempting to reduce the presence of the erotic in the consulting room, especially in the therapist. One of the subsidiary aims of this book is to place psychoanalytic practice within the context of psychoanalytic theory; to relocate psychoanalytic practice within the discovery of psychoanalytic theory concerning the universal nature of sexual desire and therefore its inevitability in the analyst. This last sentence needs an amendment. To say 'relocate' implies that, somehow, the erotic has been absent. Clearly, nothing has been further from the truth. Breuer burnt his fingers on the flames of the erotic; leading personalities in psychoanalysis like Jung, Rank, Ferenczi and many others who had sex with their patients, burnt more of their anatomy than that. Freud, though not getting burnt, was certainly singed, and by his own admission found the erotic a great difficulty.

The origins of psychoanalysis lie in the encounter of the universal sexual nature of the mind versus the analyst's attempt to extricate him or herself from its influence, to de-erotize the inherently erotic. As we are dealing with origins, it is appropriate to consider this as the primal scene of analysis. In this respect, the attempt to de-erotize the inherently erotic bears a resemblance to some of the parthenogenetic myths I discuss in a later chapter. If that is a legitimate comparison, it is to the credit of psychoanalysis since it demonstrates that the development of psychoanalytic thought succumbs to the same characteristics of the mind as does every other philosophical system, thus proving the universality of psychoanalysis and its findings. Psychoanalysis, like the Wolf-Man and everybody else, struggles both to face and to avoid its primal scene, the origins that can be neither remembered nor forgotten.

THE EROTIC LAID BARE: THE SACRED AND THE PROFANE

It is generally acknowledged that the therapist's gender is one of the most important of the 'real' attributes that the patient knows about the therapist. It would seem to me, though, that this cannot be solely limited to physical anatomy. All therapists have an erotic fantasy life even if they do not have sexual relationships. Where does this erotic subjectivity of the therapist go while he or she is with a patient? It is true we have a professional attitude, but underneath that where are the usual sexual desires and erotic fantasies which occupy such a large part of everyday life?

There has been an increasing amount of research into sexually abusing therapists. Jehu (1994) has found that something under 10 per cent of therapists have had sexual contact with their patients. This is regardless of the therapists' theoretical orientation. He also cites that 80 per cent of patients who had sexual contact with their therapist reported they were psychologically harmed by the experience. Much, or most, of this abuse is conducted by male therapists, but the evidence seems to suggest that a substantial portion of abusing therapists are women. Clearly these abusing therapists are not able to deal therapeutically with the erotic. But we cannot banish the erotic at will. Along with May (1986), I agree that the therapist must contain sexual excitement. Containment should not inhibit the therapist being aware of the passionate feelings, but he or she should not act them out.

Are the following scenarios too far-fetched? We could wonder if Freud looked at Dora's breasts. Presumably Jung looked at Sabrina Spielrein's and Toni Wolff's breasts since he ended up in bed with both. Is it just male therapists who do these things? Can we imagine Melanie Klein glancing at a nice bottom as her patient leaves the room? Or even looking at his crutch as he lay on the couch? Writing this feels like defiling hallowed ground and we have not even begun to wonder if Freud, Jung, or Klein had homoerotic or sadomasochistic fantasies about their patients; nor have we wondered about the content of their masturbation fantasies. Of course there is no historical evidence for any of these considerations. But why should not Freud, Jung, Klein, and any other therapist, have the same universal fantasies we detect not just in our psychotherapy patients but in humanity at large? Such recognition would place psychoanalysis with its finger more firmly on the pulse of the human psyche.

In a form of therapy based on in*sight*, where do therapists look? This relates to more than just inquisitiveness about the mind. This is an actual technical question. Do we observe our patients below the neck? If so, we cannot fail to notice their sexual equipment. This is even more of an issue if the therapist uses a couch, as is common practice in psychoanalytical psychotherapy. Here the therapist sees without being seen (the origins of the couch and its relation to the erotic will be explored later). What is, then, the decorum for his or her eyes? Of course, the question of where the therapist looks is not just of technical interest, but has a metaphoric meaning. Clearly, he or she needs to have access to see as much of the psyche as possible. Yet, if we explore all areas of the mind without making any connection with the body, we compound our patient's mind–body split.

My purpose in writing this book is not to present a set of facts or a manual for understanding the erotic transference/countertransference. I am not even implying these ideas are the right ones. My purpose is to allow certain ideas to be thought; in Bion's terms, to allow certain thoughts to find a thinker, to allow certain thoughts into an arena for discussion and dialogue. By articulating these thoughts I invite the reader to decide for him or herself on their plausibility or otherwise. Obviously a controversial subject matter such as this may be uncomfortable for some readers. This is regrettable but cannot be helped: it is not in the nature of the erotic to be cosy. However, it is important to open up the discussion on a relatively closed area of psychotherapeutic theory and practice.

THE EROTIC BOND

The essential nature of the erotic is that it is psychological and sometimes finds expression in the physical. The erotic concerns not merely the genital, nor is it solely about arousal and attraction. It is also an expression of underlying sexual fantasies. The following examples illustrates these points.

Mrs A is in her fifties. She came to psychotherapy after the recent death of her father which evoked anxiety and depression in her. Her profession took her into repeated contact with the dying and their relatives. Until her father's illness she had found this a satisfying job which she did very well. Since his death she had been unable to go to work.

At first she only wanted to speak about her job and her father's recent death. He had been suffering from senile dementia and she had nursed him while he was dying. His behaviour had been very difficult: he repeatedly confused her with his wife; he exposed himself and would make overtures for her to get into bed with him on the ward. This was difficult in itself, but had also stirred memories from the past.

Gradually, she revealed more of her history. Both parents were violent to each other, and the mother was violent to all the children. Father had not physically abused his daughter, but had used her for his voyeuristic pleasure: he would watch her take a bath until she was quite grown-up or force her to pose naked while he drew her. When she once tried to lock the bathroom door he had burst in saying, 'What is so special about your body that nobody can look at it?' This only stopped after her protests in early adolescence.

Her married life had been very unsuccessful, with several divorces. She had attempted to marry men very different from her father – though she realized, as she spoke to me, that each of them had in fact been an embodiment of him in some way.

In this early part of the therapy, Mrs A spoke with the intensity of somebody at last revealing a lifetime of burdensome secrets. I was aware of my position as a witness to her experience: she needed to tell her tale and her main need at this time was not my thoughts, but my willingness to listen. In truth, it was sometimes difficult for me to think. She spoke with a mesmerizing intensity that would just keep my attention to her story. I was aware that this could have been considered a transference replay of her past – the watching father as she bared herself. It was more than that, however, as I knew there was no shame or embarrassment for either of us. She said that in all her sexual experiences none of her husbands had seen her naked: she would bath with the door locked and have sex only with the light turned off. I was aware that in revealing her innermost secrets and being, she was, in a manner of speaking, psychologically naked – that this was happening with the light left on. That is to say, an erotic bond had formed between us. As she learned to trust in the therapeutic environment, she was able to reveal what she had always sought to conceal. To develop her imagery, we might say that whereas she had concealed herself from the prying eyes of those who would take advantage of her (father and husbands), she was willing to expose herself when she felt I would not take advantage of her or feel sexually stimulated looking at her nakedness in fantasy.

Ms B presented in a different manner. She was in her mid-twenties and had originally come to therapy as she was finding it increasingly difficult to cope at work, where she would burst into tears for no apparent reason. She was also suffering from headaches and exhaustion for which no physical origin had been located. She was quite pretty and mildly flirtatious, but I felt almost a complete absence of attraction to her. Though she had had a number of long-term relationships with men, she would never show her emotions with them, never get close, or love and need them as much as they loved and needed her. She told me that, for example, if she ever had a problem with a man, she would just 'dispose of it and get rid of him'. I imagined that she would be a tricky woman with whom to have a relationship. She also told me early on, and occasionally reiterated, that she was 'a man hater', always staring at me with defiance as she said this.

My first thought when she said this was to anticipate an early negative transference. In fact, that was not the case. I was slow to detect that she also made me feel a little anxious. This only dawned on me over time as we got to know each other. Once I noticed my anxiety, I began to wonder more about my own reaction. What I had felt as a mild anxiety began to feel very strong.

Before one session, I even had a sense of panic in anticipation of her arrival. I suddenly had the thought that I was frightened of being raped by this woman. This was an astonishing thought, seemingly out of the blue, and not one I had ever previously experienced. I knew this was an unrealistic anxiety and, giving my fear a name, rapidly reduced its intensity. It was some months after this that she told me she had been violently assaulted by a stranger as a child. The trauma had all but obliterated her memories of the first ten years of childhood.

Of her history, it was also significant to note that both parents had suffered psychotic breakdowns requiring periods of psychiatric hospitalization. At times, I considered her to be borderline.

One session, she arrived telling me that she had been thinking about the absence of childhood memories and the connection between this and a car crash at fourteen, when she had injured her head. She just remembered the blood running down her face. She had also begun to menstruate around the same time, and had been frightened by the blood as her mother had not properly warned her about becoming a woman. She had suddenly remembered starting junior school: she did not want to go. She vividly recalled listening to the water in the pipes that heated the school. That was like the noisy (she said 'nosy' then corrected herself) pipes at home; she could not get away from them either, even if she lay on her bed. I reminded her of earlier material about listening to her parents having sex and being excited by this. I now added that overhearing her parents, listening to their private relationship, produced guilt at being 'nosy'. She acknowledged my comment and added that the water pipes also made her think of going to the toilet. When she had had her first period she thought she was urinating blood. Blood, urine, sex and semen were all mixed up for her.

She then went on to describe a dream of the previous night. 'I was being chased by an alien in a house. I woke up anxiously looking for the alien in my room.' The alien was the one from the film *Alien*. She thought this monster was 'slimy and gross', but it had not frightened her in the cinema. Waking up anxiously in bed had a sexual significance, including listening to her parents having sex. She now joked that in the film the alien bursts out of the man's chest like a 'nasty, bloody penis'. She then felt very confused and gradually began to cry, at first slowly, then copiously. She looked towards my door saying she thought the sounds she could hear on the landing were like knocking at my door. I felt much more sympathetic and closer to her than normal. I felt like rocking her in my arms and singing a lullaby to her. I did neither, but spoke of her pain and helplessness. After I had acknowledged her pain, she found herself thinking about her cat which had once devoured a rat. She thought she saw a rat under her car this very morning, but as she got closer she realized it was just a tissue. She added, she did not know why she was thinking of this. I pointed out that she had, in fact, uncharacteristically used a lot of my tissues that day. She had scarcely been aware that she had let herself be vulnerable and cry in front of me. She said it had just felt natural to cry with me. She would not usually do that with a man. She then looked at the coloured gem stones that I have placed around my consulting room. She had heard that such stones have healing qualities and she wondered if these were healing stones. I merely commented that she was reflecting that there might be a healing process with me.

I would say that in this session full of aggressive sexual material, there was the expectation of erotic danger – penis-aliens and rats devouring flesh in intercourse. Probably at the deeper levels, this related to excitement and guilt generated by listening to her parents' sexual activity when she was in bed. She had grown up not wanting to be vulnerable or dependent on the penis of her boy-friends. In the transference, I had begun as the dangerous man who had to be kept at a distance and, if necessary, castrated and 'disposed of'. She also began to experience the transference as a primal scene, imagining noises at the door as she had listened to her parents having sex. Gradually, we both shortened the psychological distance between us. It felt as though both her sadistically sexual material and my own wariness had suddenly become sensually sexual, gentle and loving. She could now imagine a different sort of relationship with me, and I with her; perhaps the stones (note: not me as person, which was not yet safe to acknowledge) could transform her. There was a long way to go, but this was how we began together – as partners in an analytic voyage, rather than as just two people who happened to be in the same room. It was the erotic bond which launched this voyage.

The erotic is not always transformational. The following vignette is of a prematurely terminated therapy. Mr C sought psychotherapy because he had been suffering from impotence for a number of years. His mother had died ten years previously, and he had lost the capacity to have an erection the following year. He said he still had sexual desire, but this produced no effects on his body. He dismally summed this up as, 'All I want to do is go to bed to sleep'. Prior to his impotence he reported that he had enjoyed a normal sex life.

It was a curious turn of fate that his surname included the word 'dick', slang for 'penis'. I mention this because he had been born with a fairly disfiguring bodily defect. In as far as he identified himself with his name and body, his body as phallus image was as a deformed penis, malfunctioning. His metaphors while talking were replete with sexual failure: he described his life as 'all cocked up' and 'knackered' (slang for 'testicles,' but also a double meaning for exhausted old horses sent to the slaughter house).

He had split the images of his parents. Father, repulsed by his deformities at his birth, had shown no interest in him. After the death of Mr C's mother, his father had instantly remarried his long-standing mistress. This act left Mr C full of rage at the lack of respect shown to his dead mother. Mr C now thought that he could not get on with his own life until his father died. His mother had been devoted to him and had tried her best to enable Mr C to achieve the most from his capabilities. Since her death, mother had been idealized as an angel, in contrast to the father as the devil.

Quite understandably, Mr C tended to somatize his emotions. As he discussed his mother, some symptoms seemed to disappear during the session. Mother had said that he did not need to worry about his health as she was always there to look after him. Her death had shown this not to be the case; now there was no one to take the worry. The loss of his mother, and the anger with his father, had led to his inability to have an erection, and no further girl-friends after that date.

I quite liked this man, but found his tendency to talk around issues, rather than be focused, was sometimes confusing or frustrating. Everything seemed fragmented; I felt I could not get hold of him. Though he spoke willingly, my interpretations seemed to mean nothing to him. I felt Mr C was never quite in contact with me, nor I with him. There was little by way of a therapeutic engagement.

After six sessions (I actually made a typing slip on the second word and just wrote 'sex sessions' – a slip summing up how I thought about our work, which is more expressive than what I had intended to write), he phoned to say he could not make our next appointment so would meet at our subsequent session. He did not appear for this, but left a message on my answering machine the following day to say that he had forgotten; he also stated he would be at our next scheduled appointment. He did not appear for this either and ignored my letter inviting him to get in contact with me.

It has been my observation that some individuals live their life in the same way as they experience sexual intercourse; whether external circumstances are shaping sexual experience or vice versa is not always immediately apparent. In the case of Mr C, I would take the following view. His presenting problem was impotence: he could not get an erection or ejaculate. I believe the same happened with his therapy where he failed to engage and suddenly stopped. We may say he was no longer able to be firm and stopped 'coming'. The underlying erotic nature of the therapeutic experience was such that he was not able to form an erotic bond. The erotic was clearly apparent in the material, but he was no more able to achieve a symbolic creative intercourse with the therapeutic process than he was in his sexual activities with women.

EROTIC TRANSFORMATION

Unless you are a poet, it is virtually impossible to talk about the transformational qualities of love and the erotic without sounding trite and clichéd. Nor do I believe I am saying anything particularly original about the erotic. What I want to emphasize, rather than offering any final answers, is the need for a fresh approach to the erotic transference.

It is this transformational quality of the erotic transference that I believe is incompatible with the narrow view of resistance. The heart of what I am proposing is that the erotic is only explosive or a minefield when distorted by the conception of the erotic transference as a resistance. Let me be clear here. I am not saying the erotic is never a resistance nor a difficulty in therapy. In my example of Mr C, I illustrated how his impotence was reproduced in the therapy and made the clinical work ineffective. Clearly the erotic can be used by the defences as much as any other psychical activity.

In a different context, I have shown that art, which is usually seen in analytic theory as a creative process, can, on the contrary, be used for highly defensive, non-creative purposes (Mann: 1989c, 1990, 1991b and 1997). What I am saying is that normally creative activities such as the erotic or art, can clearly be used to avoid change. But just as we would not always expect this to be the case with art, the same is true of the erotic. The deciding factor is whether an individual is in a resisting or transformational stage during the therapy. If the former, the habitual defences will find expression in all aspects of the individual's psychical material. If the individual is in a transformational phase, the individuation will use all processes and materials available. All therapists know this and recognize the regressive and progressive elements, the pull and push, the backwards and forwards nature of the psyche and the analytic work. My only point is this applies as much to the erotic as anything else. In fact, because of the particular nature of the erotic, I believe it applies even more to the erotic transference and countertransference than to other elements.

Far from being a problem to be avoided it may be considered a development the patient and the therapist have been lucky enough to encounter, and though not to be encouraged, at least considered benign once it is manifest.

This last point is important to stress: the erotic should not be actively solicited as there is little difference between that and seduction. Left to its own devices, it will sooner or later emerge in most therapies, at least if the therapist is open to the process and is not subtly and unconsciously encouraging repression in either him or herself or the patient. It seems a common anxiety amongst therapists and patients that the erotic may wildly envelop either party and thus become uncontrollable. In the case of therapists who sexually abuse their patients, this clearly happens. Where this does not happen, the material is often dealt with by avoidance. Sometimes this is rationalized as the therapist not wanting to invade the patient's privacy; or therapists, like parents, deal with the erotic in an unspoken manner. This latter is fine so long as the interpretations are at least thinkable. More often, therapists and patient do not like to think about the erotic. I also think we should not see analytic metaphors as something concrete: the therapist is *not* the patient's parent and therapy is not about just doing what parents do.

To avoid misunderstanding on another point: I would like to stress that I am not advocating a 'cure by love' as Ferenczi (1926) suggests. I am not saying, as he did, that since therapy patients have had a deficiency of love, replacement love from the therapist is the solution that will compensate. Nor am I advocating Alexander's (1950) 'corrective emotional experience', where the therapist presents him or herself in the opposite way to the patient's parents.

What our patients need is the therapist's understanding in order to liberate the optimum range of their emotional experiences, so that they can have more satisfactory and loving relationships outside therapy. Their erotic fantasies need to be freed from their pre-Oedipal and Oedipal fixations. I do not see how the ability to have a more creative erotic life can be managed unless the erotic is experienced within the analysis. Unless it is experienced as a feeling or passion, the erotic remains split off and distorted (note: not sublimated) into a highly intellectual activity that is no doubt interesting, but is hardly transformative for either the patient or the therapist. Love, as Druck (1988) reviewing the literature shows, is an inherent part of the analytic work. With adults, there is no love for another which is devoid of erotic fantasy.

Cupid is the Roman version of the Greek god Eros. He is blindfolded. Love is blind, but also leads to wisdom. The spirit of inquiry is embedded in the erotic, which may be characterized by the use of penetration and receptivity – to penetrate and be penetrated. This may include the use of genitals, fingers, tongues, eyes and smells, giving access to parts of the body that are prohibited to most people, but which we only allow chosen individuals to touch. I consider that this curiosity and the willingness to explore and be explored has metaphorical equivalents. Menninger (1958) and Swartz (1967) consider that the erotized transference indicates a failure to develop a therapeutic alliance. I believe the contrary: *the erotic transference is the patient's way of forming a relationship the only way he or she knows how. The erotic is psychically binding*. As with lovers, the emergence of an erotic transference signifies the search for a new transformational object. It is an attempt to make a therapeutic alliance that may lead to a creative intercourse, guiding the patient out of his or her impasse. Lawner (1988) proposes that patients are misunderstood if viewed as seeking to verbalize new themes. Rather, they are seeking a new type of relationship. Neither testing nor resistance is a passive transferential re-enactment alone, but a disguised questioning of the analyst concerning the character of his or her potentially attainable mutual relationship.

I consider this to be so in the cases of Mrs A and Ms B. In both instances, there was an element of re-edition of key erotic experiences from their past. What was needed in the present, though, was not just a repeat performance of past trauma. What both patients sought was for the therapist to form an erotic relationship that would be different, and thereby transform the erotic fantasies into something more tolerable, detoxified of their intolerable content. In neither case was the erotic transference acting as a resistance to psychic development. Rather, the erotic was the only vehicle possible for psychical change in the search for a new transformational object.

The capacity to experience a less rigid erotic fantasy cannot merely be a developmental goal of analysis. If the erotic has not been part of the therapeutic process, it is hard to imagine how the patient suddenly develops the capacity to experience a deeper, richer, erotic life only at the end of a 'good enough' therapy or only outside the analytic situation. Rather than mysteriously going on outside the therapy, or in the advanced stages of the therapy, the erotic must be part of the process. It is the medium through which transformation occurs. Take the following views:

> The healing of the splits is a slow and painful process, but as the person begins to feel genuinely alive with access to the true self, the full range of feelings becomes available, the person feels empowered, more satisfied and competent. The individual is now ready to love another.
>
> (Setzman 1988: 132)

> Only when self-knowledge frees the patient from the endless cycles of repetitive compulsion that contaminate his adult experiences of love can he enjoy the creative or restorative aspects of love. The working through of the erotic transference has this self-knowledge and liberation as its goal. Transference love can in this sense be a preview of and a route to the creative, restorative powers of romantic love.
>
> (Person 1988: 254)

To be sure, a therapist always hopes for such a result with his or her patients, though the results are not always so successful as the ideal. However, while agreeing with the commendable sentiments, it seems unlikely to me that rather than love being an end result, the reward of the hard work, it is an integral part of the work itself – a full range of feelings is not possible unless it includes the capacity for love and the erotic. I do not see how it is possible to create the capacity for love, an aspect of the erotic fantasy life, without the erotic being part of the healing process. Nor do I see how you can make something real out of something unreal. The erotic is as much a part of the process as it is a consequence.

I shall finish this chapter as I started with reference to poetry. One of the greatest English poets, John Donne, has written some of the finest of all poetry on love. I consider that he was a man who had some of the deepest insights into the search for a new transformational object. In *The Good-Morrow* this idea is expressed thus:

I wonder by my troth, what thou and I
Did, till we loved, were we not weaned till then?
But sucked on country pleasures, childishly?
Or snorted we in the seven sleepers den?
T'was so; But this, all pleasures fancies be.
If ever any beauty I did see,
Which I desired, and got, t'was but a dream of thee.
And now good morrow to our waking souls,
Which watch not one another out of fear;
For love, all love of other sights controls,
And makes one little room, an everywhere.

Donne is not making a distinction between love and the sexual. I would combine both in the term 'erotic', though one or the other may be paramount. That said, the poet's words remind us that within the erotic is curiosity and transformational opportunities. Donne is thinking explicitly about lovers. I would think more metaphorically. Erotic processes are symbolically enacted in the analytic dyad. The erotic unconscious of both the patient and the therapist form an erotic bond. Within the erotic arena are the heightened possibilities of change and transformation with its implicit opportunities for birth and growth.

2
OF CUPID'S BLINDFOLD AND ARROWS
Erotic transference, real or unauthentic?

It is not my intention in this chapter to detail either the joys or sorrows of love fulfilled or unrequited. The reader can dip into the poetry of the world to find writers better able to do that than I. My intention is more prosaic, merely to shift the focus of the analytic view on transference love.

This chapter will explore in more depth some of the issues raised by the previous chapter. In particular, I wish to examine what I consider to be the major contradictions in the classical psychoanalytic view of the love or erotic transference. The ideas set out in Chapter 1 will be placed against the major psychoanalytic texts on the erotic transference. As this chapter is essentially a review of the literature some readers who are more interested in clinical applications may wish to turn directly to the next chapter.

Love and sex are clearly not the same thing, though there can be a close connection between the two. Freud (1915a) describes the patient's sexual and loving feelings and used these two words interchangeably. However, it is more useful for our discussion if we make a distinction between the two.

One of the most striking features in the scarce literature on the erotic transference is that most of what has been written has been done in the United States. Given that it is unlikely that patients are presenting different material simply by virtue of geography, we must assume that cultural factors are at work. The British School, while happily exploring the aggressive, seems less curious about the erotic. Perhaps this reflects a greater discomfort felt towards sexual matters and is best characterized by the British playwright Brian Rix in his farce: *No Sex Please, We're British*.

LOVE

Before the discussion shifted to America it was initiated in Germany by Freud. The article which shaped later generations of thinking about the erotic transference and countertransference was his paper, *Observations on transference love* (1915a). The background to the paper was that the reputation of psychoanalysis was being damaged by some analysts having sex with their patients, notably Jung and Ferenczi, and that analysis was being criticized as 'dirty talk'. In this paper, Freud attempts to establish that psychoanalysis is of good moral fibre.

He proposed that the analytic situation induces the patient to fall in love with the analyst, though it is not attributable to his or her personal charms. He used the term 'erotic' and 'love' interchangeably. The emergence of the erotic transference causes the patient to lose interest in understanding, being able to talk only about her love. The love is a resistance, therefore, because it interferes with the treatment. Furthermore, the patient is trying to destroy the authority of the analyst – 'bringing him down to the level of a lover'.

Freud advocates that the therapist neither has sex with the patient nor tells her to renounce her feelings. The therapy needs to be carried out in abstinence, and the patient's longings should be allowed to persist in order to impel the patient to do the work and make changes. If the therapist returns her love, he or she is acting out of what should only have been remembered, psychical material which should be kept within the psychical sphere. The love must be kept firmly in view and treated as something unreal that must be traced back to its unconscious origins and brought under conscious control; the work aims at uncovering the patient's infantile object–choice and the phantasies woven around it.

Freud continues to say that the resistance does not create this love; it finds it ready to hand and makes use of it. The issue of whether this is genuine is the crux of the therapist's abstinence. All love consists of new editions of old traits that repeat infantile reactions. What makes transference love unreal is that it has 'perhaps a degree less of freedom than love which appears in ordinary life and is called normal; it displays its dependence on the infantile pattern more clearly and is less adaptable and capable of modification; *but that is all, and not what is essential*' (my italics) (1915a: 168).

Freud continues:

> By what other signs can the genuineness of love be recognised? By its efficacy, its serviceability in achieving the aim of love? In this respect transference-love seems to be second to none; one has the impression that one could obtain anything from it.

The problem for Freud here is that every time he tries to clarify his distinction between normal love and transference love he can only demonstrate that there is no meaningful difference at all: the differences are few and 'not what is essential'. He admits that transference love has all the appearances of being genuine. However, love in ordinary life is closer to abnormal than normal mental phenomena. He continues further to explicate the differences: (1) transference love is 'provoked by the analytic situation'. I would state that clearly most, if not all love, is provoked by the situation: the presence of the loved object. Of course, not all situations are equal. There are certain kinds of relationship that are likely to foster specific aspects of love. Where there are power imbalances, as in the therapeutic setting, there will be a greater emphasis on the parent–child love. Love that grows in an unequal power relationship is more likely to emphasize the regressive parental transferences. However, such a love is not simply a repetition, but contains the desire for a new transformational object. Other forms of love where the power imbalance is not so important will also have elements of repetition. Love in the analytic relationship is as real as love in any other relationship. (2) 'It is greatly intensified by the resistance which dominates the situation.' But let us please note that most normal love is intensified by the resistance, especially if the beloved is coy or 'playing hard to get' or is not present ('absence makes the heart grow fonder' as the saying has it). (3) 'It lacks to a high degree a regard for reality, is less sensible, less concerned about consequences and more blind in its valuation of the loved person than we are prepared to admit in the case of normal love.' Here, Freud neglects the principal features of normal love which are characterized as love precisely because it has no regard for reality, sensibility or consequences, as is typified by the blindfolded Cupid. Love frequently seems to drag the lovers along, even to their own destruction, as in such famous instances as Anthony and Cleopatra, Romeo and Juliet, and many others. However, in the next sentence Freud disagrees with himself: 'We should not forget, however, that these departures from the norm constitute precisely what is essential about being in love.' In other words, Freud knows he cannot make a case for the distinction between transference love and normal love: each attempted clarification confirms they are the same.

The tangle Freud gets himself into in this article is partly due to the nature of the subject under discussion: how do you get both involved with the erotic transference and countertransference, and yet still remain detached enough to be objective? His theoretical ponderings first proclaiming the difference between transference love and normal love were followed by his disclaimers that those very differences are unessential.

However, the difficulty this poses to our theoretical understanding during the clinical work is immense. By seeing the transference love exclusively at the service of the resistance rather than as an expression of the positive transference and the patient's search for a new transformational object, Freud successfully skews both the understanding and subsequent technique. I believe that this makes the erotic more difficult and dangerous than it needs to be in clinical practice. In my view, it is because the transference love is as real as any normal love that it proves so useful in therapy.

Apart from Freud's dubious distinction between transference love and normal love, and his ensuing insistence that this can be nothing but resistance, I am in full agreement with much of what he writes. Placing the erotic in the negative transference has had an astonishingly tenacious grip on our theoretical understanding and our ability to think afresh, and this has caused more problems than necessary in connection with this challenging phenomenon. Treating the erotic as a negative transference, even when some writers are clearly pointing to its positive effects, stops the erotic being considered as a whole. If only one side of a coin is looked at or focused on, the other equally important side will not be seen at all, like the dark side of the moon.

This dilemma seems to have originated as a consequence partly of Freud's own unhappy encounters with the erotic transference, and partly of his witnessing the hapless difficulties of many close colleagues as they plunged like Icarus when things got too hot. The principal source of difficulty, though, is in the theoretical conceptualization; first, that the erotic is an expression of resistance; second, that the transference love is in some way different from normal love.

Both these problems are solved by a change of perspective. I propose that there is no difference between transference love and normal love, transference love is normal love and vice versa. This same point has been made by other writers (cf. Canestri 1993). As Freud demonstrated, normal love originates in childhood experience. To an extent, sexual partners are usually chosen, unconsciously determined, because they bear some similarity with a parent, or at least it is possible to project these similarities on to them fairly easily. However, the adult partner is usually sufficiently different for this not to create an identical situation. This stops normal love from being entirely incestuous. It also creates the possibility for a different kind of relationship to emerge, and thereby increases the potential for psychological growth and new opportunities for individuation. By and large, most patients who seek therapy come because they are experiencing problems in their loving relationships. In these cases, I have noticed repeatedly that their partner or partners bear too much similarity to one or both parents. In this respect, their partners are unconsciously chosen precisely because of the lack of dissimilarity from the parent. This is the repetition compulsion at work. Partners that would provide differences from the parents have not fallen within the patient's orbit of relationships. In other words, these relationships suffer because the infantile component of love is dominant. What I am saying here is that transference love occurs in and outside of the clinical setting and is not unique to analysis. Lovers and doctors and bosses in particular, are as ripe for transference projections as the therapist. This, too, places transference love into the realms of normal love and not something provoked simply by the analytic situation. This is not distinct from normal love. It seems to me that the idea that transference love is not real has contributed to the status of the erotic as something destructive in analysis.

What a lover or a therapist offers is sufficient difference from the parental objects. Both offer transformational possibilities because, in the best of matches or at least in the good enough relationships, the individual encounters something different from what has previously been known or experienced, a new transformational object. The old pre-Oedipal and Oedipal scenarios do not have to be endlessly replayed if the similarity with the past is not too great. That is why normal love is not pathological, because it offers the best opportunity for individual growth.

However, Freud's overall views on love are even more contradictory than those presented in his 1915 article. Here are other contrasting accounts. Freud (1916) writes: 'Side by side with the exigencies of life, love is the great educator.'

Here he appears to say love is transformational, perhaps the most transformational element of life. A few years later, he writes further:

> this transference . . . so long as it is affectionate and moderate, becomes the agent of the physician's influence and neither more or less than the main spring of the joint work of analysis.
>
> (Freud 1925)

In contrast, Marie Bonaparte quotes Freud as saying,

> One must never love one's patients. Whenever I thought I did, the analysis suffered terribly from it. One ought to remain completely cool.
>
> (Quoted in Weinstein 1988)

So love is not transformational for Freud after all.

On the other hand, the British psychoanalyst J. C. Flugel tells us that upon asking Freud why analysis cures the answer was:

> At one moment the analyst loves the patient and the patient knows it and the patient is cured.
>
> (Quoted in LeShan 1989)

So perhaps Freud thinks love is transformational after all.

Is Freud confused about the nature of love? If he is, I would say he is no more so than the rest of humanity. I would consider that he is confused about the nature of love, also about the therapist's response to it. Other writers, such as Tauber, have rightly pointed out that the classical detached therapist is himself creating a countertransference position:

> It is the therapist's fear of using himself and is directed against the therapeutic transaction; it indirectly discourages the patient's confidence and daring in respect of his own contribution.
>
> (Tauber 1979: 65)

Love, then, is dual-edged. Yes, it can be a resistance and destructive, totally blind, prone to action rather than understanding; yet surely this is not all? Love is also transformational and enriches the individual in a way with which few other activities compare. Colman (1994), a contemporary Jungian writer, also sees the erotic spirit as both divine and demonic. I feel somewhat uncomfortable at locating such a human quality as love and the erotic outside the human orbit and in the realms of gods and devils. However, he is right to highlight the dual properties. Love is blind, but it also leads to insights and greater understanding as the lovers seek to explore each other psychically as well as physically. This is hardly original thinking on my part. The idea was more cogently expressed two and a half thousand years ago by Plato in his panegyric on love, *The Symposium* (1951). Love, as Plato tells us, is the very motivation for understanding. To unravel the origins of Freud's confusion about love it is necessary at this point to make a digression to the ideas of Plato before continuing our discussion on psychoanalysis.

The platonic division of love

In *The Symposium*, Plato expresses a number of theories about love, two at least of which have caught the imagination of successive generations. The first is given to Aristophanes, the most brilliant of the ancient Greek comic poets. In real life, Aristophanes had hilariously satirized Socrates in his dramas, especially *The Clouds*, so we might perhaps assume that Plato does not want us to lay too much store in the validity of a comedian's pronouncement on love. These days, after the insights of Freud's *Jokes and their relation to the unconscious* (1905a), we might see humour containing the essence of truth. I have argued in previous articles (Mann 1989a and 1991c) that humour in an analytic setting can penetrate to the heart of the difficulty. However, whether Plato likes the myth or not, the account of the androgyne has been compelling for two and a half thousand years.

Plato has Aristophanes tell us that humanity was originally different from now. There were three sexes: male, female and hermaphrodite. Each human was rounded with two backs, four arms and legs, one head with two faces, and two organs of regeneration. Their strength and vigour threatened the gods. As a punishment, Zeus cut each in half to make them weaker, and threatened further bisection if humanity did not behave itself. The consequence: 'Man's original body having been thus cut in two, each half yearned for the half from which it had been severed' (1951: 61). An original oversight on Zeus' part meant their genitals were at the rear, which would lead to the extinction of the species; Zeus took pity and moved the reproductive organs to the front, allowing procreation. 'It is from this distant epoch, then, that we may date the innate love which human beings feel for one another, the love restores us to our original state by attempting to weld two beings into one and heal the wounds which humanity suffered' (ibid.: 62). 'Love is simply the name for the desire and pursuit of the whole' (ibid.: 64). Love will 'make us blessed and happy by restoring us to our former state and healing our wounds' (ibid.: 65). Love in this myth is portrayed as originating in loss. It is regressive because it seeks an object from the past. Only with love, though, may we become whole. The idea of the original human being cleaved is also found with the biblical Adam and the Indian Upanishads, where the primeval man, Purusu, fell into pieces to form husband and wife.

The second exposition of the importance of love in *The Symposium* is the view given to Socrates and appears to be Plato's own preferred understanding. Here, love bridges gaps. Plato starts with another myth. On the day Aphrodite was born the gods were feasting. When drunk, Contrivance was seduced by Poverty, their child was Love and became a follower of Aphrodite as they shared the same birthday. With parents such as these, Love is always poor and homeless, like his mother, Poverty, but being the son of his father, Contrivance, he schemes to get whatever is beautiful and good. However, 'What he wins he always loses, and is neither rich nor poor, neither wise nor ignorant' (1951: 82). No god desires wisdom for he is already wise. Wisdom is one of the most beautiful things so Love must be a lover of wisdom: 'The object of love is in all truth beautiful and delicate and perfect and worthy to be thought happy' (ibid.: 83). 'Love is not desire either of the half or the whole, unless that half or whole happens to be good' (ibid.: 85). 'Love is the desire for the perpetual possession of the good' (ibid.: 86). The action that deserves the name love is 'procreation in what is beautiful' – physical or spiritual. Procreation is divine in as far as it is 'endowed with a touch of immortality' (ibid.: 86). This cannot be done in disharmony and ugliness, only in beauty. 'The object [of love] is to procreate and bring forth in beauty' (ibid.: 87). Procreation is the nearest humans can get to immortality: 'Love is love of immortality as well as of the good' (ibid.: 87). There is a definite path for the lover to follow, a ladder of love: first is to begin with the contemplation of one beautiful person; next is to see beauty in the many; the third stage is to reckon beauty of the soul more valuable than beauty of the body; this leads to the beauty of the eternal which does not wither, like thought or science; from this one arrives at absolute beauty. In contrast to the Androgyne account, this love is not backward but forward looking; it is not looking for something from the past, but for something different in the future; it does not seek to heal but to transform. Of course, it is worth reminding the reader that love in Plato, in both the Androgyne myth and the 'ladder of love', refers to love between men and young boys, heterosexual and lesbian love both being devalued as unmanly. Also, when Plato talks about procreation he is referring to spiritual and not physical procreation.

Plato not only originated the mind–body duality, which would then be exacerbated in later centuries by Christianity, he also split the two motives of love – the roots from the past and the desire for transformation – playing them off against each other rather than working together as necessary.

Love and the confusion of tongues

We can now return to psychoanalytic thought. Bergmann (1982) notes that Freud was generally reluctant to acknowledge how much Plato had influenced his ideas. Though Freud makes only a few direct references to Plato, he was nevertheless very influenced: his concept of libido has much in common with Plato's Eros. Nachmanson (1915) notes that 'libido' is the Latin translation of the Greek 'Eros'. He deplores this Latinization. Had Freud retained the original Greek term, the historical connection between Plato and himself would have been more evident. In the 'ladder of love', Plato clearly describes the process of how erotic desire can be turned into something more enduring, a process Freud later termed sublimation. Another of Plato's works, *Phaedrusis*, contains an allegory of a charioteer controlling two horses, one rebellious, the other obedient. The charioteer struggles to keep control as he has a vision of love. Though Freud never cited this metaphor, Bergmann notes the striking similarities between Plato's myth and Freud's tripartite division of the personality into super-ego, ego and id.

What I find so interesting is Freud's partial use of Plato's account. Bergmann suggests transference love needs to be sublimated. I am in complete agreement with this. But it is as if Freud, though grasping the positive nature of love, could not keep a firm grip and lost sight of its transformational potential, highlighting its more problematic, resistance side. In so doing, I believe he compounded Plato's mistake. The latter divided love originating in the past (Androgyne myth) from that directed towards the future (ladder of love). Freud, while recognizing love is transformative, then divides the nature of love (normal love and transference love) and can think of it only as a resistance. In my opinion, the view of both Plato and Freud are skewed and therefore distorted on this subject. Love simultaneously contains infantile origins and hopes for the future. It is not a matter of either/or, though one may dominate. When the infantile component is too strong we may see the resistive side of love predominating over the transformational side embodied in hope.

In another article, Bergmann (1988) proposes that Freud had three distinct theories of love. (1) Love originates in infantile prototypes. (2) The second is associated with the discovery of narcissism: the self can be taken as a model for a love object, the ego ideal is projected on to the love object and love is reciprocated. (3) In *Instincts and their Vicissitudes* (1915b), Freud tried to show how the sex drive becomes love, an emotion, concluding that love exists after a synthesis of all the component instincts under the primacy of the genital and in the service of reproduction. As Bergmann wryly comments, 'The conclusion did not follow from the premise' (1988: 656).

Elsewhere, Bergmann (1980) has reviewed the psychoanalytic literature dealing with love, and detects no overall unified psychoanalytic theory or definition of love. I will summarize some of his review, beginning with two philosophers:

- Schopenhauer (1858) sees love as 'this longing that closely associates the notion of endless bliss with the possession of a definite woman, and an unutterable pain that this possession is unattainable'.
- Barthes (1978): 'I encounter millions of bodies in my life; of these I may desire some hundreds; but of these hundreds I love only one. The other with whom I am in love designates for me the speciality of my desire.'
- Abraham (1924) believes a person's character can be complete only when his or her libido has reached the stage of genital love.
- Fenichel (1945): 'One can speak of love only when consideration for the object goes so far that one's own satisfaction is impossible without satisfying the partner.'
- Balint (1956) states love is not a natural emotion but has to be taught. Culture compels the individual to fuse sex with love.
- Binstock (1973) maintains that in a happy relationship each partner vicariously experiences the other in an act of love; distinction between the sexes is not lost but heightened.
- Kernberg (1974) believes mature love is the integration of genital sexuality into a total capacity for object relations, for example, concern for the other (the loved one).
- Klein (1957) sees mature love as originating in gratitude, which makes the feeling of generosity possible.
- Fairbairn (1941) proposes that the genital attitude is essentially libidinal: in virtue of the fact that satisfactory object relations have been established, true genital sexuality is attained.
- Bak (1973): 'Being in love is a uniquely human, exceptional emotional state, which is based on undoing the separations between mother and child'.

I would add to Bergmann's list:

- Winnicott (1976) states that falling in love is 'the fantasy of finding someone who has the time and inclination to know what is needed and fulfil it.'
- Person (1988): 'Love determines one's sense of obligations and time, or transforms them. Romantic love offers not just the excitement of the moment but the possibility for dramatic change in the self. It is, in fact, an agent of change.'

Bergmann's (1988: 670) own view is that the capacity for love should not be confused with psychosexual development. Freud's views were directed at infancy yet love also looks forward. It 'consists in a hope that the lover will heal the wounds inflicted by the less than good enough early objects. That the lover should also be a healer is an important aspect of love.'

Reading this lexicon of ideas on love is rather like reading the various panegyrics on love in Plato's *Symposium* – though much more prosaic and lacking in Plato's humour. It seems to me that there will never be *one* satisfactory definition of such a complex human emotion as love. This is no surprise. Reviewing three thousand years of love poetry, Stallworthy notes:

> The evidence of the poets is as conflicting as it is voluminous . . . there are almost as many definitions of love as there are poets, because poets, like most other men and women, have something to say on the subject.
>
> (1973: 19)

The reader must either decide what makes most sense to him or her, or invent a 'new' theory.

What I like about Person's and Bergmann's quotations above is that they recognize that love, or the erotic, can be a profoundly transformational experience of intimate contact with somebody different: it heals the past and reshapes the future. In his 1980 article, Bergmann suggests that in happy love three elements combine: (1) refinding of early love objects on a number of levels; (2) improving on the old object by finding what one has never had; (3) a certain amount of mirroring of the self in the beloved.

When is love not love?

It is important to keep in mind this discussion about the transformative powers of love as we now return to the discussion of the psychoanalytic idea of transference love as both a resistance and as something different from normal love.

Other writers following after Freud have not always been so ambivalent about the nature of love, often failing to acknowledge what Freud knew to be the dual nature of love, positive and negative. Also, with only the occasional dissenting voice this view that there are two kinds of love, normal love and transference love, has continued throughout most psychoanalytic writing. I will describe some of the ideas of later psychoanalytic writers, focusing particularly on the work of Bergmann and Person as the inconsistency of the distinction is so overt in their writings.

Bergmann, after outlining the connection between Freud and Plato, goes on to subscribe to the resistance theory and the idea of the transference love as distinct from normal love. He writes:

> In real life, the infantile prototypes behind falling in love remain unconscious; while unconscious they provide the energy for the new love. In the analytic situation, these early imagoes are made conscious and thereby deprived of their energizing potential.
>
> (1982: 107)

However, if we take this distinction apart we find that, rather than describing two kinds of love, as Bergmann suggests, he is describing one type of love but two different outcomes: the lover does not seek to understand the infantile roots of his or her love; the analyst, on the other hand, does precisely that. I hope the following example, though ludicrous, will make the point. If, when standing under the balcony, Romeo heard Juliet say, 'O Romeo, Romeo! wherefore art thou, Romeo?' and if, instead of thinking in love, 'It is the east, and Juliet is the sun!', he had said something like (in appropriate iambic pentameter), 'Well, actually Juliet, I think this is more about your father complex . . . ', this might have been good analysis (or a bad comedy) and saved them both a lot of trouble, but hardly great love or tragic drama. The point I am stressing here is that, though Bergmann proposes transference love and normal love are different, he offers no suggestions about the difference only in as far as the lover and analyst deal differently with the same thing. We shall see that, as is usual in psychoanalytic writing, when authors try to designate a difference between normal love and transference love, it cannot be done. Such distinctions are usually little more than assertions (which hardly proves the case) and make sense only as long as the reader does not enquire too closely about what is said. It is also rather strange, to my mind, that a writer who can so cogently describe the positive side of love in the quotation cited earlier, should so suddenly forget this when it comes to understanding love in the analytic setting where he can view it only as a resistance. So long as we assume transference love is normal love, I can concur fully with Bergmann that 'Because erotic love impulses can be sublimated, transference love can be harnessed in the service of cure based on insight' (1982: 110).

Person, in her excellent book *Love and Fateful Encounters* (1988), details a rich account of love. However, as soon as she begins to distinguish transference love as something distinct she is lured by the idea of love as a resistance like a siren call to the rocks that already led Freud into such difficulties. She states that transference love and romantic love have much in common: they evoke similar feelings, deep connections with the other's inner most desire, powerful stimulants to change. Despite the similarities she considers there is one 'enormous *difference*':

> Transference love is far more predictable than love, such a regular feature of so many analyses that it appears almost promiscuous, whereas love in 'real' life is much more selective.
>
> (Person 1988: 248)

Now, in my opinion, this makes no more sense than the difference Freud tried to demonstrate. A few paragraphs earlier Person refers to the well-known phenomenon of patients falling in love with their doctor or nurse or sometimes with their housekeeper. She rightly states that 'rescuing or being rescued surely ranks as one of the great romantic themes' (ibid.: 244).

(Winarick (1985) makes the same point.) So it is hardly surprising, or non-selective, that love would appear in the transference. And given, as Person knows full well, that love in real life has its origins in infancy, the lover's choice of object is hardly less selective than in any other area of life.

To continue Person's case, individuals come to therapy because they are seeking to change. There is thus:

> a clear prior tendency that would facilitate 'falling in love'. . . . The analyst is the perfect foil for such fantasies because he (she) is, by and large, esteemed, respected, believed to be wise and mature, and, in the context of the therapy, the leader, therefore a candidate for automatic and instantaneous idealization.
>
> (Person 1988: 260)

I would also add other qualities here. It is not the charm of the therapist that is attractive, but what is charming about the analytic setting – being listened to and understood, accepted at our worst, not being exploited, all the qualities, in fact, we look for in a lover. What is so striking about this category of prerequisite qualities, all of which I believe Person is right to list, is that they are a prerequisite for many, if not most forms of love, especially of the rescuing type, which is not the prerogative of analysis. In other words, her distinction is not credible.

Person (1988) cites a few other distinctions which she claims are harder to come by in everyday life: (1) 'the analytic setting promotes regressive wishes', though she cancels this distinction herself by also admitting that 'part of the substratum of love is comprised of such wishes'. (2) 'There is a sense of intimacy . . . the patient feels the analyst knows her better than anyone else in the world.' Let us note here that this is probably one of the most striking features for most lovers. (3) 'The analyst remains nonjudgemental and accepting.' Though I think this is an idealized image of the therapist, it is also a common feature of normal love to be loved 'warts and all'. (4) 'Because all attention during the session is focused on the patient, there is some narcissistic gratification attached to therapy' – and, of course, it is the nature of lovers to focus exclusively on each other. (5) The interchanges of therapy are 'marked by privacy, intensity, communion, sense of mission and shared secrets'. And without my having to add how regular a feature of normal love these are, Person goes on to say, 'And, just as there is a unique dynamic characterising the transactions between each pair of lovers, every therapeutic dyad, too, has its unique rhythm and tone.'

Now, while we can certainly agree with Person that these reasons account for why the erotic or love makes such a regular feature in most therapies, with her other points we must disagree. Clearly, as my commentary illustrates, the distinctions she makes between normal romantic love and transference love are non-existent and illusory. All the features of transference love are features of normal love and no more or less predictable. Second, even if for argument's sake we allow for her 'more selective' distinction between transference love and normal love to be credible (which it conspicuously is not), her own examples illustrate it is hardly unique to analysis. As mentioned, Person has already drawn attention to the regular occurrence of patients falling in love with their doctor, nurse or housekeeper. At the end of her chapter, she adds to this list alcoholics attending AA meetings and high price call-girls (whose guidelines, apparently, resemble those of analysis! – discouraging personalization of the experience, an unwillingness to take advantage of their clients and a greater interest in other men, their pimps, than their clients). I would suggest that we might also add to the list, teachers and their pupils, and priests and their flocks. As I mentioned when discussing Freud earlier, certain power relationships are prone to emphasize the more parent–child aspects of love. For that reason, we begin to find that transference love is pretty ubiquitous and not limited to the analytic setting. The qualities that Person describes are undoubtedly the reasons why transference love is so readily stimulated both inside and outside the analytic encounter. The difficulties in maintaining the classical theory are that these qualities are the very substance of normal love. Though some situations are more likely than others to stimulate transference love – for example, analysis, a medical setting, visiting a hooker, alcoholics meetings, teaching, the church (and we could probably add more to the list) – this hardly means this love is any less normal or real than any other type of love.

I will cite one other author at this point to show the prevalence of both this view and the muddle it creates. Schafer (1977) writes:

> On the one hand, transference love is sheerly repetitive, merely a new edition of the old, artificial and regressive (in ego aspects particularly) and to be dealt with chiefly by translating it back into its infantile terms. (From this side flows the continuing emphasis in the psychoanalytic literature on reliving, re-experiencing, and re-creating the past.) On the other hand, transference is a piece of real life that is adapted to the analytic purpose, a transitional state of provisional character that is a means to a rational end and *as genuine as normal love* [my italics].

Now, as I have suggested, we are entitled to wonder about this curious duality Schafer detects in the transference: a bit of the past and a bit of the present. This sounds like the usual psychoanalytic definition of normal love. Then there is his admission that I emphasized in italics. If something is 'as genuine as normal love', how can you tell them apart? How could they possibly be anything but the same? And if this aspect of the transference love is genuine enough, as Schafer is obliged to admit, it must be normal enough. If this is the case, the reader is entitled to wonder, not only how you tell the difference in clinical practice, but also how you can even make a meaningful distinction in the theory.

Schafer goes on to acknowledge the healing powers of the transference love. He then makes a discovery (which to my mind is predictable):

> We are not in a position to disagree entirely with either conception of the transference [love], transference neurosis, and transference-laden therapeutic effects. The problem is, how to integrate the two.
>
> (Schafer 1977)

Not surprisingly, Schafer ends with a question of how to bring the two together. His problem, though, is a consequence of how the transference love is approached in the first place. In effect, he takes a unified whole, breaks it up and is then left wondering how to put the parts back together. One thinks of the Conquistadors who melted down the Inca gold and in so doing lost the map showing where they would find more gold in El Dorado. The problem of integration might be more easily solved, and the intellectual contortions avoided, by taking the more logical view that the 'genuine as normal love' is normal love, one and the same thing.

By viewing the transference love primarily as resistance, this forecloses thinking afresh about the subject. And this is despite the fact that authors cite material, and occasionally views, that are clearly not consistent with their overall theoretical explanation. In the 'hard' sciences, such as physics, theories tend to be abandoned when they collapse under the weight of incompatible evidence. I think the time is long overdue to abandon the idea that transference love, or the erotic transference, is always a resistance and an expression of the negative transference. Though it might sometimes be used as a resistance, it clearly is not the case all the time. It is an unnecessary constraint to call a whole phenomenon by the name of a single constituent part.

SEXUAL DESIRE

It is customary for writers on the erotic transference to comment on the scarce literature on the subject. It is also interesting to peruse the list of references in the articles, as the same few papers are repeatedly mentioned. It is those few influential articles that will be the focus in this section. Though the situation is clearly improving and more and more attention is being directed to this subject, there is still a striking lack of analytic curiosity towards exploration and investigation. The literature also betrays, with a few notable exceptions, a dominant attitude to the erotic transference. There appears a simple line of equation here: if transference love is a resistance and negative transference, actual sexual feelings are the same and more so. Ideas are changing and perhaps the traditional literature is no longer so indicative – though not redundant. However, the literature consistently sings a single tune, often one note with occasional variations of tone. The song is mostly that the erotic transference is a negative therapeutic reaction and is considered a resistance. As we shall see, some authors are able to maintain this view even when their own evidence contradicts it.

Erotized transference

Rappaport outlines his influential views in two articles published in the middle of this century, (1956) and (1959). Rappaport (1956) states that the term 'erotized transference' was first introduced by Blitzsten to describe an excessive libidinalization of the transference. This appears early in the therapy and denotes the patient's desire to 'overplay' the erotic component of the transference and is considered a tenacious form of resistance: 'In transference, an excess of the erotic component indicates an especially strong resistance' (ibid.: 515). This excess might be indicated by loss of reality testing: the patient does not acknowledge the 'as if' quality of things, the therapist *is* the parent. The erotization impairs ego function and the patient is borderline or psychotic. Typically, the patients' histories were with parents with whom they could not establish real contact and emotional warmth. These individuals are, therefore, hungry for what they did not get, the contact they received was invariably sexual. This desire to erotize is an attempt to make the analysis pleasurable, to deprive it of the character of a learning experience and to turn the analyst into a slave. The therapist should not become emotionally stirred as he 'will lose self-control and dignity'. The way to manage the analysis and avoid stoking the erotic fire is by scarcity of interpretations. Rappaport suggests that the interpretations should be given from the position of the analyst's authority, stating calmly such ideas as that the analyst's prestige does not require him or her to be successful with every patient and can well afford to be unsuccessful with one. The patients should be told they are playing 'cheap burlesque and that their behaviour is delusive' (ibid.: 527). Finally, it should be pointed out to them that it would do them good to admit that some inferiority is real and cannot be controlled with omnipotence. If the patient flirts, it is only 'for the purpose of teasing and frustrating the analyst'. Rappaport concludes that erotization occurs under pressure from the repetition compulsion; a corrective emotional experience is provided by the analyst acting differently to the pathogenic parent.

Rappaport returns to the theme of the erotized transference three years later in his paper of 1959. Here he outlines the therapist's own participation in the patient's production of an erotized transference which manifests itself in the first dream the patient brings to the therapy. He believes the danger exists if the analyst, in his or her appearance or behaviour, really resembles too closely a person in the analysand's past; this makes the transference unmanageable because it is too real. This is detectable if the analyst appears as himself in the first dream a patient brings. If the therapist introduces something which repeats an ancient interpersonal situation for the patient, this is not countertransference but an indication that the patient has become a transference object for the therapist, which is troublesome and illusory.

Now, clearly Rappaport writing in the late 1950s does not have at his disposal the rich understanding we now have of the countertransference. Though I think it is worth noting the moral tone of disapproval in his suggested interpretations, it is not that aspect of his theory I wish to highlight. I take issue with the type of interpretation given. I would agree that the therapist needs to be able to understand his or her feelings rather than act them out. However, as I will demonstrate later, to characterize extremely strong sexual feelings as psychotic does justice neither to expanding the diagnosis of psychosis nor to the rich and fundamentally human nature of sexual desire.

Avoiding 'Ferenczi's folly'

Saul (1962) investigates the erotic transference in a more general way and does not characterize it as psychotic. His investigation is framed in the context that the analytic situation taxes the maturity of the analyst. Patients who are provocative or hostile make it hard for the analyst to keep a 'modulated countertransference' (ibid.: 54), which is a balance between sympathy and professional objectivity. This is especially problematic if the patient is a 'young woman in full sexual vigour who has sexuality as a major channel of expression' (ibid.). Saul is plainly considering the type of woman Freud (1915a) characterized as possessing 'elemental passions', citing 'Ferenczi's folly' as an example to us all if the analyst gives way to the full heat of the patient's strongest feelings.

Saul gives four reasons explaining the folly. (1) Such a patient seeks gratification from the therapist because she has not been able to get it in real life. The analyst's task is to remove the inner blocks. Treatment is effective by diminishing the internal problem, not by giving love. (2) The transference is by nature incestuous. The adult woman may have adult sexual desires, but in the unconscious this is the child's wish for the good parent. Because the 'emotional warpings caused in children by sexually seductive or abusive parents' (1962: 58) are well known, love in analysis repeats the abuse. The marriage partner usually, in part, resembles a parent or significant other from childhood, but is also different enough to not be incestuous. (3) Unsublimated expression of the erotic intensifies the transference and makes it more difficult to resolve. Finally, (4) behind sexual desires for the analyst are repressed hostility and guilt. Here Saul cites Freud's later work, *Civilisation and its discontents* (1930), where it was shown that hostility is the cause of guilt and is co-equal to eros in neurosis, human feeling and living.

Saul then considers that 'The frustration inevitably stimulates anger and resentment and these produce guilt and masochism' (1962: 59). There is no question at this point that Saul is confusing cause with effect: if desires turn to anger because of frustration, nevertheless, the desire comes first and the hostility after. Sexual desire does not contain hostility unless frustrated. In other words, the hostility does not reside side-by-side with sexual desire, but rather follows after. Saul puts the cart before the horse. This is perhaps one of the reasons why the erotic is repeatedly seen as a negative transference or resistance, yet the order of things is fundamentally important in establishing the nature of the erotic. The frustration imposed by the necessary analytic abstinence is what turns the sexual desire into something hostile and some-times anti- or counter-therapeutic.

The resistance is, to an extent, manufactured by the analytic process itself. It is my thesis throughout this book that the erotic needs to be neither sexu-ally acted out nor simply frustrated, thereby inducing a hostile negative transference, largely of the therapist's own making. If the erotic is perceived or even welcomed by the therapist as an opportunity rather than as a prob-lem of resistance, the potential for expanding the range of the patient's emo-tional repertoire is greatly increased.

I think it is also important to address another point that Saul's work implicitly raises. The transference is by its nature incestuous, so the erotic must be dealt with carefully to avoid being abusive. However, it seems to me that speaking about the erotic cannot be avoided. In the family, except where parents are being seductive or abusive, the incestuous desire is seldom openly acknowledged and largely exists and is resolved unconsciously. One of the crucial differences between the parents and the therapy is that therapists are neither the mother nor father, and even if we think of therapy in terms of mothering and fathering qualities, these are all symbolic functions. The ther-apist will unavoidably be caught in the necessity to make conscious the incestuous desire that in the family will usually be unconscious. Saul con-cludes with a homily: analysts need to remember Lorelei and Delilah who reveal that appearances may not be reality and that what the patient puts forward may be a mask for the opposite.

I consider that Saul puts an excellent case for why the therapist should not form sexual liaisons with patients. The obvious problem with what he is saying can be briefly stated as: (1) It portrays the patient's desire, like Eve in Eden, as the problem; the therapist's co-desire to be tempted, like Adam, is not considered. (2) Saul assumes the desire is located in young women. This is wrong on two counts: sexual desire is not related to age and can be experi-enced when old, as when young. Age affects opportunity not desire (Orbach 1994 and The Hen Co-Op 1993). Secondly, sexual desire is found, unsurpris-ingly enough, in male patients, too.

The 'analyst as sex symbol'

Harold Blum (1973) also deals with the idea of the erotized transference as a subspecies of the erotic transference. His paper was the most systematic and insightful exploration of the erotic since Freud's paper of 1915. Unlike Rappaport, he does not associate it exclusively with psychotic loss of reality, but as a 'patient flooded with erotic transference preoccupations and fantasies about the analyst and hopes or expectations that the analyst shares in these feelings' (Blum 1973: 63). The erotized transference tenaciously resists interpretation and resembles 'intractable love addicts' (ibid.: 64). The origins are predisposed by early ego-impairment. Unlike most authors, Blum also discusses the homoerotic transference. He notes that many patients that erotize the transference have had childhood experiences of either overt sexual abuse or parental exhibitionism and intrusion into their privacy as children. This undermines and corrupts superego development; what later appears as ego-syntonic may once have been permitted or practised by parents. Blum considers the erotized transference to be 'relatively universal', though varying in intensity, and considers there is a continuum of feelings from affection to strong sexual attraction, 'from ubiquitous unconscious sexual transference wishes to conscious, ego-syntonic, erotic transference preoccupations' (1973: 69).

Blum disagrees with Rappaport over the therapist's role in producing the erotized transference. He suggests that though the erotic countertransference can divert tensions into shared erotic fantasies leading to deadlock, nevertheless countertransference is neither necessary for, nor a sufficient cause of, the erotic transference. The insistent erotic transference constitutes the erotized transference proper. This is a resistance to serve against hostility, homosexuality, loss, and other unconscious conflicts, whilst simultaneously representing a revival of infantile love. Refreshingly, Blum highlights that this resistance does not always mean a bad prognosis:

> It should not be overlooked that the Oedipus complex is the child's first advanced passionate love affair. A 'loving' resistance need be no more insuperable than belligerent attitudes or protracted negative transference.
>
> (1973: 70)

With this in mind, Blum writes further:

> The analyst as 'sex symbol' requires symbolic understanding. The analytic problem is not a realistic mirror resemblance, but the differentiation of past and present, fantasy and reality.
>
> (ibid.: 71)

But he then goes on to cite the resistance problems: proneness to severe regression and acting out; preference for immediate pleasure and difficulty

44

with change; fantasies of 'love cure'; the analytic situation is viewed as seductive and to be warded off by seduction. However, despite all that Blum found, as I have:

> Yet with the neurotic character disorders presented here, the defensive pleasure ego never fully overwhelmed the sense of reality and reason. These patients did not inexorably demand more time, special arrangements, or appointments, let alone sexual gratification. The imploring and insistent seduction could be tempered and tamed. The patients did not interrupt or quit treatment. When their yearnings were verbally integrated into adult awareness, they could take no for an answer. . . . It is not surprising that the disturbed and disappointed patient should want to be loved and fulfilled. The adult patient, however, also comes for help to adapt and achieve in the uncertain world outside the analytic setting.
>
> (Blum 1973: 71–72)

What is interesting in this quote by Blum, with whose views I generally agree, is that having come so close to recognizing the usefulness of the erotic he seems compelled by analytic tradition to fall back onto the formula of seeing the erotic only as a disguise for something else and as a resistance representing a defence against the analysis.

The 'sexualized' countertransference

A number of other authors shift the focus to the erotic countertransference as a tool in the analytic process, for example, Weinstein (1988) and Hirsch (1988). Gorkin (1985) shifts the focus in the theory on to the 'sexualized' (he prefers this term to 'erotic') countertransference to demonstrate that an awareness of such sexual feelings can be valuable as a means of knowing the patient and to eliminate evasion and acting out. He does so by making use of Ogden's (1979) understanding of projective identification, that the analyst is not just an empty container, a dumping ground for projections, but that the projective identification is rather a 'pulling out' or 'extracting' from the analyst. The analyst's ego enters into the interaction with the patient as a participant as well as an observer: the patient attempts to get something and the therapist responds, if only in his or her internal experience, to the patient's projections; part of the analyst's ego sinks into the countertransference, another part swims. This process cannot be avoided, any attempt to side-step the experience is a form of countertransference resistance.

Sexualization in either the analyst or analysand may serve other than sexual ends, such as narcissistic needs or hostile wishes. Sexualization is Gorkin's preferred term as it gets away from the delusional qualities associated with the erotized transference. He highlights the lack of discussion regarding the countertransference to the erotization by patients. Previous writers had highlighted the distaste evoked in the analyst. The management of the session was phrased in terms of warnings against acting out with the patient. He states that it should not be remarkable for the therapist to have some sort of reaction to intensive provocative behaviour. Gorkin believes the analyst's distaste for the erotized transference can be understood as counter-transference resistance. He gives the example of one patient, K, to whom he originally felt repulsion then a desire to do what she wanted. This was felt as a need not just to rescue her, but also himself. He came to understand this as a fusional fantasy in the service of recreating a Garden of Eden, or a 'magi-cally curative copulation' (quoted from Searles 1979). Ultimately, though, Gorkin sees this as a resistance as mutual hostility is denied. With hysterical patients, the erotic takes on an air of temptation and forbiddenness and he is surely right to propose this is a common experience in the therapist, since it is fundamentally linked to Oedipal experience in both the analyst and analysand. Failure to pick up the erotic in the countertransference causes, therefore, further repression in the guise of understanding, thus indirectly identifying with the coolly withdrawn father. The patient recognizes her sex-uality is perceived as threatening, so it never fully emerges to be worked through.

Gorkin also draws attention to the often encountered experience of thera-pists feeling castrated by phallic character patients. He rightly draws atten-tion to this as an aspect of the sexualized transference. The therapist must be made wary of becoming too submissive or castrating in return.

Of all the writers discussed so far, Gorkin comes closest to my under-standing of the erotic process in therapy. In my view, he rightly emphasizes the usefulness of the sexualized countertransference and highlights how this mutually interacts with the patient's pathology. He places the erotic where it belongs, as part of the expected responses within analysis. Even so, his views and mine differ in two important areas. Despite his subtle insights into the erotic, he is still in the tight mould of analytic tradition and cannot see beyond the idea that the erotic can be anything other than resistance; the erotic, in his view, is still a defensive concealment of something else, usually hostility, and therefore essentially negative. My other disagreement is that Gorkin still insists that the sexualized countertransference is only a response, via projective identification, to the patient's projections. While I do not doubt this is clearly the case sometimes, nevertheless, it contradicts the idea of the therapist as an originator of his or her own erotic desires.

What I would emphasize here is that, as we all know, the therapist pos-sesses his or her own sexual desire, which does not come into existence only as a response to the patient's material. The fact is that many therapists main-tain a sex-life, or if they do not have lovers they will, like any human being, nevertheless have sexual fantasies, either conscious or repressed. This, and the fact that they dream or engage in sublimated activities, all demonstrate the presence of the therapist's own sexual desires. Given these considerations, it becomes strategically impossible to maintain, as Gorkin does, that sexualized or erotic countertransference is merely a response to the patient. Sexual fantasies are not merely 'pulled out' or 'extracted' from the therapist. Since they are human, they too possess an erotic subjectivity. Most therapists are quite capable of pulling out or extracting their own sexual fantasies.

A woman's desire

Eva Lester (1985) writes about the erotized transference to the female analyst. She explores why female analysts with male patients get fewer erotic transferences. She proposes that women therapists get more pre-genital issues and that the 'fear of the powerful pre-Oedipal mother' threatens and inhibits expression of strong erotic fantasies. Now, clearly, as a male therapist, I am not in a direct position to doubt this claim. However, it has been my repeated observation from discussing the erotic transference with women colleagues and supervisees, and also from the reports given during my workshops on the erotic transference, that woman therapists do experience frequent erotic transferences from male patients, and indeed from women patients, too.

I am also doubtful about other aspects of Lester's claims. Even if there are issues about the powerful pre-Oedipal mother inhibiting erotic desire, this does not explain why material towards the erotic Oedipal mother does not emerge once the pre-Oedipal issues have been worked through. Lester proposes that by then the analysis is fairly advanced so strong erotic transferences do not emerge. This is a highly doubtful claim in my opinion, as Oedipal material will eventually emerge whatever the stage of the therapy.

Lester is also assuming that the pre-Oedipal mother is not erotic. This seems to me to be an idealization of the mother–infant myth, that the pre-genital mother–child relationship is not erotic. In fact, the term 'pre-genital' is a rather curious phrase to be used in the literature, with a latent meaning implying a 'before genital existence' which is a contradiction to the biological facts. Recourse to explaining the lack of erotic transference by the pre-eminent issues about the powerful pre-Oedipal mother does not marry well with other observations. I am thinking here of the often cited (usually socioculturally explained) phenomenon of men habitually sexualizing relationships: how many times do we hear women say, 'All he wanted was sex' or, 'Men confuse sex with intimacy'. If that is the case, why is it so absent in the literature and in the erotic transferences to women therapists? My view on the reason for the relative paucity of reported erotic transferences between male patients and female therapists is that it is partly socio-cultural, with women therapists particularly reluctant to articulate their male patient's desire, as this might be understood as sexually forward and perhaps inviting trouble.

I also think the matter is deeper than this. The erotic and the nurturing functions of motherhood – the mother–baby relationship – have been split in analytic theory as elsewhere, as is seen in the widespread use of terms such as 'pre-genital' or 'pre-Oedipal', which imply there is no eroticism in this early stage, when I believe the reverse is true. Compounded to this is the incest taboo. Father–child (usually daughter) incest taboos are spoken about often enough. Mother–child (usually the son) is much more problematic. Historically, this is the oldest incest taboo, because for many generations paternity could not be proved, and in many societies the male role and the function of semen were not understood in the reproductive process.

I also think that the incestuous desire of the erotic mother is imbued with the greatest psychological erotic horrors and on the scale of things is considered an even greater taboo than father–daughter incest. Ultimately, the erotic mother is perceived as a threat to individuation and differentiation, her sexual desire may voraciously swallow the child, subjecting him or her to the loss of a separate self which is incorporated inside the mother. Equally the child's incestuous desire for the mother, the allure of losing all separateness and returning to oneness, is a desire that must be resisted if the progressive, developmental parts of the child's personality are to prevail. Thus there are several reasons which combined make it difficult for women therapists to interpret the erotic transference, especially with male patients: the woman therapist's reluctance to go against socio-cultural taboos, plus deeper layers of splitting and desexualizing the mother's role and the prohibition on the mother's sexual desire for her child. Both the patient and the therapist may prefer to avoid the psychological horrors of the mother's incestuous desire.

The erotic as a gold-mine and minefield

Person (1985) has made a detailed study of love and the erotic transference in a number of publications. In this article she also notes that, though universal, it is variable in expression. Following on from Lester (1985), her article makes the distinction between how male and female patients express the erotic in the transference. She proposes that women utilize the erotic transference as a resistance, while with men the resistance is to the awareness of the erotic. This distinction is phrased in terms of transference resistance and resistance to the awareness of the transference respectively. Overt expression varies not only according to the particular unconscious conflicts and personality structure, but also depends on the sex of the patient vis-à-vis that of the analyst. The problem of resisting the erotic transference for male patients is that it perpetuates the instability of their capacity to form enduring love relationships, the inability to merge sexual and dependency yearnings. The erotic is resisted because the male fears dependency connected to sexuality. The difficulties may be compounded with a woman therapist who, because of cultural impediments, may be embarrassed to bring the erotic fantasies out explicitly. It is important to state that this view has not been confirmed by other women writers such as Silverman (1988), Wrye and Welles (1994), Maguire (1995) and Schaverien (1995). However, Silverman, too, sees the erotic as resistance. Wrye and Welles emphasize the transformational qualities.

Person elaborates further. The erotic transference and transference love are used interchangeably and refer to the mixture of tender, erotic and sexual feelings that are part of the positive transference. She rightly notes that the erotic transference is generally viewed by therapists as tainted by unsavoury associations and considered as slightly disreputable. Even so, she considers 'It remains both a goldmine and minefield' (1985: 163). What is striking in Person's accounts is that, even though recognizing the erotic as a potential goldmine opening up new possibilities in the patient, she still maintains its status as resistance. The source seems to be located in the sentence, 'When the erotic transference is experienced, but not fully analysed, it becomes the resistance to the analysis' (ibid.: 168). Now, we might be able to go along some of the way with this conclusion. But Person does not think through the logic of her proposition: most erotic transferences are not fully analysed precisely because the predisposition to view them as a resistance makes the analysis incomplete. The erotic as resistance becomes a self-fulfilling and perpetuating prophesy. To expect the erotic to pose a resistance forecloses the situation and makes it very hard for the therapist to mine for gold profitably. Often the very act of treating the erotic as a resistance causes it to become a resistance. The point I am emphasizing here is that the erotic is a mixture of cure and ailment, good and bad, positive and negative. To focus on only one aspect of the nature of the erotic is to leave it insufficiently analysed and understood.

'Observations on transference love revisited'

A more recent view of the erotic transference is to be found in a collection of articles edited by Person (1993). I will treat these ten articles as one on the same basis as in clinical work, when a patient has two or more dreams in one night, they are best understood as a unity. So, too, these ten articles, though different in many respects, have a unity. Each takes as its starting point Freud's 1915 paper on transference love.

In her Introduction, Person highlights the widespread power and threat which has always existed in psychoanalysis concerning transference love. I think it is safe to say that this power and threat is apparent in all the articles in her book in varying degrees of intensity. This is clear in the way some of the authors write about the subject: transference love is a hot and passionate phenomenon and by definition is an interesting subject. Yet Eichoff (1993) can nevertheless produce a remarkably dull review of the limited literature, and Wallerstein (1993) seems to find the subject so difficult to focus on he makes a long, meandering digression off the subject and brings himself back to the point only with some difficulty. The impression is that it is extraordinarily dangerous material, too hot to handle or look at; material that must be desiccated before it can be considered. This is consistent with Freud's own view when he makes the analogy that the analyst working with transference love is like a chemist working with explosives. This view is further reinforced by most of the contributors seeming to fear to give examples from their own practice. Indeed, Betty Joseph (1993) is the only contributor to make her points more alive by including material from her own clinical work. The editor's comment about how transference love is seen as a threat is nowhere more confirmed than by the fear of the subject exhibited by the eminent writers in the book itself.

Another striking feature about the articles as a whole is the varying degrees to which they advance our thinking in the years since Freud's original paper. In this respect, only the papers by Schafer, Gill, Canestri and Stern really add anything new to our understanding of transference love.

Schafer (1993) looks at Freud's paper from five angles, or readings, as he prefers to call them. Along with Stern and Canestri, he demonstrates the muddle in Freud's mind about the distinction between transference love and normal love. He sums up the confusion rather humorously:

> He [Freud] presented transference love as both unreal and genuine and suggests that, technically, it should be treated as unreal, even if it is basically genuine.
>
> Schafer (1993: 78)

Yet, technically, we should allow for a new attachment – that is, the patient relating to a new object.

Gill also takes up the supposed distinction between transference love and normal love. He again shows how Freud mistakenly thought he had eliminated himself as a co-participant once he abandoned hypnosis. Gill writes:

> Probably the greatest obstacle to analyst's recognition of their participation in the analytic situation is the assumption that the analyst can choose whether or not to participate. The point is that he participates whether he likes it or not. His participation will be experienced by the patient in all the shades of gratification and frustration.
>
> (1993: 127)

Gill also makes one of the few remarks in this book that comes close to seeing anything positive about transference love, since he concludes that genuine love includes consideration for the beloved's wishes.

Canestri (1993) takes up the issue of the reality of transference love as well by exploring another of the striking metaphors from Freud's paper: that an exclamation of love by the patient is like a cry of 'fire' in the auditorium during a play. Canestri shows that the use of fire and explosive imagery is important, paraphrasing Hippocrates, that there can be no cure except by fire. Even so, Canestri shows that Freud underestimated the role of passion in analysis. He concludes that transference love is normal love.

Finally, Stern's (1993) article introduces some very interesting empirical data about the origins of love, demonstrating that most of the characteristics of adult lovers find their prototypes in the mother–child relationship. Physical qualities of lovers, like kissing, mutual gaze, synchronized movements, and so on, are established by the fourth month of life. The intrapsychic features of love also begin early – the exclusive focus on one person, the sharing of meanings, etc. – these preconditions of adult love are registered as motor memories, not as symbolic knowledge. Therefore, he concludes, acting out may be a form of remembering.

I have emphasized how some of these authors acknowledge the positive characteristics of normal love. This is important, because the manifest position of all the authors in this book is to follow Freud's view in seeing transference love as a resistance. Some, like Joseph and Cesio (1993), are more firm in this conviction than other contributors. But, nevertheless, this remains the underlying conviction of all the authors of this book. This is very important for a number of reasons. For example, the widespread perception of transference love as a resistance is an indication of how threatening it feels to psychoanalysis. And yet, as I have illustrated here, a number of the authors show transference love is indistinguishable from normal love. Are we to conclude, therefore, that normal love is a resistance? This is a patently absurd proposition. The contradiction between the evidence and the theories attempting to explain the evidence is like a gaping chasm. However, having exposed the confusion, none of these authors can disentangle him or herself sufficiently from the basic theoretical and clinical assumptions to make the break with Freud's views that is necessary if we are going to avoid an impasse for the next eighty years. The tendency to see transference love as a resistance, and therefore as something negative interfering with the psychoanalytic process, indicates more about the fear and resistance in psychoanalysis than it does about what the patient is actually doing.

This raises all sorts of problems for psychoanalysis, both theoretical and practical. Not the least of these was Freud's concern to avoid the analytic dyad ending as a sexual relationship. Freud's 1915 moral and theoretical strictures, far from curtailing professional sexual relationships, merely drove them underground and has intimidated analysts from healthy disclosure to colleagues and supervisors which might have gone further in stopping the abuse of the therapeutic relationship.

In my opinion, this collection of articles edited by Person (1993), though a worthwhile contribution in the endeavour to give the difficult subject of transference love a place in constructive debate, nevertheless raises more problems than it solves. What is clear is that our understanding of transference love has not developed very far since Freud's 1915 paper. Transference love is still a muddle for psychoanalysis. This in itself suggests we need to give the matter much more thought.

The erotic and hostility

Perhaps the analyst who has written most about the erotic is Robert Stoller (1975, 1979, 1985). He proposes that hostility is an integral part of the erotic:

> It is hostility – the desire, overt or hidden, to harm another person – that generates and enhances sexual excitement. The hostility of eroticism is an attempt, repeated over and over, to undo childhood trauma and frustrations that threatened the development of one's masculinity or femininity. The same dynamics, though in different mixes and degrees, are found in almost everyone, those labelled perverse and those not so labelled.
>
> The following, then, are the mental factors present in perversions that I believe contribute to sexual excitement in general: hostility, mystery, risk, illusion, revenge, reversal of trauma or frustration to triumph, safety factors, and dehumanisation (fetishization). And all of these are stitched together into a whole – the surge of sexual excitement – by secrets.
>
> (Stoller 1979: 6)

Stoller sees sexual excitement as a defence against anxiety, by turning anxiety into a 'melodrama'. The ultimate danger in sexual excitement is the threat to one's sense of maleness or femaleness.

Now, I am in complete agreement with Stoller as a description for perversion. Most, though not all by any means, of his clinical material is drawn from individuals with perverse states of mind. It is not clear in what precise quantities of 'mixtures and degrees' Stoller considers these components to exist in non-perverse states of mind. Though he proposes a continuum with 'less use of hostile mechanisms' (ibid.: 31) at one end, to more frequent use in psychotic and perverse at the other, he remains imprecise about what we might encounter in the middle. While I am ready to admit the possible presence of hostility in most sexual desire, it cannot be ascribed as always the most dominant feature. Often the hostility is subservient in importance to tenderness, affection, intimacy, compassion, the wish for the other's happiness, all of which find expression in sexual desire as well as love. Stoller considers they appear only infrequently in sexual excitement. In addition, though, it seems inevitable that sexual development contains frustrations if not traumas, the nascent sexual development also encompasses experiences which enhance and promote sexuality. Sexual experience and desire are life-enhancing as well as sometimes being a process of traumas defensively reworked. Stoller acknowledges this, but prefers to focus on the trauma–hostility aspects. He has a negative outlook and does not appear to consider the erotic as transformational:

> My theory makes sexual excitement just one more example of what others have said for millennia: that humans are not a very loving species – especially when they make love. Too bad.
>
> (Stoller 1979: 35)

To be sure, some voices have said this across the aeons. Other voices, not mentioned here by Stoller, have said the opposite. In other words, Stoller defines the whole by half of its parts. I am sure he would be the first to agree that this is both a hostile and, albeit very slightly so, a perverse way of thinking. I would also add a 'chicken and egg' point of view. If, as it is generally considered, the erotic contains or conceals a hostile sentiment beneath, this cuts both ways. Frequently hostility conceals the underlying erotic. Fairbairn (1940) in particular has made this point regarding schizoid individuals who rather incur hate than love. I have noticed that hostility obscuring the erotic occurs more widely than just in schizoid personalities.

Given the above, Stoller's view of the transference and the erotic in therapy is predictable enough. The erotic transference is problematic: 'Erotic excitement felt for the analyst is not so easy to analyse' (1979: 76). In his lengthy case study of Belle, 'Her resistance was overtly shaped more by sadomasochism than by anything else' (ibid.: 113); the erotic would be a 'hindrance unless insight intervened' (ibid.: 97). Belle would try to draw him into her fantasies and make him a victim as she was in her erotic scenarios. She would try to excite or seduce him. Stoller tells us that only towards the end of her analysis was Belle able to admit she needed him to be her analyst and observe her dispassionately. Stoller does not use my phrases, but I would define it thus: the erotic transference, in as far as it was a resistance, employed hostility to hide the more meaningful erotic fantasy underneath, the wish to be loved, warts and all. He was never quite trapped by her:

> I do not see how an analyst can for long feel himself a victim if he is serious, he will be too busy thinking about why the patient is doing this, which precludes his believing he is the real object of the sadism.
>
> (Stoller 1979: 117)

This is important, and fundamentally what makes therapy different and not just a re-edition of the patient's past. I would, however, modify Stoller here and add that sometimes, even when we as therapists are 'serious', the patient will necessarily pull us into the transference orbit totally and for longer than we might wish. Stoller and Belle seemed to have had an extraordinary effect on each other: he on her, for the clear benefits and improvement their work brought to her life; she on him, to be such an evocative muse to stimulate a whole book about sexual excitement. Despite the professed pessimism of his earlier quote, their analytic encounter is more a testimony to the transformative effect of sexual excitement.

CONCLUDING REMARKS

In the preceding pages I have discussed in detail my criticisms with the classical psychoanalytic views of love and the erotic transferences. I will conclude with a final quote by Lear who argues for the pervasiveness of love in human relationships. He writes:

> Love runs through human nature, and it is through the transactions of love as incarnated in humans that individual persons come to be.
>
> (Lear 1990: 186)

'Come to be' refers to the psychological, as well as physical, creation of the individual. As I noted in Chapter 1, anthropology has not confirmed the existence of love as a universal phenomenon. However, the erotic is, and if we substitute the word 'erotic' in Lear's passage we will derive the meaning that the erotic is an essential feature of the human condition, and the source of its individuation. There are many paths leading to a new transformational object. In my view, the most significant of these paths are offered by the erotic transference. The erotic transference is then utilized by the patient in the quest for a new transformational object that will produce intrapsychic change.

3

THE PSYCHOTHERAPIST'S EROTIC SUBJECTIVITY

WOODY ALLEN   I realize it's just transference doctor but these days, I'm
     madly in love with you.
WOMAN ANALYST   *Just transference*! With legs like mine you think it's
     Just transference?

(Woody Allen)

Woody Allen's joke, like all jokes, touches something fundamentally true in the analytic process. In this instance, the joke refers to the underlying erotism that exists in the analytic setting.

This paper is about the therapist's erotic subjectivity, by which I mean all the therapist's conscious and unconscious sexual thoughts, feelings, physical sensations and fantasies toward the patient. This aspect of eroticism, like humour, receives scant attention in psychoanalytic discussion. It is as if the analyst must not admit to anything which might be considered pleasurable. Actually, though, erotic fantasies in the therapist give little pleasure: they are more likely to induce guilt, shock or embarrassment.

TABOO AND EROTIC DESIRE

The dyadic relationship between patient and therapist is often likened to a parent–child relationship; at other times the emphasis is considered in terms of creative discourse. I think both these descriptions are important, but for the present communication I wish to focus on another kind of couple: the sexual relationship. Two is the number for intercourse and procreation. Whenever two people are together there is the possibility of a sexual encounter whether they like it or not. This may or may not occur depending on the particular sexual morals and taboos that lead either to repression or expression of sexual desires. The couple forms the sexual basis for the human race and most of the creatures in the animal kingdom. I wish to propose that the analytic encounter shares this erotic nature as any other encounter between two people.

In some respects this is well-known analytic knowledge. The area of

55

erotic transference is a well-investigated and common phenomenon: patients may fall in love with their therapist and have erotic fantasies about the unobtainable person behind the couch. In stark contrast, the area of erotic countertransference is much less investigated. Tower, writing in 1956, noted: 'Virtually every writer on the subject of countertransference . . . states unequivocally that no form of erotic reaction to a patient is to be tolerated' (quoted in Searles 1959: 285). In many respects this is still true forty years later. As Dahlberg (1970) writes, it is a subject 'too hot to handle'. At the start of the question period when this chapter was first read at a conference in 1992, some of the audience immediately began talking about another subject altogether. The topic was evidently to hot to pick up straight away! Often, such references that are made to the analyst's sexual feelings to the patient are frequently clothed in moral or professional disapproval, rather than in an attempt to apply any scientific understanding. Though it is now easier for therapists to discuss erotic feelings to their patients, a comparison can be made between the relative difficulty of our profession to engage in more frank discussion and, in our society at least, parental reluctance and guilt about admitting erotic feelings towards their children. To an extent, the incest taboo that silences the parent also silences the analyst. The fact that we know that some analysts and analytic psychotherapists do have sexual intercourse with their patients is in itself evidence that the current approach to dealing with the analyst's erotic desires; that is to say, avoiding looking at the issue scientifically is clearly not working

Erotic desires and fantasies are so fundamental in human experience as to be almost continuously present. This view firmly supports the need for elaboration and clarification of the therapist's erotic subjectivity in psychoanalysis and psychotherapy. Consideration of this process need not be limited to examples of pathological countertransference. Unless we take the view that all erotic desire and fantasy is a perversion or neurotic, and psychoanalytic theory tells us this is clearly not the case, then the therapist may experience healthy erotic feelings and these may be useful in the analysis if the therapist deals with the desire appropriately; if the therapist remains unconscious of the desire and does not analyse it effectively, then the erotic feelings are more likely to bring an unhealthy distortion into the work. It would seem that anything less than an open recognition of the analyst's erotic subjectivity leaves psychoanalysis in the illogical and untenable position of seeing the ubiquitous pervasiveness of sexual fantasy in everybody else except the psychoanalyst!

Some psychoanalytic procedures can be thought of in terms of the incest taboo between therapist and patient. Two are particularly so. First is the fact that, although in the last forty years most commentators on countertransference have seen increasing value in using the therapist's feelings as a therapeutic tool, there is still (with some notable exceptions) a marked inclination not to apply this to erotic feelings (e.g. Reich 1951; Greenson 1974). The level of prohibition suggests just how pervasive erotic desires actually are: the intensity of a prohibition is proportional to the intensity of a desire. There is no point banning something which people do not want to do. From this we must assume that most analysts and therapists feel erotic desires for their patients at some time or another. The second procedure is the prohibition against physical contact, which can be partly understood as minimizing the sexual temptation not only of the patient but also of the therapist. The tenacity with which the psychoanalytic method adheres to this taboo, which I personally think is essential, is also an indication of how strong the temptation can be for both; the analytic setting is a cauldron of intense primitive emotions, phantasies and desires for both participants. A lengthy training analysis does not stop the therapist having unconscious phantasies but should put him or her in a better position to be able to analyse and utilize them in the patient's interest. It is precisely because of these heightened and intense feelings and phantasies that analytic boundaries, which I am suggesting are extensions of the incest taboo, should be maintained. The analytic setting encourages the patient's transference on to the therapist: in this way the patient re-experiences the original struggles with the parent. By the law of talion (Racker 1968), the therapist will experience not only a reactivation of their own childhood experiences, but also him or herself as a parent in relation to the child. The incest taboo serves not only the purpose of initiating the child into civilization but also of protecting him or her from abuse by the parent; in this sense the incest taboo serves to constrain the parent when the child is too helpless to protect itself. (I have discussed the role of the father's aggression to his son elsewhere, cf. Mann 1993a.) The therapist, no less than the parent, will experience the full force of erotic and aggressive desires, as the experience of Laius and Jocasta, the parents of Oedipus, fully indicates. Yet it is on the successful working through of incestuous desires that healthy maturational development depends. The child needs to be able to internalize and identify with the beloved parent of the opposite sex. In so doing the child acquires the parent's ability to contain, but not deny, incestuous desire.

Kumin (1985) proposes the term 'erotic horror' to describe the impending awareness and accompanying discomfort as the patient feels the erotic transference. According to Kumin, erotic horror stimulates intense defences against this awareness. Erotic transferences are therefore seen as a resistance and a form of negative transference and their unpleasurable effect is evidence of aggressive drive derivatives. But the analyst may also feel erotic horror as the analytic situation excites both participants and the rule of abstinence imposes on both the inevitable frustration of the ultimate fruition of these desires. Kumin states that the analyst must have an appreciation of what both the patient and he or she desires. Only an accurate perception can diminish the desire. Citing Bion's famous caution against memory and desire, Kumin says: 'Thus we might conclude that the patient's desire for the analyst does not present the most pernicious resistance to the analysis of the transference, but rather the desire of the analyst does' (1985: 13). The author concludes that only the correct interpretation reduces desire and resistance. This interpretation does not necessarily have to be spoken, but does need to be thought. Once made, the analyst is in a position to return to his neutrality. For Kumin, the erotic horror for both the patient and the analyst is almost inevitable but is seen as an obstacle to analytic progress.

Searles (1959) in his paper, 'Oedipal love in the countertransference', takes a different view. He notes that, towards the end of an analysis, he usually felt erotic desires and a wish to marry the patient. He came to believe that, before an analysis can be worked through, the analyst should experience the patient as beloved and desired not only at an infantile level but also at an Oedipal genital level. Real maturation and growth derives from the renunciation of incestuous goals by both participants. From this, it follows that erotic feelings augur well, rather than ill, for the therapeutic outcome. Like Kumin, Searles states it is the analyst's own inner awareness of these feelings which is crucial. Some patients, particularly schizophrenics, can benefit from the therapist's disclosure of these feelings. He writes: 'If a little girl cannot feel herself able to win the heart of her father . . . how can the young woman who comes later have any confidence in the power of her womanliness?' (ibid.: 296). The same, of course, is true for the little boy with his mother. Searles considers that Freud's view that the Oedipal phase results in a severe and forbidding superego is a description of neurotic or psychotic development. Changing the emphasis, but not contradicting Freud, Searles considers that healthy ego development results from enhancement of the ego's ability to test inner and outer reality. In his view, every individual patient indicated that their ego impairment was due to the beloved parent repressing his or her desire for the child, chiefly through unconscious denial of the child's importance to the parent.

My points of agreement and disagreement with Kumin and Searles are these. Both authors consider that the essential ingredient is for the analyst to recognize their own desire, failure to do so leading to difficulties in the analysis, and with this I am in total agreement. With Searles, I agree that erotic desire is not to be considered simply as an obstacle, as Kumin states, but that it has a positive contribution to make. I disagree with Searles in that, as Kumin shows, erotic desires can emerge at any point in the therapy and not just in the termination phase. I am also sceptical about the merits of the analyst revealing his or her desires to the patient.

I would like to suggest that erotic desire in the therapist needs to be reconsidered. It seems increasingly inadequate simply to dismiss it as a neurotic disturbance in the analyst or as a consequence of insufficient personal analysis. I would like to propose that erotic desire in the analyst needs to be considered in terms of the Oedipal triad. As such it is part of normal and healthy development, but like any other stage of development, it can go wrong with the failure of a good enough working through.

EROTIC SUBJECTIVITY

Following on from Natterson (1991), I would suggest we need to go beyond the term 'countertransference' in describing the therapist's feelings. The problem with the term 'countertransference' is that: (1) owing to the historical development of the term it is not free from the implication that what the therapist is feeling is somehow a neurotic distortion; (2) countertransference implies that what the therapist feels is merely a reaction to the patient's material, which seems to negate the fact that therapist's have their own emotional and fantasy life irrespective of the patient. For these and other reasons, Natterson proposes we view the therapeutic encounter as an intersubjective process whereby the analyst's internal world meets the patient's internal world and there is an interaction between the two. What I am suggesting, therefore, is that analysts' erotic desires are part of their own psychic world, and not just something patients make them feel. Analysts have their own sexuality like everybody else, and they bring it with them into the analytic setting. Yet there is an important difference that should be stressed: analysts and analytic psychotherapists need to scrutinize their erotic fantasies with analytic methods rather than act upon their desires.

Erotic fantasies and desires need be no more detrimental to the analytic process than any other feelings such as jealousy, rivalry, hate, compassion, love, etc. I would suggest that it is not the existence or experience of these feelings that is problematic. Rather, they are for the therapist to scrutinize in self-analysis so they can be utilized in the analytic relationship in the interest of the patient. In my opinion, the hasty denial or repression of erotic desires is more likely to have a detrimental effect. As our theory tells us, repression simply takes the fantasies away from where they can be accessible for analysis. I would hypothesize that it might be more accurate to suspect a disturbance in the therapist by the absence of conscious erotic fantasies and desires. This may be an indication of severe repression or guilt, thus causing erotic desire to be unconscious. More research would need to be done to test this hypothesis but I believe that a variety of analytic disturbances, the most gross of which is sexually assaulting the patient, and among the least of which can be listed difficulties in managing the erotic transference, are due to the therapist's difficulty in analysing his or her erotic subjectivity. The whole point is that the therapist has got to contain these feelings and desires and subject them to thought.

Winnicott in his seminal paper on 'Hate in the countertransference' (1947), distinguishes three types of hate that may exist in the analyst:

1   Abnormality in countertransference and set relationships and

identifications that are under repression in the analyst . . . it is evident here that the analyst needs more analysis.

2 The identifications and tendencies belong to the analyst's personal experiences and personal development which provide the positive setting for his analytic work and make his work different in quality from that of any other analyst.

3 The truly objective, or the analyst's love and hate in reaction to the actual personality and behaviour of the patient based on objective observation.

These demarcations may usefully be applied to the therapist's erotic desires towards the patient. The main task of the therapist in these circumstances is to be able to have erotic desires objectively. That is to say, the therapist should feel but contain them. It is this containing function in the desired parent that the child needs to be able to internalize. Feelings, especially prohibitive incestuous feelings, can be experienced; they do not have to be acted upon or repressed, neither of which is in the interest of the child's healthy development.

Discussion of erotic countertransference raises the spectre of sexually abusing the patient. Freud (1915a) had been aware of this misuse of the analyst's subjectivity and cautioned against the analyst becoming seduced by the transference. He writes:

> This experimental adoption of tender feelings for the patient is by no means without danger. One cannot keep such complete control of oneself as not one day suddenly to go further than was intended. In my opinion, therefore, it is not permissible to disavow the indifference one has developed by keeping the countertransference in check.

But it seems to me that this is the problem. The analyst's unanalysed desires are where the dangers lie. If the analyst loses control of them they have not been analysed. I would understand the sexual abuse of the patient to be an exploitation of the transference. However, one effect of this fear of the abusing analyst is to lead to an almost complete stifling of discussion about the erotic subjectivity. I would suspect that its occurrence is more widespread than is openly acknowledged: the effect of a taboo is not to stop it from happening, only to stop it from being talked about.

A perusal of the literature highlights some of the difficulties analysts face in trying to deal with their erotic subjectivity. Loewald (1988) describes an account with a schizophrenic woman who had a long-standing sexual relationship with her father. At one point during a session the transference suddenly became concrete: she beckoned Loewald over saying, 'Come over'. At this point there was no difference for her between her father and her analyst. The psychotic spell was broken with a chance interruption by a drug salesman opening the consulting room door. Loewald then describes how, having chased the man away, both the patient and he laughed with relief. Unfortunately Loewald does not give us the reasons why he personally felt relief; we can only imagine that the patient's proposition felt both frightening and exciting and therefore posed a tabooed temptation. His relief may therefore be understood as a defensive avoidance, he had been let off the hook of having to acknowledge and deal with his own desire.

The Jungian analyst Samuels (1985) highlights a different response. He makes the point that the absence of the erotic may mean that transformation cannot take place. The incest impulse and the incest taboo are natural to each other. If the analyst is cut off from his or her own unconscious he or she is unable to use the countertransference. Samuels gives two clinical examples. The first led to him initiating a sexually exciting embrace with a young, unmarried, female patient. He later extricated himself from this difficulty by telling her that, although he could see them both in bed together, it was never going to happen and that they had to work towards accepting this fact. His own analysis of this event led him to describe the countertransference as acting out because he had been denying sexual feelings towards the patient. His second example took the form of a fantasy. He imagined he was in an enormous desert and felt a great thirst. He told the patient this and she replied it was a desert where, during the war, her father met the man who became his lover and then her mother's lover. This led to discussion about lack of erotic feedback from her father and how this made it difficult for her to relate to men as anything other than as a seductress. Samuels' first example illustrates the opposite pitfall to that of Loewald: a strong desire may be acted out and expressed if not repressed. I agree with the conclusion of his self-analysis and can sympathize with the difficulty that his acting out engendered: his patient was required to help him with his countertransference. I do not think, however, that his second example illustrates his point: the fantasy of the desert was not an erotic reaction to the patient though it did lead to erotic material via the patient's associations.

Freud seems to have struggled with his erotic subjectivity from the beginning of his career. In his *Autobiographical Study* (1925) he gives an account of a woman patient who, as she emerged from a hypnotic state, threw her arms around him. Only the chance entrance of a servant, presaging Loewald's encounter, relieved him from painful discussion. In the long term, Freud was able to utilize this event as it led him to explore the transference rather than his own personal irresistibility. In the short term, he solved the problem by avoiding hypnotizing the patient. Another example from Freud illustrates a further difficulty. Natterson (1991) cites several literary critics of psychoanalysis who have described the contribution of Freud's fantasy life in his work with Dora (1905b). He quotes Jane Gallop's contention that Freud's interpretations to Dora were 'titillating, coy and flirtatious' and Toril Moi's (1990) contention that Freud's fellatio fantasy in Dora was more probably his than hers (Natterson 1991: 111). I suspect that the truth is more likely to be that the fellatio fantasy was both Dora's and Freud's. We might further add that if Freud had been able to recognize his own erotic subjectivity to Dora, whom he describes as in 'the first bloom of youth – a girl of intelligence and engaging looks', which I interpret as Freud saying she had engaged him and he found her attractive and desirable, this recognition might have led to greater insights. In this instance, his erotic desire for Dora was Freud's identification with Herr K in the countertransference. In his 'Postscript' to the case, Freud felt the treatment had been broken off prematurely because he had not comprehended the transference in good time – namely, he had not listened to her warning that she would leave treatment as she had left Herr K. In the transference, he was now Herr K and no longer her father. He reprimands himself saying:

> I ought to have said to her, 'it is from Herr K that you have made a transference on to me. Have you noticed anything that leads you to suspect me of evil intentions similar whether *openly or in some sublimated form* to Herr K's?' [my italics].

(Freud 1905b)

With hindsight we might now interpret this in terms of transference and countertransference. We may now wonder if Dora was indeed receiving 'some sublimated form' of sexual message indicating Freud's fellatio fantasies about her. Freud's would-be interpretation suggests that he, too, was dimly aware of this possibility. Had Freud grasped the countertransference issues as well as the transference, and in so doing recognized his own erotic desire and identification with Herr K, Dora might have seen him less as an embodied repetition of Herr K and thus might not have prematurely terminated.

In his paper, 'The schizophrenic's vulnerability to the analyst's unconscious', Searles (1958) gives the example of his work with a paranoid woman who had the frequent hallucinatory experience of being raped and impregnated in her stomach. Searles came to see that this experience of hers correlated with his own dissassociated desire to impregnate her. In one session, unusually warm with sexual undertones, she suddenly became anxious and demanded to know if he had put something into her stomach. He said, 'No', but a few nights later he dreamed he was impregnating her. Prior to this, he had been unaware of this desire towards her, though he had felt an erotic urge in response to her seductive behaviour. Searles comments that he cannot prove her impregnation experience was a reaction to his disassociated desire, but it was his impression that there was a connection. Another patient, a hebephrenic woman, had intense fear of being raped. It was only after several months' work that Searles realized his powerful urges to rape her. So powerful were these urges he had to confide them to the director of psychotherapy. He realized that the patient's responses were, in part, a reaction to disassociated states in him. This led him to realize that data in the transference suggested that her early relationship to her father was coloured by his long struggle against just such unconscious desires towards her. Both these examples suggested to Searles that the danger to the patient is not that the analyst has sexual desires, but that the desires are not consciously owned by him or her.

I would suggest a review of the work by the various analysts just discussed indicates that, no matter how experienced the analyst may be, it is the area of erotic subjectivity that most find difficult. The twin dangers are: on the one hand, to repress, deny and split off feelings thus leading to displacement or projection on to the patient; or, on the other hand, to be overwhelmed by the feelings thereby leading to acting out with the patient.

CLINICAL EXAMPLES

The following clinical examples serve to illustrate some of the issues described so far. The purpose of the examples is not to show that specific erotic fantasies are essential for treatment. Rather, I am endeavouring to demonstrate that erotic fantasies always occur in analysis and may be utilized by the therapist.

D is a woman in her early forties. She presented herself for treatment because she was feeling blocked in her career and relationships. At our first consultation, she described being unable to enjoy sex with the man she loved, but could in casual encounters. Her solution to this was to have a considerable number of affairs. During the initial meeting I was struck by her appearance which was very untidy and uncoordinated: her striking black hair seemed uncombed for several days; she had holes in her jumper and jeans and all the various colours clashed loudly. Though she appeared unattractive to me, it was clear she was attractive to other men. For my part, I felt no attraction or erotic desire and was left wondering why this was. Another part of me was critical that I should have such thoughts: my internal censor was saying, 'I shouldn't think this kind of thing about a patient and, besides which, I sound sexist.' I decided not to push the thoughts out of consciousness, but elected instead to wait and see if future developments made them clearer.

This situation continued for some months. Then, one session, I suddenly found myself thinking, 'Yes, perhaps she was attractive': I could see what other men saw in her. The following session she reported for the first time that she had had an incestuous relationship with her father. She then said she was extremely embarrassed to tell me she had sexual fantasies about her father. She could not enjoy sex with men she loved so she would fantasize it was with her father and this enabled her to orgasm. Her need to resort to these fantasies to achieve sexual satisfaction was a tremendous source of guilt. This was analysed in terms not only of her identification with her father's promiscuous behaviour, but also of erotic horror – father was hated, but desired, for the exciting feelings he generated.

My understanding of this sequence of events is as follows. In the early part of our work her eroticism and sexual desire were heavily censored because of guilt and apprehension about what I would think. For my part, I experienced her inhibition almost as desexualization. I found it hard to imagine how this unattractive woman maintained an extensive sex life. Gradually, over the course of months, I became more aware of her sexual qualities. This stimulation of acknowledged erotic desire in me was then followed by her revelations of an incestuous relationship and erotic fantasies about her father. We could say an erotic bond had suddenly emerged: my awareness of her as a sexually viable person created the situation that allowed a more free expression of the patient's sexuality and experience. At another level, my erotic desire for her can be seen as an identification with her father; but unlike her father, I never expected her to cope with my desire by transgressing appropriate sexual boundaries. We were then able openly to explore in the transference her fear that, like her father, I might not be able to keep my sexual boundaries, and so abuse her. This, in turn, led to further developments in the work: her excitement at the possibility of having father as a sexual partner and, in the transference, the excitement at the possibility of having sex with me. A little while after these disclosures, she revealed she had once sexually abused a neighbour's young child. In the transference, this took the form of wanting to excite and seduce me. My own erotic desire could now also be understood as being receptive to her wish to invite me into the horror of a tabooed, but exciting and elicit, relationship. I would suggest that being aware of my erotic desires in these sessions greatly enhanced my empathic possibilities with the patient.

A second example may illustrate how erotic desires might be a gauge of therapeutic closeness and intimacy. E was twenty when she arrived for her first consultation. She presented with a long history of incestuous abuse, from the age of eight till thirteen, by her brother. She was the third youngest of four siblings. Her family background was complicated. She was the product of an affair her married mother had with her employer. One consequence of this was that she was never totally part of the family. This was also used by her brother as a justification for his abuse, claiming she was not really his sister. At the age of eleven, she began calling herself by the name of E, an identification with an important woman friend. The whole family seems to have agreed to this new name and have called her by it ever since. The change of name was linked to the incest and provided the method for massive disassociation: it was the other little girl, not E, who was being abused. She was seeking treatment for chronic depression and alcohol abuse, and problems at work and in her relationships. At first she denied being apprehensive about seeing a man for analysis, but it soon emerged that she was terrified I would be like her brother. Her sessions were characterized by considerable acting out: she frequently missed sessions; she was mostly late for those she did attend and sometimes arrived drunk. My attitude to the latter was that it was better to see her drunk than not at all, though I told her it was better to come sober. There was something in her behaviour that was testing to see if I could take her at her worst. The beginning of a session was filled with a tense prolonged silence, which would begin to ease towards the end of the fifty minutes

Unlike the previous patient I described, E was very attractive and looked like a model. She always wore smart casual clothes and sometimes arrived wearing a mini-skirt. Despite the considerable difficulties she had in coping with her life, she always tried to dress well and 'make an effort', as she put it, for our sessions.

I had two distinct, but related, fantasies during our sessions. The first was that our sessions were like the ancient Greek minotaur myth. That is to say, trying to find a way through her elaborate defence was like trying to find a way through a labyrinth. I felt that the little girl, who had changed her name to become another person who was not abused, was hiding somewhere in the darkness. Here was a disassociation between a true and false self to a massive degree. And somewhere was the psychic minotaur – which for her was her own aggressive and sexual feelings that terrified her. I had the impression that I was like Theseus trying to rescue the innocent human sacrifice. We might say this represented the benevolent therapeutic aspect of my subjectivity. The reverse was also true. The minotaur was, of course, symbolic of my own would-be identifications with her aggressor.

The second fantasy I would have was more openly erotic. I imagined us both on holiday in Greece – where I normally take my holidays. I was swimming in the Mediterranean. E would be on the rocks, reluctant to get into the water. I would be encouraging her to swim. My associations during self-analysis revealed how much I felt her life to be 'on the rocks'. I wanted to encourage her into the sea, the therapeutic setting, thereby simultaneously symbolizing both psychological coitus and rebirth. I understood this latter fantasy as the opposite of the minotaur: here was the desire for a non-abusing experience.

Both fantasies were sensitive to the fundamental schizoid split in E's personality. The therapy was like hide-and-seek: lost and found only to be lost and found again. In this respect, both fantasies were an accurate barometer of how close or hidden E was at any one time; sometimes she would want to be found and during these occasions I felt I was more likely to have the sea fantasy. At other times her defences were higher than usual. It was then she tried to remain hidden and I would think of the labyrinth myth. As such, these fantasies may be understood as an empathic understanding of her longing for closeness along with her but fear of the abuse that emotional proximity might entail. The erotic fantasies in particular alerted me to her terrible fear, but also to her pleasure during incestuous encounters, and the subsequent guilt she experienced at enjoying aspects of sex with her brother. In addition, by recognizing my own erotic interest, I could analyse it in terms of identifications with her brother which prevented my unconscious acting out, including needlessly mistaking and projecting my desire as hers. As I have discussed in several previous publications (Mann 1989b, 1995; Mann et al. 1990), this latter is of especial importance when working with incest survivors; the therapist needs to be clear about boundaries, and this begins with knowing what belongs to him or her and what belongs to the patient.

It is hoped that the above illustrations give some indication of the therapeutic value in recognizing erotic desires and fantasies in the therapist. Erotic fantasies in themselves are neither benign nor malignant – as Freud said, 'no one can be slain in *absentia or in effigie*'. In the analytic setting, what tips the balance one way or the other is how open these desires are for analysis. I suggest that erotic fantasies that are suppressed or ignored, because they are thought incompatible to a personal or to a professional attitude, are more likely to become malignant and lead the analyst into a countertransference that disturbs and hinders the patient's development. Erotic fantasies and desires, like any other feelings the therapist may experience, can be used in the service of the analysis if they can first be analysed. It follows that erotic desire forms a natural part of the therapist's 'ordinary' feelings towards the patient. As such they may be of extreme importance at some moments or stages in the therapy, and relatively unimportant at other times when different feelings and fantasies are dominant. The intensity with which they impress themselves on the therapist is the most useful indication of their importance at any one time.

In my opinion, erotic fantasies should not be shared with the patient. The analyst must deal with these either in self-analysis, supervision or discussion with colleagues. It seems to me, that to expect the patient to deal with the analyst's erotic subjectivity is analogous to expecting the child to deal with his or her parent's incestuous feelings. The burden of dealing with erotic desires must fall on the therapist, as it does on the parent. It is through the ability to contain and not act out incestuous desires that the beloved parent helps the child to introject and identify with the successful experience of the forbidden, without it being acted on or repudiated and repressed.

The erotic implies transgression into the sacred and the profane, into the secret, into the closest possible intimate contact. The erotic, therefore, takes us from where we feel safe and secure and places us full square into what is uncomfortable and exciting. It is the area of the unknown where innovation can come into being – links can be loosened or forged. In this way it takes analytic work away from the predictable exchange of associations and interpretations. In the uncertainty, new possibilities, new ideas are given birth. Out of erotic desire, two people have intercourse and something new is created. This is as much a model of psychic development as it is of biological conception. A recognition of the therapist's erotic desires contributes to the creative intercourse that is the analytic setting. The ability to experience erotic desires that are objective – that is to say, do not impinge upon others – is an indication of healthy ego functioning and development, and mature awareness of differentiation between the self and others.

4

VARIETIES OF EROTIC COUNTERTRANSFERENCE

This chapter will focus on the therapist's responses to the erotic transference. I will first describe current psychoanalytic views about the countertransference and then explore how this particularly relates to the erotic countertransference. The model developed will relate to the therapist–parent response to the stage appropriateness of the patient–infant. Parenthood and psychotherapy are both activities which generate ambivalence. This will be explored in depth with clinical material relating to four varieties of erotic countertransference: the erotic pre-Oedipal mother, the erotic Oedipal mother, the erotic pre-Oedipal father and the erotic Oedipal father.

THE COUNTERTRANSFERENCE

For many decades psychoanalysis tended to regard any erotic feeling in the therapist as an indication of a neurotic blockage in him or her that needed further personal analysis. As I showed in Chapter 2, this view has been changing in more recent years. However, even with more radical writers who have seen the inevitability and usefulness of the erotic countertransference, there is a tendency to view it as the patient's creation: the therapist feels something because the patient put it there or pulled it out using the primitive mechanism of projective identification (e.g. Gorkin 1985; Wrye and Welles 1994).

Strikingly, though there have been major advances in the psychoanalytic understanding of countertransference overall, the application of this general understanding to the universal nature of the erotic countertransference has moved at a slower pace.

Before discussing the erotic countertransference in further detail the current psychoanalytic understanding of countertransference in general needs to be considered.

Contemporary psychoanalysis has, for the most part, moved away from the idea of the therapist as an objective blank screen, or even from the belief that what the therapist feels is entirely the patient's creation – as Heimann (1950) in her revolutionary paper suggested. These days, there is general acceptance that the analyst's countertransference can be a crucial source of information about the patient, for example, Abend (1989), Maroda (1991), Searles (1959), and many others. Some writers go further than this and see the countertransference as, not just a source of information, but as an important part of the working through in the mutual analytical transformational process, for example, Symington (1983), Carpy (1989). I am very much in agreement with this latter view.

In an excellent summary of the literature on countertransference, Gabbard (1995) notes that, broadly speaking, there is a growing recognition in all quarters that the analyst is 'sucked in' to the patient's world through an ongoing series of enactments that dislodge the analyst from the traditional position of objective blank screen. Bion (1962) describes how the analyst will feel coerced by the patient into playing a role in the patient's fantasy life. Joseph (1989) talks of how patients 'nudge' the analyst to act in a manner corresponding to the patient's projection. Gabbard (1995) highlights that for such a mechanism as projective identification to work it requires a 'hook' in the recipient of the projection to make it stick – for example, the nature of the recipient's intrapsychic defences – and conflicts and self-object affect constellation will determine whether a projection has a 'good fit'. This applies even if the therapist experiences these sensations as sweeping over him or her like an alien force. If a good fit is not present projected representations may be shaken off by the analyst. Bion (1959) and Ogden (1983) also emphasize the ability of the recipient to be enlisted by the patient's internal world.

Sandler's (1976: 76) idea of 'role responsiveness' describes a similar process:

> Very often the irrational response of the analyst, which his professional conscience leads him to see entirely as a blind spot of his own, may sometimes be usefully regarded as a compromise-formation between his own tendencies and *his reflexive acceptance of the role which the patient is forcing on him* [author's italics].

The idea of countertransference enactments that has been introduced by ego-psychologists may also prove useful to our understanding here. Countertransference enactments refer to a subtle interlocking of the transference and countertransference. Chused (1991: 629) describes enactments as 'when an attempt to actualize a transference fantasy elicits a countertransference reaction.' A panel discussion at a psychoanalytic conference (Panel 1992) noted the similarity between enactments and projective identification. Implicit in the idea of projective identification is that any analyst would respond more or less the same to a specific behaviour or material in the patient, because the analyst is seen as being a virtually empty receptacle for the patient's projections. Countertransference enactments, however, assume that the intrapsychic meaning of an interaction by different therapists could be totally different in response to the same material from the same patient. Gabbard (1995: 480) notes:

> The analysand evokes certain responses in the analyst, while the analyst's own conflicts and internal self- and object-representations determine the final shape of the countertransference response.

Such countertransference enactments are inevitable, though not all analysts agree about their usefulness. Gabbard cites Eagle (1993) who describes a transference–countertransference enactment which appeared to cure a symptom by disconfirming a core unconscious pathogenic belief. This led to symptom remission without insight. Chused (1991) emphasizes the value in the new understandings that may be produced by enactments. In that respect, Renik (1993) argues that countertransference awareness can only emerge after a countertransference enactment. He shares Boesky's (1990) view that analysis can only proceed if the analyst gets emotionally involved in ways that he or she had not intended. Analysts of the social constructivist school (e.g. Gill 1991; Hoffman 1992), emphasize that enactments are inevitably happening all the time, and the analyst must be aware that he or she is unconsciously participating in an internal script from the patient. This process cuts both ways, of course, in that the analyst's behaviour influences the patient's transference. It follows, therefore, that the intrapsychic and the interpersonal realms cannot be divided from one another. Mitchell (1988) draws attention to the idea that the therapist cannot escape 'assigned roles and configurations within the analysand's relational world'. Even if the therapist is desperately trying to stand outside the patient's world, he or she still plays a part. This is not only unavoidable, it is also desirable: without entering the patient's relational world the analytic experience cannot be maximized. The experience of the analyst is not an exact replica of the patient's intra- or interpersonal world. The analyst's own conflicts or repressed material add a new element to the recreation of the past with the present.

Gabbard (1995) draws attention to the common ground in psychoanalysis that now sees intersubjectivity as the crucial element in the analytic process. This may be best summarized by two authors. Bollas writes:

> In order to find the patient we must look for him within ourselves. This process inevitably points to the fact that there are 'two patients' within the session and therefore two complementary sources of free association.
>
> (1987: 202)

Ogden, paraphrasing Winnicott's famous dictum on the mother and baby dyad, writes:

> There is no such thing as an analysand apart from the relationship

with the analyst, and no such thing as an analyst apart from the relationship with the analysand.

(1994: 63)

In this present chapter, I wish to stress that I am of the view that the countertransference is a joint creation. This is also true of the transference. By emphasizing the analyst's material, I draw attention to countertransference positions that can be denoted as typical as a consequence of dealing with particular material from the patient. This assumes that, with individual variation, most analysts feel something broadly similar given the same material from the same patient. I would stress, though, that I see scope nevertheless for a very wide variation of responses. There are as many ways to respond as analyst–parent as there are varieties of different mothers and fathers. The point is that parents and analysts are dealing with the reconciliation of ambivalent feelings.

EROTIC COUNTERTRANSFERENCE

It is a theme of this book that therapists possess an erotic subjectivity which is neither neurotic nor solely a response to the patient, since everyone has an erotic fantasy life which, like it or not, is brought into the clinical situation and has a bearing on the therapeutic transaction. If it is neither repressed nor denied, but subjected to the rigours of analytic thought, it can be utilized to the patient's advantage. Along with Gorkin, I agree that these erotic feelings and fantasies will do less damage to the therapy and the patient if the therapist is aware of them. Better still, they can be turned into something useful. The habitual notion that erotic material represents resistance in therapy, primarily signifies resistance in the therapist to recognizing ego-alien erotic desires in the patient and in him or herself.

Let us consider for a moment the erotic countertransference as an expression of the therapist's difficulties. In as far as the erotic transference denotes a neurotic problem in the therapist, this does not in itself make the clinical work impossible. We need to make a distinction between chronic and fleeting neurotic manifestations (Racker 1968). For example, if the therapist is habitually feeling aroused with all his or her patients we should have no doubt that this is neurotic countertransference that is interfering with the work. On the other hand, if an erotic feeling or fantasy is occurring with some patients and not others, though it may well be an expression of difficulties in the therapist, it can be turned to therapeutic advantage if the therapist is able to consider questions such as: 'Why has this feeling/fantasy emerged now at this stage in the therapy with this particular patient?' Placed in such an interactional context, the therapist's difficulties can be seen as part of the combined analytic transference neurosis that affects both participants. As such it is a joint creation. If the therapist works through this, he or she may find an interpretation useful to the patient whilst also making some personal movement. If therapy has a transformational effect on one of the participants, it must inevitably have a resonating effect on the other. (This distinction between chronic and fleeting feelings applies, of course, to all countertransference feelings, sensations and fantasies and is not applicable solely to the erotic countertransference.) My assumption here is that the therapist's countertransference is indicative of the human situation; that is to say, what is going on inside the therapist is what happens to people generally. The erotic countertransference is, therefore, a mixture of original material from the therapist's own erotic subjectivity in interaction (initiating and responding) with that of the patient. Some of this will be a result of the patient's projective identification. The rest of the therapist's erotic experiences is a mixture – as in most people – of healthy and neurotic sexual material, conscious and unconscious.

By and large, most of the therapist's erotic experiences are not usefully understood as a hindrance to the clinical work. There are clearly innumerable ways in which to structure how we understand the erotic in the patient and the therapist.

Racker (1968) takes the position, correct in my view, that all adults, including analysts, are still children and neurotics underneath the surface. With this in mind, he describes countertransference predispositions as neurotic vestiges of the analyst's Oedipus complex. Thus, female patients are partially reacted to as the analyst's Oedipal mother and male patients as the Oedipal father. However, Racker emphasizes the aggressive countertransference and does not especially focus on the erotic. He is also inclined to explore the countertransference from an Oedipal, and not a pre-Oedipal, perspective. In that regard, I would say that the female patient may also be seen as a pre-Oedipal mother, and similarly a male patient as a pre-Oedipal father.

Searles (1959), whose work stands almost alone in the library of psychoanalysis, relates the erotic countertransference to the renunciation of incestuous longings. He argues that the presence of erotic feelings in the analyst is auspicious. The patient's self-esteem is increased by knowing that he or she is desirable in the eyes of the analyst. This relates to the need the daughter has to be attractive in her father's eyes in order to have confidence in her womanliness. Searles advocates disclosure of sexual countertransference; some other therapists, particularly Maroda (1991), agree with him. I do not, as I fail to see how it can be anything other than seductive and bruising – in effect, saying to the patient, 'I might like you but you can't have me'.

Gorkin (1985) explores the erotic countertransference (he prefers the term 'sexualized' to 'erotic') as a response to particular character types met in analysis. He lists four types: the erotized transference, the female hysteric, the female masochist, and the male and female phallic characters. Each type of patient will elicit a different type of erotic countertransference in the therapist. When the therapist feels sexually interested as a response to the erotized transference, this can be seen as activating his or her omnipotent and grandiose wish to be the all good, symbiotic mother. Mutual sexual fantasies are in the service of creating a mutual Garden of Eden, 'a symbiotic oneness'.

With the female hysteric, the erotic countertransference is different. The hysteric tries to avoid the emergence of sexual feelings towards the analyst while simultaneously creating an atmosphere replete with romanticism and sentimentality. The countertransference is, typically, that the analyst becomes timid of, and avoids, the sexualized response. The analyst evades his fantasies as the patient evades hers. An additional danger is that the therapist may then become the seductive possessor of psychological knowledge. The hysteric experiences the process of making *known* her sexual fantasies in precisely the biblical sense: revealing material is in itself an act of sexual intimacy. The best guide for the therapist is to be aware of sexual feelings towards the patient which diminishes the danger of acting them out.

The female masochist includes those patients whose sexual feelings towards others take on a character of punishment and injury to the self. Frequently, these women have had incestuous experiences where sexual excitement was mingled with punishment. Punishment and wounding are therefore entwined in the sexual experience. Typically, the countertransference is aggressive and sadistic.

The last of the character types Gorkin outlines are the phallic characters. In men, this manifests as pronounced, swaggering assertion of their masculinity; in women it is an exaggerated form of assertiveness infused with aggression, alongside a corresponding disparaging of their feminine traits. These patients wish to be seen as highly potent and will frequently engage in 'phallic jousting' with the analyst, attempting to demonstrate that the analyst is not potent and enviable after all. The countertransference is that, in some measure, the analyst will experience him or herself as castrated: robbed of potency and effectiveness. The danger is that the analyst will either fight back or become submissive. Gorkin notes that analysts who, by disposition or intellectual persuasion, have gravitated towards Kernberg's (1975) recommendations for treatment of narcissistic personalities tend to err on the side of taking up the joust with phallic characters; on the other hand, analysts disposed to Kohut's views (1971, 1977) are more apt to err on the side of submission. In Gorkin's opinion, the analyst needs to be aware of, and work through, the induced sense of being robbed of his or her effectiveness.

An additional feature of working with phallic characters is that, with women patients, the analyst may have the fantasy of being the passive partner, the one who is possessed. The male patients may fly into *Don Juanism* to defend themselves against homosexual longings and may try to arouse the analyst; under the guise of a 'macho' sharing of sexual prowess are feelings of mutually exciting homosexual sharing.

Gorkin's categories are extremely useful in thinking about the erotic countertransference, and what he describes can frequently be seen in clinical practice with these character types. The only difficulty I have with this is that he sees the therapist as merely passively responding to what the patient brings. The therapist has feelings or fantasies put in or plucked out of him or herself. In this model, the therapist is merely a container and what emerges in the countertransference is entirely of the patient's making.

Classical object relations theory has tended to focus on the nurturing side of the mother while ignoring the erotic aspects. Wrye and Welles (1994: 34) take up this neglect. They emphasize the sensual bonding or 'body loveprinting' between mother and baby. This forms the basis of all eroticism. These two authors locate the origins of erotic experience in the contacts dealing with body fluids: after the amniotic fluid comes milk, drool, urine, faeces, mucus, spit, tears, perspiration. The seminal and vaginal fluids of adult erotic play are a symbolic extension of the earliest sensual fluids. The mother's ministrations of these fluids create a sensual adhesion to the relationship. The maternal erotic transference and erotic countertransference recreate the sensual erotic contact between mother and infant; the maternal erotic transference is a positive and necessary transforming phenomenon in psychoanalytic treatments.

Wrye and Welles distinguish four related narratives:

1 Birth of desire: body-based aspects of the self. Infants seek sensory stimulation. These early interactions enter analysis in a wordless form, pregnant silences, primitive emotional relating.

2 Anal eroticism: permutations of desire. This includes fantasies of anal containment or expulsion, anal spoiling or valuation and cloacal birth. In analysis this can be represented as making something special for the mummy–analyst; sometimes it is experienced as a core belief that the patient is not worth anything.

3 The sensual matrix in the formation of object relations. This is the patient's attempt to rework a primitive fractured narrative into an integrated view of the mother–analyst as a living whole object. The therapist is often dreamed of as a container and reflects the child's development of integrating parts into a whole, especially loving and hating sides of the mother. In the transference, this appears as fractured imagery – separate parts of the therapist's body or rapid fire themes which become a blur.

4 The solidification of gender identity through erotic experience. This oscillates between pre-Oedipal and Oedipal phenomena. In boys, closeness with the mother is fraught with loss of masculinity through merger with the pre-Oedipal mother. With girls, it includes Oedipal disappointment as she turns her attention back to her mother.

Wrye and Welles emphasize that it is crucial for the therapist to metabolize countertransference phenomena in order to enable the patient to work through the parallel transference. The pursuit of transformation returns the patient to an identification with and immersion in the early mother's body. In this search, desire is born. Here the bodily sensations are not symbolic of sexual contact – they are the contact. The relation is to the body of the analyst, but not as a differentiated 'other' body. The 'body' includes the analyst's whole room.

Wrye and Welles emphasize the importance of the maternal erotic countertransference. Mindful of the dangers with countertransference reactions, these authors make the point that patients experiencing pre-Oedipal maternal erotic transferences evoke powerful and primitive wishes and defences (including manic, depressive, obsessional, schizoid or paranoid elements) in the analyst. The problem for analysts is less one of behaving themselves than of allowing participation. Involvement in the pre-Oedipal erotic experiences is not about genital sexual intercourse; it is more diffuse, relating to fantasies about feeding, bathing, diapering, and perverse variations of these wishes. The patient longs for contact with the early mother's voluptuous body. Both participants in the analytic dyad may face the longing and terror engendered by the wish to be one person in the same skin. Unconscious erotic countertransference impoverishes or derails the analytic process. Erotic feelings fused with aggression are particularly prone to inhibit experience and expression within analysis. Wrye and Welles write, 'The greatest danger to analyst and patient alike is they may fail to recognize early eroticism' (1994: 86).

In fact, conscious erotic awareness is often unrecognized precisely because it does not present as an organized genital excitation, but is diffuse, pertaining to the whole body and carries a positive and negative valence. Wrye and Welles conclude:

> A typical response to the heat of this conflict is to douse the fire and become deadened. The task in hand, then, is to tolerate the 'heat' without fanning the flames and allow the erotic transference to unfold.
>
> (ibid.: 87)

If conscious, these feelings can be worked through and enable the patient's corresponding material to be understood. Brenman Pick (1985) and Carpy (1989) also propose that it is not possible to experience a countertransference fully without minimally enacting it in the treatment.

Before the work of Wrye and Welles, countertransference reactions to maternal erotic transferences had not been described in the literature. They propose that there are four defensive constellations used by analysts when faced with primitive erotic material.

1 Grandiose fantasies, where the analyst believes the patient will be completely reborn through treatment with a 'magical breast'. The therapist is seductive, with cooing words that soothe rather than advance treatment.

The core fantasy is that intimate physical contact or sexual union will heal the patient. Wrye and Welles do not cite the work of Gorkin. However, it is to be noted that this countertransference bears a strong similarity to Gorkin's description of the response to the erotized transference.

2 Anaclitic–depressive countertransference. A depressive response is revealed by the analyst's unwillingness to 'let go' of a patient, preferring to hold the view that the patient is needy. A patient seeking merger may regress, thereby causing the analyst to defensively introduce the father with penetrating interpretations.

3 Erotic horror and schizoid distancing. This is a distancing from the patient's material to avoid his or her consuming wish to invade the therapist's body. This may produce a 'perverse misalliance' and a reluctance to deal with erotic material. This, too, has a similarity to the countertransference to female hysterics described by Gorkin. Wrye and Welles describe a process not detailed by Gorkin with this group, namely one in which the patient may focus on minute aspects of the analyst's person in order to reassemble these bits internally. The analyst must tolerate being cut to pieces, even though both participants may feel this as an intensely destructive voyeuristic process. Another consequence of this may be that the therapist colludes by phobicly avoiding the patient's sexual impulses, especially perverse wishes. Here, too, is a description strikingly similar to Gorkin's experience with female hysterics in which the therapist also avoids naming erotic material.

4 The therapist's gender and maternal erotic countertransference. The ego ideal of most female therapists is represented more like Mother Theresa than the pop singer Madonna. As a consequence, they may be more comfortable in the role of nurturer than the sexually seductive mother. On the other hand, they feel less threatened by regression into a boundaryless state. In contrast, male therapists are more able to see themselves as objects of Oedipal sexual feelings, but may have more difficulty tolerating regression and bodily longings of the pre-Oedipal mother.

Like Gorkin, Wrye and Welles also emphasize the patient's use of projective identification to account for loving, hurtful impulses and perverse wishes (or defences against them) in the countertransference. They note, too, that erotic countertransferences can occur in relation to forms of transference that are not primarily erotic, but are contained in responses to projective identification.

Finally, these two authors declare that there are two principal ways the analyst can prevent a paralysing countertransference: first, is the ability to view him or herself as the erotically sensual pre-Oedipal mother; second, is the analyst's ability to experience, contain and make accessible the patient's potential eroticism, including perverse aspects. I am in total agreement with

Wrye and Welles on both points. I would, however, extend the development of eroticism to entail more than just the contacts dealing with body fluids, as these two authors suggest. Recent infant research, some of which is cited by Wrye and Welles, highlights the early sensual, erotic attachments between mother and baby. Stern (1985) cites numerous examples. For instance, new-born babies see things best at a distance of about ten inches, the usual distance from the mother's eyes to the eyes of the infant positioned at the breast. This ensures the infant a full array of human stimulation in parental social behaviour. MacFarlane (1975) demonstrates that three-day-old babies show a sensory preference for their mothers and select by smell the breast pads of their own mothers over those of other nursing mothers. The evidence given by Stern suggests that it is more than just transactions concerning body fluids that lubricate the erotic nursing couple. Making a note that psychoanalysis has tended to look right past the mother and baby social interaction and only see the biological functions he writes:

> The tasks of eating, getting to sleep, and general homeostasis are generally accompanied by social behaviours by the parents: rocking, touching, soothing, talking, singing, and making noises and faces. These occur in response to infant behaviours that are mainly social, such as crying, fretting, smiling, and gazing. *A great deal of social interaction goes on in the service of physiological regulation* [my italics].
>
> (1985: 43)

Later Stern adds:

> Different feelings of vitality can be expressed in a multitude of parental acts that do not qualify as 'regular' affective acts: how the mother picks up baby, folds the diapers, grooms her hair or the baby's hair, reaches for a bottle, unbuttons her blouse. The infant is immersed in these 'feelings of vitality'.
>
> (ibid.: 57)

In my view these pre-verbal interactions would also form part of the erotic dyad and may also gradually find their way into the analytic couple.

What is striking when we compare the observations of Wrye and Welles with Gorkin is the substantial overlap of material despite differences in theoretical position and understanding. Doubtless there are many contributory factors at work here. In my opinion, one of the main sources of confusion comes from the over-use of the concept of projective identification which these authors employ. The issue is one of ownership of affects, sensations and fantasies. By and large, what tends to be described as projective identification are those qualities that conflict with the ego ideals of most therapists. There might be sound professional reasons for wanting to locate sado-masochistic or perverse fantasies as being caused by or originating from the patient. Most therapists, especially in published reports, are cautious of being labelled neurotic (or worse) by colleagues if there is a hint of anything less than benign neutrality in the therapist. It seems to me, however, that because therapists possess an unconscious they will inevitably bring their own material to the clinical work. This can sometimes produce problems for the work, especially if it goes unrecognized, but it is also reassuring that therapists are human, too. It is this common humanity that makes the analytic work possible.

THE THERAPIST'S AMBIVALENCE

The context for this chapter is the parent–therapist model. Just as the child has incestuous and homicidal phantasies towards the parents, so, too, the parents have incestuous and homicidal phantasies towards the child. I have explored the paternal filicidal phantasies in an earlier article (Mann 1993a). In this chapter, I will be focusing on the erotic countertransference from the perspective of the parent towards the child. I delineate four countertransference positions: the erotic pre-Oedipal mother and the erotic Oedipal mother; the erotic pre-Oedipal father and the erotic Oedipal father. These demarcations are not limited by the gender of the therapist.

The parent's emotional state is not the creation of the child, however, the infant's stage of development will influence how the parent feels about the child. The experience of parenthood tends to activate various unconscious processes in the parent. The baby recalls (consciously and unconsciously) the parent's own experience as a child: in that sense the parent sees something of him or herself in the infant. In addition, the infant reminds the parent of his or her own experience and quality of parenting from their mother and father. For example, during a feed the baby may cry. This cry stirs a constellation of ancient memories of the mother's own mother's response to a crying baby, such as 'this crying baby is always making unbearable demands'. Depending on the quality of parenting they have themselves received, the mother and father will either wish to emulate or wish to avoid the mistakes of their own parents.

The reason why I am stressing the parental internal world as it is experienced when dealing with both the pre-Oedipal and Oedipal child is because there is a parallel process for the countertransference.

This is worth stressing, particularly in the light of recent infant research which emphasizes the reciprocal initiating and responding patterns of infant and parent interaction. For example, infants seem to prefer high-pitched sounds to low-pitched talk (cited in Chamberlain 1987). As parents and carers change their vocal pitch to a higher frequency when making 'baby talk', babies are eliciting precisely what they need. Papousek et al. (1986) studied playful interactions between two- to four-month-old babies and their parents. Most infants (91.7 per cent) engage in vocal play, and did so more often with age. The majority of these episodes (82 per cent), were initiated by the infants themselves and were characterized by audible expressions of pleasure. Rheingold (1983) identifies the infant as the 'prime mover' changing the lives of parents – teaching them how to be parents, modulating and refining their caretaking. Infants can 'tell' parents when they want to eat, sleep, play, be picked up, have their position changed. Babies amplify tenderness and compassion in most adults. I would also point out that babies may also bring out the worst in some adults. In 1994, more than 1,300 children were murdered in the USA, mostly by their parents (figures given on the *Today* programme, BBC Radio Four, 10 July 1995).

Infants are sensitive to changes in their mother's appearance. Cassel and Sander (1975) asked mothers during a single feeding on the seventh day after birth to wear a mask and remain silent. The infants were clearly disturbed by this change and drank less milk, scanned the room anxiously when put back in their cribs and had disturbed REM sleep. Chamberlain cites various experiments that have observed similar reactions when experimenters asked mothers to become silent and 'still faced' for just three minutes. He writes:

> Infants recognise this strange behaviour and in just 15 seconds begin trying to influence the situation with inquisitive looks, vocalizing or reaching out as if to elicit a normal response. Depending on their age in weeks, they use a varied repertoire to try to gain her attention but if unsuccessful they will withdraw. Even worse effects have been observed when mothers were asked to look 'depressed'. These older babies (three months of age) cried in protest, looked away, and days later still acted wary of their mother (Tronick et al. (1982); Fogel et al. (1981)). Note that language is not part of this interaction; perceptive looking provides the information which has such a profound impact.
>
> (Chamberlain 1987: 58)

What I wish to highlight, particularly from this last example, is the extent to which the infant tries to influence the mother's mood and behaviour. A baby will generate behaviour in the parent that is appropriate for the child's stage of development. When the parent does not respond in the appropriate way, the baby becomes disturbed or withdrawn. Stern concludes:

> The social presence of an infant elicits variations in adult behaviour that are best suited to the infant's innate perceptual biases; for example, infants prefer sounds of a higher pitch, such as are achieved in 'baby talk.' The result is that the adult's behaviour is maximally attended by the infant.
>
> (ibid.: 73)

Bell (1974) makes a distinction between maturity and competence. The parent is obviously more mature and capable of intentional acts, but may not be as competent as the infant at eliciting a certain level of responsiveness. Neonates have highly effective behaviours which are compelling in bringing about support and protection. Most people comment that they find an infant's cries especially difficult to ignore and, if intolerable, have to remove themselves from earshot. We may also add that such cries sometimes bring out the most malevolent response in the adults entrusted with the child's care.

If we accept the parallel process of mother and baby as a model of therapeutic transaction between analyst and analysand (and this model is integral to the Object Relations School), then it becomes clear that we cannot work with pre-Oedipal or Oedipal states in our patients without a correlated significance of identification with the parent in relation to the pre-Oedipal or Oedipal child – especially since infant research shows that babies make sure their parents experience something! That is to say, not put in or pulled out by the baby, but the parent's own material. We might say then that patients make sure their therapists feel something.

This brings me back to the erotic in therapy. The erotic implications of this for the countertransference have not produced the level of interest we might consider the subject warrants. In my own workshops on 'Working with the erotic transference and countertransference', some therapists of both sexes have reported difficulties identifying material relating to the erotic mother, especially the erotic pre-Oedipal mother. I will discuss shortly how the apprehension of the pre-Oedipal mother is that she is engulfing, and that she threatens the therapist, patient and the child with loss of a separate identity. We cautiously approach this material for fear we may be permanently sucked in. Clearly the therapist faced with erotic pre-Oedipal or erotic Oedipal material from his or her patient will experience a variety of countertransference emotional states. These emotional states, although in response to the erotic stage of the patient as it is manifest in the transference, are clearly not solely attributable to the patient's creation, though this undoubtedly plays a part. The therapist, like the parent, will also have his or her own erotic reactions to the erotic pre-Oedipal or Oedipal child–analysand.

Therapy, like parenthood, is a matter of ambivalence. This ambivalence is not pathological or out of the ordinary. It is the stuff of the human condition and interpersonal relationships. As a matter of fact, it is usually the use of primitive defences to eschew ambivalence that creates pathology. Christie and Correia (1987) identify the repression of deep ambivalent feelings as a major obstacle preventing mothers (and I would include fathers) from relating deeply and genuinely with their children. Further, the denial of hate (and I would also say the erotic) does not help the child. For full functioning entails some integration of ambivalent and erotic feelings. A number of writers (Widlocher 1978; Joseph 1978; Dreyfus 1978) have stressed the need for the analyst to be aware of feelings incompatible with the ego ideal.

In as far as parenthood for a 'good enough' parent is an ambivalent occupation, the erotic countertransference will also contain a mixture of pleasant and unpleasant, positive and negative, qualities. These reactions fall within the normal range of emotional experiences, rather like Winnicott's (1947) eighteen reasons why a mother may justifiably hate her baby. In the parent–therapist model that dominates psychoanalysis, we might extend these ideas to say these negative reactions go hand in hand with the benign feelings the therapist has, and form part of the general ambivalence he or she has towards the patient. Therefore, this therapeutic ambivalence is best considered as available for creative therapeutic usage, and not simply as perverse or pathological.

Winnicott had been concerned with hate induced in the therapist because the patient's illness has made him dislikable. I do not doubt though that all the therapist's hate cannot be attributable simply to the patient being dislikable. The therapist, like the mother, may have his or her own subjective reasons to hate no matter what the patient is like. When reading Winnicott's list of eighteen reasons why a mother hates her baby (Winnicott 1947: 201), it is an interesting exercise to substitute the word 'patient' for 'baby' and 'therapist' for 'mother'. The list then contains remarkable parallels with the analytic process. The following is a list of my own describing some of the reasons why a psychotherapist may hate the patient in the erotic transference and countertransference, even if they are paying a good fee:

- Patients pour negative projections on to and into the therapist and expect these to be absorbed without retaliation. As an aspect of the erotic transference, this may almost be likened to rape as the patient forces part of themselves into the therapist. I am reminded of the fact that 'therapist' is sometimes written as 'the rapist'. Though in the analytic setting the patient may also take this role.
- Patients activate the primitive layers of the therapist's unconscious and ignite intrapsychic conflicts and repressions in the therapist. This is particularly so regarding unresolved erotic phantasy in the therapist.
- Patients may verbally abuse, denigrate or show intense rivalry with the very people the therapist loves most: their spouses and children. In other words, those individuals to whom the therapist has an erotic attachment may be subjected to intense hatred and envy.
- Patients burden therapists with the expectation that the therapist must succeed where so many others (parents, lovers, friends, children, bosses) have failed them and let them down. The therapist is expected to be an omnipotent breast or penis, full of magical properties. At its crudest level, therefore, the therapist's own sexual organs are expected to symbolically produce a miraculous performance.
- Closely related to this last item, patients demonstrate that the therapist is not an omnipotent healer, and deal narcissistic wounds to the therapist by drawing attention to his or her limitations. Each patient thus confronts the therapist with the reality that they do not possess a magical breast, vagina or penis.

- Patients immerse the therapist in the misery of life. On a daily basis, therapists hear stories describing the worst of human behaviour, the worst of what some people are capable of inflicting on others. Listening to this relentless stream of misery continues for eight hours a day, five days a week, year in and year out.
- To a greater or lesser extent, most therapists have come to be interested in psychotherapy out of a wish to have their own wounds healed. At some level, the therapist is hoping that each patient will allow him or her an opportunity to work through some unresolved personal issue. Thus, therapists are narcissistically defeated as the patient does not allow the therapist to 'get better'.
- Other people (lovers, spouses, bosses, family) in the patient's life may get the benefit from changes in the patient; the therapist may still have to deal with the worst side of the patient's life. Ultimately, the patient drops the therapist and goes off with another man or woman, rather as the parent watches the child marry and leave home.
- The patient rekindles the therapist's unresolved pre-Oedipal and Oedipal issues, in terms of the child's intrapsychic complexes and experiences with parental (or significant other) failure. This is particularly important as the experience with the patient will touch the heart of the therapist's erotic subjectivity.
- And to paraphrase Winnicott's final reason, patients excite and frustrate the therapist – and the therapist must neither eat nor trade in sex with the patient. The patient thus comes to represent the parent of either sex that is not available for incestuous consummation.

With a 'good enough' therapist, these reasons for these erotic disappointments are kept in check by the benevolent reason (the therapist's love) that makes the difficult task of psychoanalysis a worthwhile occupation.

We may think, therefore, in terms of: the positive and negative aspects of the erotic pre-Oedipal mother; the positive and negative aspects of the erotic Oedipal mother; the positive and negative aspects of the erotic pre-Oedipal father; finally, the positive and negative aspects of the erotic Oedipal father. Each of these will have their own countertransference equivalents. In terms of the countertransference reaction, I believe it must be stressed that most of the patients seeking psychotherapy come because of problems with their personal relationships. Usually, taking a detailed history reveals that most of our patients have had something much less than good enough parenting, if not outright abuse. This will be reflected in both the transference and countertransference. As much as the therapist may wish to avoid the mistakes of the patient's parents, some acting out is inevitable. In that respect, though ultimately the therapist's good intentions must win out, the insistence on a 'benignly evenly hovering attention' may be used as a defence against recognition of the more ego-alien aspects of the countertransference response to the negative aspects of the father or mother, especially regarding the erotic and sado-masochistic aspects.

Perhaps this is the place for a word of caution: any attempt to classify or organize material will inherently be limited and unintentionally rigid; nor are clear-cut distinctions encountered in a pure state in reality. I do not wish to imply that my descriptions are the only facets of the phenomena under discussion. I hope that drawing attention to some of the qualities of the erotic opens up a way of thinking about the erotic process rather than prescribing a set list of characteristics.

THE EROTIC PRE-OEDIPAL MOTHER

Typically the pre-Oedipal mother is seen in terms of good enough nurturing qualities. This has been well discussed in analytical literature. Winnicott (1956) sees the pre-Oedipal mother as providing primary maternal preoccupation, 'ego-relatedness', which lets the mother feel herself into her infant's place allowing a process of disillusionment (1960). There is also room for negative feelings and hate (Winnicott, 1947) towards the baby, but the 'good enough' mother keeps this safely contained and the infant will remain unaware of her feelings.

Bion describes a different image of the pre-Oedipal mother: how she provides a container for the infant's distress. She detoxifies the anxieties and, in so doing, hands back to the child something of the ability to learn how to do the same; the mother in her reverie thus allows the child to develop his or her own thinking capacities. The mother's inability to take the child's projections is experienced by the child as a destructive attack by the mother.

There are two striking characteristics to these images of motherhood. The first is a considerable degree of idealization of maternity. For example, neither Winnicott nor Bion seem to allow much room for maternal failure as a consequence of unconscious intent. The second characteristic, and very much related to this issue, is the notable de-erotization of the mother. Raphael-Leff (1984) also proposes that the myth of the 'devoted, selfless, sexless, "mater delorosa"' is represented by Balint (1939) and Deutsch (1945).

For a representation of the more negative side of the erotic pre-Oedipal mother, we find her many faces in numerous myths. Wieland (1991) points out that in *The Odyssey* Homer presents images of the endless struggles of man against woman and her engulfing presence. After escaping from the Cyclops, Odysseus encounters woman in all her phantasied power. In Antiphates' wife, he encounters the man-eater woman. In Circe, he encounters the seductress who enjoys trapping and humiliating men. In the Sirens and Scylla and Charybdis, he faces engulfing feminine forces. Calypso is a more benevolent, gentle goddess, but nevertheless one who would keep him from regaining his kingdom. Wieland notes that 'It is remarkable that all the forces of regression in Odysseus' travels are represented by women or female forces which he will have to defeat, overcome or outwit' (1991: 136). We find similar representation in other figures such as Medusa. Medusa had begun her career as one of three beautiful sisters. One night she lay with Poseidon in a temple dedicated to Athena. Athena was so enraged that, as a punishment, she turned Medusa into a monster with serpent hair whose gaze turned men into stone. Thus Medusa's monstrous appearance is directly linked to female sexual appetite and the desire to transgress holy boundaries. Interestingly for our purposes here, she was slain by Perseus, who was having difficulties of his own with his pre-Oedipal mother, Danae, fighting off her suitors – his erotic rivals for his mother. Only after killing Medusa was he then able to fall in love with the helpless Andromeda as she lay naked, chained to a rock to be sacrificed by her parents.

We might add one more example to the list of erotic pre-Oedipal mothers: the biblical Eve, the prototypical seductress.

These pre-Oedipal mothers are united by their self-interest, the needs of the other are subsumed by their own primitive desires. What is engulfed is the separate identity and autonomy of another. The engulfing feminine is that part of the mother which cannot experience the baby's mind as separate. The capacity for empathy (primary maternal preoccupation) becomes 'non-good enough' mothering when the mother, for her own reasons, incorporates the infant's mind as an extension of her own. The other's needs are not identified or are ignored. The baby is then inappropriately erotized. Not simply the formula, baby equals penis, but baby equals any erogenous zone or erotized part of the mother's body, such as the hair.

The mother's erotized engulfment will not be identical for the boy and the girl. In all probability, the boundary lines will be more blurred with the daughter, who is perceived as similar to herself from the start. With a boy, the difference – represented by his penis – may to be denied or disavowed. I have discussed this in considerable detail in a previous article on castration desire (Mann 1994a).

Recent research on the erotic pre-Oedipal mother has revealed interesting observations. Most mothers seem to agree that breast feeding, while being a nurturing activity, is also an erotic experience. Olivier (1980) cites a number of studies that show mothers make a distinction (probably unconscious) between baby boys and girls. Belotti (1976) showed that girls are for the most part weaned earlier than boys. Brunet and Lezine (1965) found that mothers stop giving the breast to girls, on average, in the twelfth month, and to boys in the fifteenth; the feed is longer for boys – at two months, forty-five minutes against twenty-five minutes for girls. Olivier considers these findings demonstrate that mothers do more for boys than girls. Such research is open to numerous interpretations. I suggest that the erotic experience of the baby boy at the breast is more acceptable because of its heterosexual nature. With the daughter, there must inevitably be a stirring of homoerotic desire and its ensuing defences against the experience. However, whatever the explanation, the erotic nature of the pre-Oedipal mother is well illustrated by these observations.

Analysts from different orientations have observed that infants at the breast like to interrupt a feed and play with the breast and explore their mother's face and clothing. I would add that this suggests the feed to be as much about erotic, sensual contact as it is a nurturing feed. Ainsworth and Bell (1970) found a correlation between attachment behaviour of one-year-old children placed in an unfamiliar situation and the extent to which they had been permitted to be active partners in the feeding situation. The mother's conception of the relationship with the baby as a partnership affects the development of both attachment and exploration. Indeed, Hamilton considers the infant's most primitive notion of permanence arises in the context of the mother's almost constant physical presence and holding (which includes mirroring, echoing and imitating) which increase the familiar patterns of communication. She concludes:

> The idea of a primary affectional bond and of an intense, loving relationship between mother and infant was (in the 1930s), and still is today, novel to the *psychoanalytic* theory of early infancy [author's italics].
>
> (1982: 91)

We find the clinical equivalents in mothers who do not allow their children much autonomy. We also see it in what Stern (1985) calls 'misattunements'. The following vignette is a case in point.

Ms F was in her late thirties. She suffered from a progressively deteriorating physical disease which, when I saw her, was not posing too many constraints on her mobility, though she carried a walking stick. She had gynaecological problems that made sex painful, which she insisted was not psychological. Her presenting problem was depression related to her hair, which was curly. This was distressing to her as she longed for straight hair because she believed this was more attractive. A few years earlier she had gone to a hairdresser to have her hair straightened. This was not successful and, at the time, had caused considerable hair loss. Although, to my eyes, she appeared to have a normal amount of hair, she was still obsessive about it falling out and how this affected her looks. Her worry was that curly hair made her unattractive; her fantasy was that if she had straight hair men would be more interested in her. I related this to her doubts about being sexually viable, being lovable. She then revealed her deep desire – which was to have somebody with whom she could wash her hair. She went on to describe the trust involved in letting somebody run their fingers through her hair, and the experience of her hair with water running through it. It further transpired that her mother was also obsessive about her own hair, and for forty years had had her hair washed twice a week only by a hairdresser. She had deliberately passed on some of this hair anxiety by buying Ms F a wig when she was thirteen.

Ms F knew her parents' sexual relationship was unsatisfactory. Her mother, on the pretext of not liking her husband's snoring, had slept in a separate room for twenty years. Father had told Ms F that he now made 'special arrangements' for his sexual interest, which Ms F understood to mean either affairs or prostitutes. Mother was experienced as not at all understanding. For example, when Ms F phoned to tell her mother about breaking up with a boy-friend, the mother took his side and saw it from his point of view, not her daughter's. An early memory at four-years-old was on similar lines. She remembered seeing her mother lying on the floor and being hit by her father for causing her mother to faint.

Soon after Ms F and I started working together she began a short unsuccessful affair with a man whose first name was the same as mine – David. At first, I understood this as an Oedipal erotic transference being enacted outside the sessions – what she wanted was a sexual relationship with me.

I began to change this view as it gradually dawned on me that maternal issues were dominant. I sometimes find it useful to day-dream silently about a patient's material, especially his or her use of metaphors or dream images. Day-dreaming in this way often throws up surprising and uncensored imagery. I then reflect analytically on my own unconscious associations. Even if the day-dream has produced material I recognize as typically my own, I find it can be useful to wonder why it has come up in this particular context, with this particular patient at this particular moment. That is to say, I refer to the notion that countertransference is nearly always interactional.

My conscious thinking about Ms F began to change when I began to day-dream about her hair-washing fantasy and asked myself, would I like to wash her hair? I instantly thought 'No!' I then took the day dream further and wondered if I would like her to wash my hair and surprised myself by answering in the affirmative. The fantasy of washing hair was sensuously sexual for her, and she had already related her anxiety that her curly hair reduced her sex appeal. However, she had also linked this fantasy to her mother's phobia with hair washing, thereby establishing her sexual preoccupations with identification to her mother. As I thought about this, I reflected on our experience during sessions, which seemed mutually frustrating. Specifically was the difficulty in trying to mirror Ms F's experience. The following exchange was typical. Ms F was talking about compliance and the need to be liked:

Ms F My sister told me I was really naughty at fourteen and fifteen. I don't remember that or what it was about. Mum apparently told me off rather than trying to understand.

DM   In your attempts to be liked, it is striking that you can't recall a period when you were more rebellious.

Ms F   I can recall, I've not forgotten staying away from school.

What I wish to draw out from this example is that, when I tried to use some information that Ms F had given, attempting to make some sense out of it, Ms F would then deny having said it in the first place or would insist that she had meant something different. This kind of interaction would go on four or five times a session over a number of weeks. It confused and clearly frustrated us both: I felt I could not understand her, she felt misunderstood. I came to believe that what I was experiencing was maternal misattunement: no meeting of minds or empathy, but two minds going off at a tangent. My fantasy of not wanting to wash her hair but wishing her to wash mine summarized the erotic misattunement: I wanted her hair/head/mind on my terms, but not on hers. Having understood the hair washing as representing the sensual–erotic meeting of minds with the mother, I was then better able to interpret back to Ms F the misattunement during the therapeutic process. In other words, erotic Oedipal material to the father disguised the issues around the erotic pre-Oedipal mother. Her hair-washing fantasy was symbolic of intimacy in both sexual intercourse and the therapeutic process. Wondering about this fantasy and identifying with her mother by thinking about my hair being washed made explicit the underlying erotic misattunement of mother.

THE EROTIC OEDIPAL MOTHER

In many respects, the Oedipal mother shares characteristics with the pre-Oedipal mother. In the 'good enough' manifestation, the erotic Oedipal mother reflects and validates her son's sexual viability (Searles, 1959) in such a way as the father does with his daughter. With her daughter she represents the fecund model of what is desirable to men (the father); she is the representation of voluptuousness and the enjoyment of sensuous and erotic contact in her own right.

What distinguishes the pre-Oedipal from the Oedipal is triangulation and the advent of rivalry between all three participants. In myth, this is best represented by the mother of Oedipus, Jocasta. Another figure is Medea who destroys her husband, Jason of the Argonauts, when he takes another wife. Threatened by her rival, Medea then destroys her own children and the rival, and hides her children's bodies so Jason cannot mourn them properly. Other images of the negative erotic Oedipal mother include such displacement figures as witches and step-mothers in fairy tales. This is illustrated, for example, by the Queen in *Snow White* who has a magic mirror and asks of it: 'Mirror, mirror on the wall, who is the fairest of them all?' So long as the mirror says it is the Queen herself she is narcissistically gratified. When the mirror replies 'Snow White', the Queen is enraged. She will tolerate no sexual rivals: no one can be more desirable than she is, and Snow White is no longer safe.

It is not that the erotic Oedipal mother, like the pre-Oedipal equivalent, knows no boundaries, it is more that, for either conscious or unconscious reasons, the boundaries are ignored. Jocasta ignores the characteristics of the man who has defeated the sphinx to win her hand in marriage. Knowing the prophesy that the child she bore will kill his father and marry her, nevertheless, she ignores the fact that he is the age her son would be, he bears a family likeness, and his very name draws attention to the place where her son had been wounded – 'Oedipus' means 'swollen foot', because his feet had been spiked as a baby. All this is ignored or denied, possibly consciously, at least in the Sophocles version of the myth in which Jocasta knows the truth and tries to dissuade Oedipus from finding it all out for himself:

> Nor need this mother-marrying frighten you;
> Many a man has drempt as much. Such things
> Must be forgotten, if life is to be endured.
> (Sophocles King Oedipus)

How conscious is Jocasta? Sophocles implies that Oedipus is little more than an incestuous toy-boy for his mother's desire.

Naiman (1992) has made the interesting point that there is a distinct difference between the Jocasta portrayed by Sophocles and that portrayed by Freud. Freud (1900, 1928) makes no reference to Jocasta's desire: the Oedipal rivalry is conducted by the males for the woman, rather like mediaeval knights jousting for a maiden – the woman's preference for one man or the other is not considered. The Jocasta of myth, however, is active. She rapes her husband when he is drunk and, unlike Oedipus, she realizes early on that there is a familial connection in the second marriage. Jocasta knows the oracle's prophesy and that if Laius has children he will be killed by one of them. From that perspective, raping Laius is intimately connected to his murder and her preference for her offspring rather than her husband. Of course, we seldom encounter the overt behaviour of myth in the clinical situation, but we do encounter its ordinary, everyday manifestation. This aspect of the Oedipal mother, which I would specifically call the erotic Oedipal mother, has, as Naiman notes, seldom been described in the analytic literature. The erotic Oedipal mother favours her children over her husband, whom she is willing to sacrifice for the exclusive relationship with her offspring.

We may also emphasize that the erotic Oedipal mother is competing with her husband for the son. The daughter is experienced as a rival for her husband. When love mollifies the hate, the Oedipal mother will allow her husband a more-or-less fruitful and benign erotic relationship with his children. The mother relinquishes some of her hold over her son to allow his negative

Oedipal wishes to identify with his father. In this sense, the boy must make his escape from his mother. This is a less problematic manoeuvre if the mother is prepared to relinquish him to her rival, the father. With the daughter, the mother must be able to concede that her daughter will also be an object of erotic desire for her husband. Some writers take the view that the girl's sexual identity is forged in her relationship with the mother (e.g. Chodorow 1978; Eichenbaum and Orbach 1982); other writers see the father as the key protagonist in the development of the girl's sexual identity (e.g. Olivier 1980; Wieland 1991). It is not my intention in this chapter to investigate the origins of sexuality and gender formation. I have explored the significance of the father in the psyche on a number of other occasions (Mann 1989b, 1993a, 1993b); the role of the mother is discussed in Mann (1994a). I suspect that in practice it is not an 'either/or', but a 'both/and'. I take the view that both parents are important and are represented in the child's mind by the primal scene.

It is important to mention that there is a correspondence between what I describe as the qualities of the erotic Oedipal mother, and what Gorkin describes as the countertransference with female hysterics and Wrye and Welles describe as erotic horror and schizoid distancing. The essential ingredient is a reluctance to experience the erotic presence of self and other.

The erotic Oedipal mother will have a countertransferential equivalent.

Ms G is in her late thirties. She is single and an only child and has lived all her life with her mother. She loved animals and felt her pet dog was like the child she never had. Mother was very clinging and had been attending a psychiatric out-patient clinic for many years. Ms G reported that it was difficult to leave mother alone; in recent years, on the pretext of noisy traffic, mother had moved her bed into the quieter bedroom of Ms G, which they now shared. From the descriptions I heard, Ms G's mother seemed to be extremely destructive to her daughter's confidence and made any moves towards independence almost impossible. For example, mother would scream at her that she wished her daughter had never been born and that she had wasted forty years slaving for her. Any reply Ms G made, such as, 'I didn't ask to be born', was countered by mother saying, 'That's a terrible thing to say'. Through it all, Ms G always found justifications for staying with her mother (for example, that she could not afford the rent of another house). It was clear they formed a mutually co-dependent couple. In fact, my impression was that they were like a quarrelling married couple who could not do without each other. In that respect, Ms G was given something of the role of fulfilling a husband replacement to her mother: her father had been dead for a number of years. Mother had come to idealize the marriage and complained to her daughter that she would have preferred his company to hers. Ms G recalls that the marriage had not been good, with much arguing and shouting, Ms G always taking her mother's side against her father.

Ms G had never had a sexual relationship. Her only boy-friend had been in her teens and he had been keen that she should move into his house. Mother had made a point of driving him away and breaking up the relationship. In the face of such maternal disapproval, Ms G had not attempted to find any further boy-friends. Mother was clearly jealous of any men that might find Ms G attractive. Early on, while I was seeing her, she had a visit at home from an official from the DHSS. He had asked her out for a meal, but she had seen the need to consider his invitation was not serious and turned him down.

For my own part, I was not aware of having had a single thought about her sexual identity for many months. The absence of any such thoughts was brought to my attention quite suddenly during one session. Ms G reported that, before she had left home, her mother had mockingly said, 'So you are off to see your young man?', and had ridiculed her daughter about not tidying up her appearance before she came to see me. Ms G added that her main concern was to not let mother see that her jibes were getting to her. What had surprised me, however, was that, as Ms G was relating her mother's comments about coming to see her young man (sic!), she did so with a twinkle in her eye and I realized she was flirting with me. This had well and truly taken me by surprise. As she left at the end of the session she again talked about going home to her mother's ridicule about 'her young man'. I spontaneously made a rather fatuous comment about it being nice to be considered young, and knew as I said it that this was neither an interpretation nor reciprocal flirting, but something falling miserably between the two. However, this transaction was extremely illuminating and important.

As I reflected about the session, I came to realize I had been seeing Ms G as asexual, a sort of doll with no signs of sexuality, nor a woman's desires. If not that, my impression had been to see her as a poor castrated husband-substitute for mother: they shared the same bedroom and argued like mother and father had done. They were like an old married couple. I realized that the failure to see any erotic potential in Ms G had itself been a countertransference reaction. Like mother, I had not allowed the image of Ms G as a viable sexual individual to fully emerge. Mother had not only seen off all potential suitors as rivals, she had also attempted to stop Ms G from being a full woman. Thus, rather like the Queen in *Snow White*, she could not tolerate another woman competing with her. In some stories the young woman is allowed her charms, but locked away where they will not be seen (for example, *Cinderella*, or in the story of Perseus' mother who was locked away in a tower). Ms G's mother had gone further and had attempted to demolish any of her daughter's knowledge of her own sexual self, as well as keeping her from the eyes of suitors. Ms G did not want anything that would interfere with her relationship to her mother. She avoided rivalry with mother as the only significant person in her life. This was a failure of working through the Oedipus complex with both parents, especially the mother who would not allow father a chance to participate. Not seeing the repressed sexual side of Ms G was thus an embodiment of the mother in the counter-transference, as I, too, was denying her sexuality.

I was then able to bring this self-analysis into the therapy. This led us to discuss her psychosomatic symptom of her stomach swelling when she was under stress. I interpreted this as representing her desire to be pregnant, have children and a partner. She initially strongly denied this but then reported feeling dizzy. I replied my comment had sent her into a whirl and had opened the way for a more conscious acknowledgement of her sexual desires.

Typically, characteristics of the erotic Oedipal mother are found in inces-tuous families. I have worked with a number of mothers whose children were sexually abused by the husband. These mothers expressed surprise at the daughters' revelations when the incest was exposed and brought to the legal courts, all strongly asserting they had had no knowledge of the incest occur-ring. Amongst the issues going on for these mothers was an inability to see their children's sexual identity, which did not exist for them in a real way.

THE EROTIC PRE-OEDIPAL FATHER

To speak of the erotic pre-Oedipal father is virtually a linguistic contradic-tion in terms. How can a triangular (Oedipal) relationship exist when using terms like 'pre-Oedipal' means a pre-triangular period? I think we may begin to think about this in terms of the infant engaging in two or more dyadic pairs: not a triangular configuration of infant and mother and father, but infant and mother, or infant and father, or infant and grand-mother, etc. – a kind of serial monogamy. Wrye and Welles (1994) note that the pre-Oedipal father may be either a loud, overpowering intruder in the mother–baby closeness, or a reassuring other during separation–indi-viduation. Burlingham (1973) and Machtlinger (1984) see the pre-Oedipal father's role in promoting gender identity in the period preceding the Oedipal phase proper. Wieland (1991) considers this is especially the case for the little girl. Tyson (1982) notes the pre-Oedipal father enables the boy to develop a core masculine identity that can then withstand the rivalry with the father during the positive Oedipal phase.

The pre-Oedipal father helps to diffuse the intensity of the erotic bond with mother, but in so doing also introduces a further erotic relationship into the baby's life which the child must negotiate.

Recent infant research gives some interesting food for thought. Fathers can be as equally attuned as mothers. Chamberlain cites research on motor synchrony involving anticipation captured by photographing a new-born and his father. He writes:

Slow motion reveals that as the father's head began to move *down* to look at the baby, the baby's head began to look *up*. Also when the father's *right* hand began to move *up*, the baby's *left* hand moved *up*, so the two hands met and the baby grasped his father's finger! These moves involved the eyes, motor system and anticipation of the correct movement needed to bring them together in space from opposite directions. . . . It boggles the mind as to how synchrony of this sort can exist.

(1987: 41)

But the pre-Oedipal father is also different to the mother. Gerrard (1992) cites Benjamin (1988) who describes research showing that fathers play with their infants differently from mothers:

They are more stimulating, less soothing – offering more arousal in early interaction – jiggling and bouncing. Benjamin says 'the father's novelty and complexity, as opposed to mother's smoother, more contained play, has been characterized as an aggressive mode of behaviour that fosters differentiation and individuation' (p. 102). Fathers tend to offer more exciting play, and so from the beginning they represent what is outside and different. Mothers are more likely to soothe, nurse, *contain and hold* their infants. Benjamin goes on to state 'perhaps parents will ultimately integrate the aspects of holding and excitement. At present, however, the division between the exciting, outside father and the holding, inside mother is still embedded in the culture' (p. 17).

The erotic pre-Oedipal father embodies several aspects best illustrated by mythology. In emphasizing the erotic over other characteristics of the pre-Oedipal father I would draw attention to the father's phantasy of the infant as his creation. This clearly runs as a parallel experience to the mother's phantasy of the baby as her creation, which finds ultimate expression in the virgin-birth stories. There are comparable myths for the father. Principal amongst them are myths of male parthenogenic birth. The two best known examples are probably that of Zeus giving birth to Athene – who sprang fully armed from his head – and to her half-brother Dionysus. He was carried by his mother for six months until she died after seeing Zeus in his full godly aspect. Zeus then took the child and stitched him into his own thigh and carried him for the remaining period of gestation. In the biblical tradition, it is God (always considered male) who makes the first man from clay without a woman's aid, going on to make the first woman in a dual parthenogenic creation: a male god making new life from a male rib. There are other variations on this theme: Pygmalion, a mortal, by-passed the limits of male generative power by sculpting his ideal woman in clay, which then came to life. In Norse mythology the creator is a giant called Ymir. Out of his left armpit emerge the first man and woman while he is asleep. When Ymir is slain, his decapitated body is used to make the earth, sea and sky. There is a comparable myth from the aboriginal Australia, in which the first men grew from the armpit of an earth father called Karora as he thought of his wishes and desires.

The erotic pre-Oedipal father can be seen, therefore, as centred around a phantasy of the omnipotent penis, all powerful, magic and life creating, needing nothing but itself to create a new life.

Clearly infants enjoy some sort of relationship with their father. However, in the clinical setting, it can be extremely difficult to identify material relating to the pre-Oedipal father. Locating the pre-Oedipal father in the transference–countertransference matrix is further compounded by child-rearing practices where fathers are, indeed, frequently absent in the child's pre-Oedipal years (and often much later). An additional difficulty is that often the patient reconstructs the pre-Oedipal father from memories derived from the Oedipal stage. Further, in actual practice the pre-Oedipal father usually blends smoothly into the Oedipal father (as the pre-Oedipal mother usually blends seamlessly into the Oedipal mother), thus making a distinction in parenting, and in clinical practice, extremely difficult.

There is a similarity of description here between the erotic pre-Oedipal father and the 'grandiose fantasies' and 'erotized transference' described by Wrye and Welles and Gorkin respectively. The essential feature is the fantasy of magical intercourse that will dissolve the problem and bring the ultimate transformation. The phallus represents both the curative penis–wand and the feeding breast with its sustaining semen–milk.

The following vignette illustrates something of these issues in the therapeutic transaction.

H was fifteen when she was encouraged to see a therapist by her mother and GP. The presenting problem in the initial referral was that she was feeling sad and panicky at the same time, and had been treated with anti-depressants during the past year. Her doctor had found it difficult to elicit exactly how she was feeling and it was hoped psychotherapy might be useful.

Our first session was rather a shock and mutually difficult. It was at the height of a very hot summer ('the drought of '95') and the fashion amongst some teenagers was to wear very low-cut, tightly-fitted, scanty tops revealing a large part of the midriff; this would be worn with extremely short mini-skirts. H, a very attractive and physically well-developed adolescent, arrived for her session wearing just such an attire. While she was undoubtedly dressed as many fashion-conscious teenagers were at the time, I had never encountered any patient coming to psychotherapy so scantily dressed. The way she sat on her chair did not leave much of her anatomy to my imagination: she looked lovely. My sexual interest was further aroused by her opening words that she was feeling depressed because she was bothered about being a virgin; she did not want to be a virgin any more and she hoped I could help her with her depression. She left it rather vague as to what way she thought I might be of help to her. She was not sure how she would feel different if she had sex, but said that losing her virginity was a milestone she was desperate to cross. The erotic atmosphere felt intense. As she spoke, she would frequently lapse into silence, break eye-contact and then give me what I considered rather coy, longing looks. I found my own sexual imagination running riot during our first meeting. I thought, 'If it is just one sexual experience that can put everything right for her, I can provide that!' I imagined us coupling on the floor between our chairs with me initiating her to the pleasure of sexual intercourse. H reported several times that complete strangers would just stop her on the street and ask her out. She felt irresistible. I did not see her as an innocent virgin (even if she was), but as an experienced Siren who knew how to press the arousal buttons in men and lead them into danger. Although she was seductive, I am not locating the arousal as simply her stimulus: we must all take responsibility for our desires and this particular desire was my own. I considered the option of referring her on, but was reluctant to do so until I was clearer about my countertransference reaction. I was also aware from the history I had gathered that she had had a succession of nine boy-friends (mostly eighteen- and nineteen-year-old boys) over the last year, and had been rejected by everyone of them: I was reluctant to be yet another male who could not cope with her and wanted to get rid of her.

After this first session I was sufficiently concerned about the intensity of my own sexual reaction to seek immediate advice. I promptly spoke to two female colleagues, saying I was at a loss to know how to work with this seductive fifteen-year-old virgin. I was also hoping that in 'confessing' (because that was how it felt – desiring sex with a girl who knew herself to be under-age) my erotic interest to other people, they might hold me to a boundary if I felt myself slipping.

Speaking to my two colleagues was immensely helpful. This was partly because they had some good ideas. Mostly though, it enabled me to reflect on my own processes. I realized that, in seeking female advice, I was attempting to triangulate my relationship with the patient; that is to say, I was seeking to bring in the mother. I realized at that point just how much both parents need the other to defuse the intensity of the primitive feeling generated by incestuous desire: parents need each other to help deal with the Oedipal scenario. In other words, the pre-Oedipal issues felt so intense, I unconsciously acted out my anxiety by making them amenable to Oedipal triangulation. The intensity of her relationship with the pre-Oedipal father (blurring into the Oedipal father) came to light after a few sessions when she told me that her father had been accompanying her to and from our sessions. I thought this indicated both a male rivalry (Oedipal issues) and also a reluctance to let her engage in a relationship with another – in other words, to experience a triangulated relationship (pre-Oedipal issues).

I understand our first meeting as me falling hook, line and sinker into her fantasy of magical intercourse. She believed that one act of sex would solve all her problems, take away all the sadness and depression, and raise her self-esteem. It would show her that she was desirable and that boys and men did want her. I, too, had the fantasy that that was all it would take, and imagined myself as the older male initiating her into sexual womanhood. I would be the omnipotent lover, or analyst, taking all her difficulties away and bring her total joy. In this description there is something of what Racker (1968: 134) calls concordant identification: the 'recognition of what belongs to another as one's own ("this part of you is I") and on the equation of what is one's own with what belongs to another ("this part of me is you")'. Racker is inclined to squeeze all material into an Oedipal scenario. In my experience, the emergence of concordant material relates to issues of fusion and merging and is therefore better understood as relevant to pre-Oedipal sources.

As I thought about the implications of my erotic arousal with this patient, the excitement almost totally disappeared. In our subsequent sessions, she was always dressed the same, but my reaction was very different, almost the reverse. I became aware that this young woman (I can hardly think of her as a girl), so desperate for sex, was in fact all but impenetrable. I realized I knew little of her fantasy life; her childhood was difficult to explore as she just insisted it had been good. I was able to elicit she had bouts of anorexia. My experience with anorexic patients is that they treat therapy like food and will starve themselves rather than let any of the nutrition or goodness enter, be it food or its symbolic equivalent with analytic interpretations. I realized that some of my initial reaction of helplessness was also due to feeling powerless, impotent, unable to get through to her. This virgin was something of an iron maiden. My experience of her was then confirmed when she related an attempt at sexual intercourse with her current boy-friend. The tip of his penis had entered her but she found the experience too painful and, after several failed attempts, he eventually lost his erection; for her part, she was not sure if it was the penetration or his jeans rubbing her legs which hurt. After a few months' work, H said she felt only a bit better. However, outside the therapy, things did seem to improve. She had a new boy-friend and this relationship was lasting more than just two weeks. Eventually, she was able to lose her virginity with him, but was surprised this did not relieve her depression. After this, we were able to do more effective work. I am not entirely sure that, in helping an under-age girl lose her virginity, therapy is being efficacious. However, having sex with her boy-friend certainly dispelled her fantasy of the 'curative penis'. Psychologically, this also made her more open to therapeutic input. Some months after this, one of the colleagues that I consulted earlier reminded me that she had said that if H and I were able to work together successfully, H would be able to have a more stable relationship outside therapy. I do believe this was the case.

What I wish to highlight from this example is the nature of the erotic pre-Oedipal father: the omnipotent fantasy of the child as his creation which is his property to treat as he pleases. The fantasy of the magical curative penis is sometimes found in both promiscuous men and women. The 'magical fuck', as one of my patients called it, is the elusive search for the intercourse that will transform all the pain into ecstasy, separation will dissolve into union of bodies and minds.

THE EROTIC OEDIPAL FATHER

The pre-Oedipal mother and Oedipal father are the parental positions most discussed within analytic literature. The erotic component has long since been recognized with regard to the Oedipal father, unlike with the pre-Oedipal mother. Within psychoanalysis the Oedipal father is most often discussed in terms of either his role as a dangerous authority figure to whom one must surrender, such as described by Freud (1921), or as the embodiment of 'The Law' as proposed by Lacan. His other frequently-discussed aspect is as an incestuous abuser. In his more benign aspect, he is seen as the third party who helps the infant separate from the mother (Abelin 1975) and brings the child into the wider social world (Loewald 1951). This function has also been emphasized by Chasseguet-Smirgel (1981) and Benjamin (1988). In a previous article (Mann 1993b), I discussed the absent father in psychosis and the ensuing defensive need to create a fantasy figure of the father to make reparation for the supposed patricidal murder. Some writers, for example, Wieland (1991) and Samuels (1985), give him a key place in the development of sexual identity.

The father as an incestuous abuser is not only preferring his children to his wife, but is also sometimes representing the grandiose phallus that penetrates everything, reducing all before him to a similar status.

While, clearly, the father will have other qualities than those of persecutor, it is striking that mythology does portray a preponderance of figures of the destructive type. There are some positive father–child relationships – for example, Odysseus and his son Telemachus in *The Odyssey* – but it does seem that fathers are represented more in their negative aspect, especially in relationship to the son. Clearly, fathers possess other qualities. In a previous article (Mann 1993a), I proposed that one of the qualities of the 'good enough' father is that he contains his destructive potential and allows his son and daughter certain victories (excluding taking his life or usurping his place in the marriage bed), thereby allowing the child a more realistic idea of his capabilities and ensuring that he does not appear phantastically omnipotent. Allowing his offspring to have some victories also enables the child to develop a sense of him or herself as a winning agent, rather than just as a loser in the Oedipal contest.

However, even with the good enough father qualities must take account of the aggressive and rapacious side of masculinity. The prototypical Oedipal father is Oedipus' father Laius who begins his claim to notoriety by raping his host's son while on a visit. He is often credited as being the first pederast on record. It is important to note that it was not the homosexual nature of this act which was reviled at that time, but that it was done without the boy's consent. The boy's father then lays the famous curse on Laius that he will be killed by his own son who will then marry his mother. To defy his fate, Laius abstained from further sexual encounters. As I noted in the section on the erotic Oedipal mother, his wife Jocasta rapes him when he is drunk. Neither parent wished to be directly culpable of infanticide, hence the reluctance to kill the boy outright. Differing accounts attribute the abandoning of their child on the hillside as the work of Laius, or of Jocasta, or both. Piercing the child's feet so that he could not crawl away appears to have been Laius' idea. Later, on encountering a lone stranger (Oedipus) at a crossroads, Laius sends the overwhelming might of all his bodyguard to kill the traveller who, astonishingly, defeats them all and takes Laius' life in revenge. What is clear from the myth is the selfish brutality of Laius, who will attempt to enforce all to bend to his will. He tolerates no rivals and will use all the power at his disposal to gain advantage.

Because the erotic Oedipal father has been fairly well described and understood, I see the purpose of this section as being one of describing a particularly extreme form of a common clinical situation. I found myself describing this patient to a colleague in the following terms: 'You know that Greek lad who killed his father and married his mother? Well, he's registered at the GP practice I work in and I saw him last week!'

Mr I had been referred for short-term, time-limited psychotherapy to deal with his depression and apathy. He was in his thirties. He told me that he had lost his interest in life. He had been a 'keep-fit fanatic' going every day to the gym, but now he could not be bothered to go. For many years, he had also been into martial arts, at which he was an expert. Towards the end of our work, he revealed quite a violent history and a fear that his uncontrollable rage might result in his killing someone. When feeling violent he would always look to fight the biggest people he could find; in most cases he won the fight.

He described what appeared to be a ritualized and rather obsessional collection of routines in his life. He had had a few girl-friends, mostly unsatisfactory as he was drawn to 'the wrong sort of girl'. Invariably his girl-friends were already married. His last girl-friend had been married and the daughter of his boss, with whom he got into conflict about the relationship. He lived with his mother and had always done so. He declared there was no precipitating cause to his change of mood that had begun some months earlier. In response to my questioning about what was going on in his life at the time, it emerged that his depression had begun shortly after his mother's surprise party for her birthday. He had a really good relationship with her and she looked after him: 'She has always been there for me. She's an angel.' My comment that his mother's birthday had left him depressed because he was worried that she would not always be there for him, and that he was depressed about the prospect of her getting old and dying, proved to be accurate in describing the precipitating event. What I wish to highlight is that his whole life revolved around his mother. They did everything together like husband and wife, holidaying and socializing – everything, that is, except sexual intercourse. At a later point in the therapy, he himself suggested they were like a married couple. He was concerned that he would go mad and become a down-and-out after she died.

Of his more distant history, he described a number of significant events. He had been born with a congenital illness. At four and a half, he entered hospital for an operation after which he was told he would only lead a 65 per cent normal life. He had got into physical health fitness to prove the doctors wrong and was proud he had done so. He recalled mother's constant presence, and father's total absence, while in hospital: 'He was a drinker and away having affairs while I could have been dying in hospital.' Mr I was very angry with his father. He hated his father and could not sit in the same room as him. He recalled a row during his adolescence resulting in violence because father wanted him to join his old regiment in the army; Mr I wanted to go where the action was with the marines. When his parents divorced, Mr I took his mother's side and shunned his father. A few days after the decree, father returned to the family home with a shot gun to kill mother and son; on other occasions, father tried to run mother and son over with his car. Father's life deteriorated into chronic alcoholism which eventually brought him to the brink of death. The hospital thought a liver transplant would be worthwhile, and Mr I was found to be the only suitable donor. When asked if he would donate part of his liver, Mr I declined, saying, 'Father would only go straight back on the booze and be back in hospital in six months.' With that decision there was no hope left for his father, who died a few days after this. Mr I felt glad he had died and squandered his inheritance in a few weeks.

I want to limit the discussion of this material to what is relevant to this chapter. In his psychical constellation, Mr I had killed his father when he had not acted to save his life, thereby putting a death sentence on him. This parricidal Oedipal triumph led to the Oedipal reward, an exclusive relationship with his mother in which they were both happy for him to usurp his father's place. By his own admission, he had married his mother.

My countertransference was focused around my dislike for Mr I. Although I found him interesting, he was not readily likable. I hardly ever dislike my patients, but Mr I was an exception. With his history of violence and mistreatment of women, I thought of him as a 'nasty piece of work'. I was immediately wary lest my dislike should influence my work with him, so I monitored my own feelings quite carefully. As I did so, I became aware that my own reaction to him was more complicated and richer than I first thought. I found myself thinking contemptuously and disparagingly about the physique of this man of violence, who took pride in his physical prowess and fitness. For example, despite his attention to his body, he looked neither especially strong nor attractive. Early on, he had initiated shaking hands at the end of our sessions and I had been struck by how feeble his handshake was. I imagined I could crush his hand in mine. My fantasy was clearly omnipotent: Mr I was much taller and stronger and had been trained to a high level in martial arts. Yet, despite his 'real' advantages, I imagined I could force him to his knees and humiliate him.

Because this therapy was time-limited to twelve weeks, a number of issues were barely explored. One of these was the fear of his latent homosexual feelings. Mr I described how, at the gym, he and his friend would goad each other to lift heavier and heavier weights, saying such things as, 'Have you become a limp-wristed poof or something? Why can't you move that?' Being strong and stereotypically masculine was a defence against recognizing any homosexual thoughts. As he described this, I found my own fantasies take the form of sadistically sexually humiliating him in the very ways he was most fearful of.

My understanding of this transference–countertransference matrix is as follows. Mr I had a history of a murderous relationship with his father: father had paid no attention to him while he was seriously ill at four and a half; they had fought for male superiority in his teens; father had lost the rivalrous competition and had attempted to shoot mother and son and run his car into them; later Mr I condemned his father to death by withholding a donor-organ transplant. His Oedipal rivalry continued with father surrogates: picking fights with bigger men or getting involved with married women (like his mother) thereby trying to triumph over married men (like his father). In that sense, my own hostility to Mr I can be understood as my identification with his father. The negative side of the erotic Oedipal father is completely to dominate or even to destroy the son who is experienced as a competitor, which found expression in my sadistic fantasies of wanting to sexually humiliate him. One of the positive aspects of the erotic Oedipal father is that he usually does not use all his advantages to crush his son (Mann 1993a).

Therapeutically my work with this man had been reasonably successful, given the short period of analytic intervention. He reported the lifting of his depression and had begun discussing with his mother his fears about her eventual death, a previously unthinkable subject. I think that the therapeutic work we had achieved was made possible entirely by my being conscious from the very beginning of the analysis of my sadistic fantasies towards this patient. This kept my fantasies in check and stopped them from unconsciously influencing the work in a destructive manner. Such a process has been noted by Searles (1958), who describes the damaging effects on the patient who is sensitive to the therapist's unconscious processes. Accepting such negative thoughts about Mr I, which clearly derived from a countertransference position of the negative erotic Oedipal father, was ultimately the most that could be done in this short therapy to allow it to be helpful.

CONCLUDING REMARKS

It has been suggested in this chapter that the therapist can expect a range of positive and negative erotic feelings as a consequence of working with pre-Oedipal and Oedipal material in the patient. Working with the model of the patient–therapist transference–countertransference matrix as a parallel process to the infant–parent dyad, the parent and therapist alike will experience a range of erotic responses in the presence of the relevant stage of infant. I have outlined some of the characteristics of the erotic pre-Oedipal mother, the erotic Oedipal mother, the erotic pre-Oedipal father and the erotic Oedipal father. These ingredients found in the parent will find a corresponding countertransference equivalent in the analytic setting. If the therapist can become aware of these unconscious erotic attitudes, the clinical work is enriched and allows the patient to begin to work through the same material. The analytic couple become increasingly genuine and whole as unconscious ego-alien erotic material is incorporated into a conscious ambivalence that is the hallmark of mature relationships, in which the sadistic exists but is tempered by the love.

5

THE HOMOEROTIC
TRANSFERENCE–COUNTER
TRANSFERENCE MATRIX

The homoerotic transference–countertransference matrix seems to pose particular difficulties within the broad range of erotic transactions in analysis. Freud (1937), Glover (1955) and Greenson (1967) have stated that, in the analysis of males by male analysts, a major source of resistances are the passive homoerotic wishes towards the analyst. Lester (1985) also emphasizes that passive homoerotic wishes by the female patient directed at the female analyst become an equally important cause of resistance. I would also stress that the countertransference equivalent is a frequent form of counter-resistance in the analysis.

If the erotic transference in general is considered a major obstacle and difficulty in the analytic work, the homoerotic seems to push the buttons to a whole lot of alarm bells seemingly unique to itself. The reason seems self-evident: for some psychoanalysts the status of homosexuality is that of a perversion. To me, such an understanding does seem to place morality in front of clinical understanding. Limentani stated the difficulty very succinctly when he wrote:

> The development of psychotherapeutic measures enabling us to deal
> with the many kinds of homosexuality that we encounter in the course
> of our clinical work has been slow, and marred by influences derived
> from moral, social, and even religious prejudice.
>
> (1994: 50)

Freud was very liberal minded regarding homosexuality, which he specifically said was not a perversion. However, for decades, many of his followers could write about homosexuality only in what is little more than a homophobic manner (e.g. Socarides 1979). I am of the opinion that this is a countertransference reaction that tells us more about the analyst than the patient.

An example from my own practice may serve as a useful illustration here. I had just begun working with a young homosexual man, an artist whom I found interesting and with whom I had developed a good therapeutic alliance. He had been attending for just a few weeks when, on arrival for his session, he smiled and commented on my appearance as I opened the door, saying,

101

'You're very blue today', referring to my jacket and tie. Then, as usual, we walked silently to my consulting room and the session began. I instantly found myself thinking of caressing my wife's breasts, a very pleasing thought. I had the image of her body and my hand clearly in my mind's eye. After a while I realized I had been thinking about this for some minutes at the expense of being able to focus on what this patient was saying. I attempted to concentrate on the session. The fantasy of my wife's breasts then became more intense: the more I tried to banish it from my mind the more insistent it became. By now, a full five minutes had passed and I could not recall a word my patient had spoken. Only at that point did I consider I might be having a countertransference problem and I began to wonder what it was about. I tried to focus on my reaction to the material. It was then that I realized I had obviously experienced my patient's appreciative words about my appearance as, rightly or wrongly, a sign of homosexual interest; to this I had defended myself with a quite compulsive heterosexual fantasy, specifically what he could not provide – breasts. Only after seeing my own resistance to the homoerotic was I then able to begin to listen to what the patient said.

My aim in this chapter is quite specific: I do not intend to explore the aetiology of homoerotic desire, nor am I focusing on technique when working with homosexuals. My view is in line with Limentani's points that psychotherapy may be an effective intervention with: (1) 'latent heterosexuals' (Limentani 1977) who agree to use analysis to achieve changes in their orientation; (2) bisexuals whose uncertain sexual aims lead them into personal difficulties in work and creativity; (3) overt homosexuals seeking therapy for their depression whilst insisting nothing should be done to alter sexual orientation. I am also in agreement with Isay (1986) that the analyst's role with a homosexual patient is to help resolve the neurotic conflicts that prevent the establishing of stable, loving relationships. Isay cites Friedman (1988), who shows that research indicates there is not significantly more psychological disturbance in the homosexual community than in heterosexuals. This is a particularly surprising finding given that cultural persecution often intensifies existing personal tendencies towards low self-esteem, depression or paranoia. I also prefer the term 'homoerotic' to that of 'homosexual'. The former relates merely to a kind of erotic desire and does not imply a compulsion to express itself in action. I use the term 'homosexual' to refer to overt homosexual activity. Having stated this, I will proceed with my main concerns in this chapter.

My interest here is to explore some of the issues of homoerotic desire as it relates to the transference–countertransference matrix. At issue is the proposal that therapists need to be able to utilize heteroerotic and homoerotic identifications in the child's relationship with both parents; related to this are the heteroerotic and homoerotic desires of both parents towards the child. The homoerotic desire will clearly have relevance to both the transference and the countertransference.

According to Freud (1905c), we are all born polymorphous perverse, meaning without a sexual aim: the individual is born with both heterosexual and homosexual desire in addition to incestuous desire. With the internalization of taboo and the formation of the superego most of us renounce both incestuous and homosexual goals. Freud wrote:

> psychoanalytic research is most decidedly opposed to any attempt at separating off homosexuals from the rest of mankind as a group of a special character. . . . all human beings are capable of making a homosexual object choice and have in fact made one in their unconscious.
>
> (1905c: 145)

From a clinical point of view, we might imagine that the existence of homoerotic desire as an expression of pre-Oedipal polymorphous perversity, and as an aspect of the Oedipal scenario (the negative Oedipal), have both an important and frequent expression within the therapeutic transaction of transference and countertransference. Any extended therapy will eventually reveal the presence of homoerotic impulses, either conscious or unconscious. For the most part, these relate to latent homoerotic desire rather than to overt homosexual behaviour. Indeed, the complete absence of homoerotic material is usually an indication that important psychic material has not been covered by the analysis. Bibring (1936) makes the point that of all the 'real' attributes of the analyst which have an effect on the patient, gender must be the most important. I agree and would also add that, of all the 'real' qualities of the patient, gender must be the most important to the analyst. The implication here is that the sex of the other in the analytic dyad has a direct impact on the erotic unconscious of both participants and finds a resonance in the polymorphous perversity of pre-Oedipal and negative Oedipal issues. Thus, the heterosexual or homosexual character of the dyad is an issue from the beginning of the analysis.

LITERATURE

Though little has been written about the erotic transference and countertransference, most of what there is has been written by men. Women writers have entered the debate much later. However, when men have discussed the subject, it is nearly always in a mixed-sex analytic dyad, usually female patient with a male therapist (e.g. Freud 1915a; Samuels 1985; Bolognini 1994). I do not make myself an exception here: Chapter 3 of this book was originally published as a journal article, written in 1992 and published in 1994 (Mann 1994a), and contains the same heterosexual emphasis. Usually male writers do not discuss the homoerotic countertransference. For example, Bollas (1992) writes a sensitive chapter on *Cruising in the homosexual arena*. He makes no reference at all to the therapist's reaction if the patient is a homosexual addicted to casual relationships. Given the status of homosexuality, it is difficult to imagine a therapist having no affects at all with such a patient. Occasionally the homoerotic countertransference is discussed in passing – for example, Gorkin (1985) in his discussion of work with phallic character men (see Chapter 4). Women writers, on the other hand, though they have written about the erotic less than their male colleagues, have made the homoerotic a much more integrated part of their discussion (see below). At the very least this would suggest that women are more comfortable with the homoerotic transference–countertransference; by the same token, male therapists feel particularly threatened by homoerotic desire and are more cautious about publishing their explorations. This probably accords with the legal status of homosexuality, which for so long was a crime between men; homosexual acts between women have not been subject to the same punitive legislature. From that point of view, homoerotic desire has been the focus of much prohibition, which not surprisingly contributes as a silencing force in analytic investigation and honesty. I am not sure that homosexual therapists have an advantage here. Cunningham (1991) talks about the homosexual therapist's need to resolve his or her hatred and envy of the opposite sex in order to be capable of a depressive concern for the internal parental couple. It has been my casual observation, and I freely admit I do not know how generally it applies, that homosexuals have as much if not more anxiety at their heteroerotic desires than do heterosexuals at their homoerotic ones.

Most heterosexual therapists are probably more comfortable dealing with a heterosexual erotic transference than a homoerotic transference. The crux of the distinction is to be found in the countertransference. The homoerotic transference stirs and reactivates the therapist's homoerotic desires, which in turn leads the therapist to feel more threatened both interpsychically and intrapsychically.

As noted, the literature on the homoerotic transference–countertransference matrix has mostly been considered by women writers. As far as the female analyst with the female patient dyad is concerned, Lester (1985) suggests a strong erotized transference to the phallic mother is possible because of the circumstances of female development. The long pre-Oedipal attachment of the girl to the mother may induce a regressive stance in analysis, which activates infantile omnipotence in the female patient without threatening gender identity. This leads to a particularly tenacious erotized transference in this dyad leading to erotic phallic fantasies with a strong loving and murderous content. She describes a female patient who, at various times, perceived her, the therapist, as having a penis or totally nurturing breasts, and a fusional fantasy was underscored by her insistence on calling the therapist 'my lady'. The fantasy of 'the lady' became a transitional experience, a space between fusion with mother and separateness from the therapist. Lester regards the intensity of the erotic (homosexual) wish existing concomitantly with regression and almost psychotic distortion in the transference. It is of interest to note that Lester gives hardly any countertransference information regarding what it was like to have such a patient in therapy.

Person (1985: 165) takes the view that, if a heterosexual woman with a woman therapist develops an erotic transference, 'the manifest, predominant Oedipal role 'assigned' the woman analyst is usually that of the rival mother not the erotic object. . . . the predominant erotic feelings are more often directed onto a real or fantasized male figure outside the analysis'. Within the analysis, the erotic is not explicitly sexual but is expressive of affection, tenderness and the wish for intimacy. They are explicitly homosexual transferences only as manifestations of a negative Oedipal complex or erotized components of pre-Oedipal material. Now, as I indicated in Chapter 1, other women writers (Maroda 1991; Wrye and Welles 1994) have not confirmed the absence of erotic transference among women patients. Also, as Wrye and Welles and I indicated in Chapter 3, the pre-Oedipal period is highly erotic. Person notes that homosexual women may develop intense erotic transferences, but she does not develop her discussion of the significance of this.

Regarding the male patient–male therapist dyad, Person considers that this erotic transference is also muted, both with heterosexual and homosexual patients, and if sexual thought occurs it is ego-alien. If the erotic transference is too strong it leads to 'massive anxiety and well known homosexual panic' (1985: 173). The paucity of homosexual erotic transference confirms the male resistance to the experience of the erotic transference. It is interesting to note that, while Person gives clinical examples to illustrate both the heterosexual analytic dyads (male patient–female therapist, female patient–male therapist), she gives no examples at all for either of the homosexual dyads. There could be, I am sure, many reasons for such an omission, one of them possibly being another indication of fear of the homoerotic in analytic discussion.

In Person's view, erotic manifestations are greater in heterosexual dyads, while rivalrous constituents are more prominent in same sex dyads. This seems confirmed by Limentani who notes that, with overt homosexuals there are strong resistances against acknowledging the degree of hatred and hostility hidden behind activities which are claimed to be simply erotic. However, hostility and murderousness can be analysed comparatively safely in latent cases.

Limentani cites a number of transference and countertransference implications when working with homosexuals. He considers that many of the anxieties felt by the therapist are often a derivative of the patient's anxieties which are not yet fully conscious, often issues about power, aggression and sado-masochism. However:

In many cases it will be difficult to pinpoint the transference with any degree of precision, because the patient will use projective identification means to get rid of his masculinity or intolerable femininity. Shifts in the transference appear in rapid succession when the analyst is asked to fulfil a male or female role, according to the patient's whims. This is of course a reproduction of those very common exchanges occurring in male and lesbian couples acting within direct sexual context when flexibility and turn taking is a prevalent feature of the relationship.

(1994: 57–8)

I agree with Limentani's description of the shifts in the transference as difficult to detect, but I disagree that it is always the consequence of projective identification, as it seems to me that the therapist will enter the therapeutic transaction with his or her own anxieties about this material.

The issue of homoerotic desire emerging in a heterosexual analytic dyad is a problematic subject. While it is not difficult to imagine a male therapist experienced as a mother, or a female therapist experienced as a father, sifting the homoerotic components from an erotic transference is no easy matter. Karme (1979) wonders whether a negative Oedipal transference by a male patient with a female analyst is possible. She considers that the fear of the phallic in the transference blocks the development of passive homosexual urges towards the analyst. Lester makes the point that Karme leaves unclear the distinction between pre-genital maternal transferences and phallic mother, and negative Oedipal transferences. I think that accurately summarizes the situation. Nevertheless, however much we may be able to make a theoretical consideration of this issue, in clinical practice such a distinction is inordinately difficult.

I wish now to make a consideration of the positive function of the homoerotic in psychic development. In the last chapter I dealt at length on erotic pre-Oedipal issues. I will now broaden our focus.

In the usual course of development, identifications with the same sex parent play an important function. For Freud, the negative Oedipus complex meant the boy identifies with the mother and passively desires the father. In *The Ego and the Id* (1923), Freud draws attention to the structuring effects of the Oedipus complex on bisexuality. Psychic homosexuality is at the heart of Oedipal structuring. Classically, the homoerotic was seen as a defensive flight from castration anxiety assumed in heterosexuality. Blos (1985) amongst others has criticized this idea. Ross (1982) highlights the importance in boys of an early identification with the generative father, which still contains a residual homosexual wish. Benjamin (1988: 106) finds the prototype of ideal love in the boy's rapprochement love for his father, 'the homoerotic love affair with the father, who *represents* the world' (author's italics).

Bokanowski (1995: 793) highlights that for many analysts psychic homosexuality is an essential reference point in men, especially regarding the structuring role of passive homosexuality towards the father. He goes on to suggest that psychic homosexuality is 'most usefully considered not as a singular entity but as a set of plural entities'.

Hopcke (1988: 67–68) describes what he considers as the 'positive functions homosexual relations serve in society, for example, the educative function of homosexual relationships between older and younger men or the fostering of a true exchange of intimacies between "high spirited, intellectual" women'. This view draws much from Plato, though, as in ancient Greece, such relationships are susceptible to exploitation. It is worth noting that societies which culturally sanction homosexual activity do so with the expressed view of the older generation helping the younger generation to develop their masculinity. This attitude was propounded in ancient Greece. Stoller (1985) describes a cross-cultural study he undertook with a tribe from New Guinea. This tribe lives in a particularly harsh environment where a fierce masculinity in men is necessary for survival. However, the route to this survival is through institutionalized homoeroticism for all boys from childhood until marriage. As part of their initiation rituals young boys between seven to ten years of age are required to learn the secret of maleness: to drink as much semen as possible. These boy must perform fellatio as much as possible with postpubertal boys precisely to acquire the masculine strength ascribed to semen. As he gets older the boy then becomes the person who is sucked. The practice stops when the older boy marries. It is not acceptable for a bachelor to fellate other males. Stoller reports that neither youths nor men express any impulses to such penises. Interestingly, heterosexuality is the only accepted behaviour. Homosexuality is negatively sanctioned and a man who insistently indulges would risk being called a 'rubbish man' (ibid.: 109). Typically, the men of this tribe desire women for the rest of their lives without ever forgetting the homoerotic joys of their youth, and this is despite superstitions about the debilitating effects of vaginal fluids on a man and the fact that white juices of certain plants are frequently drunk to replace the semen lost during sexual intercourse. Stoller highlights that, although an aggressive heterosexuality is indeed necessary for this tribe's physical survival in hostile conditions, the homoerotic has a valued place in their society to help the younger generation develop its masculine identity. Stoller's research suggests that a strong sense of masculinity is not undermined, or even necessarily made problematic, by either homoerotic desire or even overt homosexual experience.

We may deduce from current thinking and research that the homoerotic serves positive functions in the personality generally. If this is true of psychic development, it follows that we might expect to find similar positive functions of the homoerotic in the analytic situation. I will describe two vignettes, the first of which was with a practising homosexual.

CLINICAL VIGNETTES

J was in his early thirties when he first came to see me. He reported having considered himself a homosexual ever since boarding school. He had two long-term relationships, the first of which he described as the love of his life but which he broke up for no apparent reason other than fearing it might come to an end some day. Currently, he was living with his partner of nine years' standing. His lover, a successful business man, was quite a bit older. J took on the cooking and cleaning role in the couple, which he greatly enjoyed. He felt they were mutually dependent on each other. He had previously had periods of promiscuity, but this finished when he decided to commit himself to his current relationship. He had come to analysis for his depression and his chronic underachievement, intellectually and creatively. He declared that he did not wish to have his homosexuality analysed, but he did want to work on his depression which had begun seven years earlier. I pointed out that we might at some stage want to look at why he foreclosed such a major area of his life. He actually related this to a frequent habit of blocks descending on his mind. Many months later, he spoke of an image that summed up his life: he is in a high-walled garden, full of undergrowth and with no visible gate or door leading in or out. This wall spoke of many things, including rigidly segmenting areas of his life from each other.

He had been born and brought up in an ex-British colony. He described relationships with his mother as good but that he was a clingy child. Father was busy at work most of the time and was reported by J as being an absent, shadowy figure in his early years. This was a striking admission, as I always had a much clearer picture of father than of mother from his descriptions. There were two strong memories associated with mother from his childhood. The first was being asked by her if he wanted to go into town with the family. J said no, but changed his mind at the last moment and came running out of the house to find his mother driving off and not noticing him running behind the car. The other memory concerned his first day at nursery school. His mother had shown him how to use the zipper-fly on his short trousers when he went to the toilet. This he duly did until he was embarrassed to realize that the other boys did not bother with the zip but lifted up the leg of their shorts to have a pee. J recalled feeling intensely embarrassed that his mother did not know how boys would go to the toilet. He felt the second of these memories indicated that mother did not know what boys did with their 'willies'; if father had taught him how to go to the toilet things would have been different. I found both these memories incompatible with his espoused good relationship with his mother.

Father was considered an insensitive man who suffocated the life out of his family. J was sure that mother was a naturally lively person who had been subdued by her husband. Father was described as a 'typical white settler: racist, patriotic and emotionally blocked'. There was not a lot of physical violence, but what existed was memorable. Mother would give mild slaps. For more serious offences, father would use an old whip used in the slave trade made from coiled rhino-hide. On one occasion J was beaten for untidying his bed. He immediately wrote in an exercise book: 'I will not allow my father in my room again'. He promptly rubbed this out. Some years later he found the book and could still see a trace of where the writing had been; he was amazed that he could have felt so angry at his dad.

J attributed all his problems as originating with his father. There were two recollections that seemed to characterize his feelings about the man. The first was that his parents recalled father going off to climb a mountain as soon as J was conceived. J was sure that this was symptomatic of father's remoteness. The other recollection concerned a photograph of J's christening. The photo showed J in his mother's arms; he is arching back and reaching out for his father, grabbing him by the lapel of his jacket; father is looking at the hand on his lapel, not at J.

J was insistent that he did not want to use the couch in his analysis. He felt he needed the eye contact as a way of keeping personal contact with me. Father gave nicknames to J and his two older sisters. At first he could not decide whether to call J after the brand name of a make of batteries, or 'Donk', short for 'donkey'. Father settled on the latter. This seems significant – a battery, his boy J is a source of power, whereas a donkey is merely a beast of burden. The choice of nickname seemed to reflect J's experience of his father disempowering him. All these vivid memories conveyed an image of a father who was indeed powerful and destructive, but also very present and not distant in the way J considered him to be.

The first dream J brought reflected his experience of emotional isolation: he is on a rock looking down into a pool of still water. Two friends (his partner and another man) are swimming under the water. The other man is reaching out for reefers as they sink to the bottom. Associations included the distance he habitually feels between himself and others; the water is like a sheet of glass he sometimes feels is between others and himself; the other friend is himself reaching out in rather the way J had for his father in the christening photo; the friend is also me, being a significant other in his life. The 'reefer' is both cannabis but also a coral reef, dangerous but alive. This was my view of his father: distant but at least alive, especially compared to the fondly remembered but totally obscure mother, who seemed completely emotionally absent: with father there was hostility and therefore a relationship; with mother there seemed to be nothing binding them together. In this regard, J reported that, as a child before the age of ten, he would frequently wander off by himself and get lost in a daydream. The fantasy was always of being on another planet, sometimes there were animals, often not. There were never any people. I had been seeing him for about eight months when I suddenly began to feel confused, vague and disorientated during the sessions. At times I felt desperate and empty. This continued for several weeks

109

before I came to realize this as a projective identification experience of his childhood feelings. I eventually told him of my feelings of confusion and emptiness and imagined that this was how he felt as a child. J immediately felt the void of his own childhood open up and began to experience how emotionally impoverished it had been. This significantly changed his way of relating to me which became more trusting. Whereas previously in the transference, I had been seen as his rather silent, unsharing and distant father, in our relationship now there was something more alive. A short while after this I found my mind wandering again in another session: I thought about the first man on the moon, Neil Armstrong, and his famous words, 'One small step for man, but a giant leap for mankind'; my mind then rang to a song by the pop group *The Police*, about walking on the moon. I wondered why my mind had been wandering and this made me aware that J, though he had been speaking, had been doing so in a particularly distant and remote manner. I then recalled his frequent childhood fantasy of dreaming of uninhabited distant planets. Again, I understood my day-dreaming as my becoming immersed in his childhood experience since, like him, I dreamed of an empty moon. I said nothing, but merely thinking this to myself seemed to change the interaction that day. Minutes after my realizing the source of my day-dream he began to describe feeling like two people, an old him and a new fragile him. He was worried that this new self might be a big mess. He then had the spontaneous fantasy that if his lover were a woman, and had a phantom pregnancy, J would copy his symptoms. This was a complex image that brought the erotic openly into the therapy for the first time: if his male lover were a woman it would be a phantom pregnancy, not a genuine one, and this seemed to be correlated to J's idea of possessing a non-potent, infertile penis; his false self had no power and his new self felt too fragile to be strong.

The sense of feeling split seemed to create a crack in his habitual defences. This allowed more discussion about his mother which, along with his homosexuality, he had more or less tabooed from discussion. He noticed details around my room, the presence of new ornaments like Russian dolls which I had brought back from holiday. For the first time he began to be curious about me, my training, what I would say my therapeutic orientation was, where I took my holidays and if I lived with anybody. Discussion about his new-found curiosity led him to admit he had these queries early on but felt he could not ask questions; this related to the father transference where it emerged he had not been able to ask his father about his occupation. He had another lifelong image of himself standing outside a door not daring to knock or enter; curiosity was not something he had felt could be satisfied. He was quite shocked to realize he could project qualities of his father on to me. This admission was also his first acceptance of any transference interpretations. A year after this discussion, in the third year of his analysis, he mumbled something I could not understand about his father. When I asked him to repeat what he had said, as it seemed he had wanted to tell me something without my hearing it, he then said that his father and I shared the same christian name, David. With that acknowledgement, his use of me as a transference figure for his father was completely acknowledged. He wondered if he hated his father because he has 'a classic Oedipal complex and wanted him out of the way or do I hate him because he never showed me he loved me?' He talked of needing a caring, reliable father – in effect, a father who would show him how to go to the toilet when wearing short trousers, a father who would tell him what to do with his 'willy'. He recalled that, in adolescence, the only advice that his father gave him about relationships was that he should be careful not to get a girl pregnant. J took this to mean he should not have a potent penis.

His image of the primal scene was pertinent to this last point. He could not imagine his parents having any sex and that, even if they did, neither, especially his mother, would enjoy it. When I queried what he knew about his parents' sexual activities he reported two memories. The first was in his early teens, looking around his parents' bedroom while they were out. He had found some condoms on his father's side of the bed, but was inclined to think his parents did not use them; many years later he recalled mother telling him she did not enjoy sex. His denial of the evidence before his eyes that the condoms were a testimony to the existence of his parents' sexual activities had been further reinforced by understanding his mother's statement to mean they had no sex at all. Again, rather like his image of his partner having only a phantom pregnancy, J had no image of a creative coupling, either literally or metaphorically.

His experience of his mother's sexuality seemed to influence his view of the heterosexual women he knew. During one session, he described the activities of a few of the women in the office where he worked. It seemed to me they were flirting and were attracted to him. I said as much in what I intended as a casual remark. J strongly denied the possibility that they fancied him and saw no reason why they should as he offered no encouragement or reciprocal flirting. I proposed that perhaps he could not see himself as an object of female desire because he had not felt himself desired by his mother. This interpretation was totally rejected as self-evidently preposterous, and he added that the women he worked with were merely being friendly. I felt that the intensity of his rebuttal suggested I might not be totally wrong, but this line of investigation was very difficult to pursue.

This discussion brought us more directly to the homoerotic transference which was never very overt in this analysis. I consider that this was largely due to him foreclosing his homosexual side from the analysis. However, though it lacked in intensity, it seemed to exert a continuous presence throughout the therapy. In his first dream of his two friends swimming in the pool, one was his lover, the other possibly myself. Thus he linked his lover and me together. Yet he is sitting outside, uninvolved, relating neither to his lover nor to me. On returning from my summer break in the second year of his analysis, he reported that he had started a deep platonic relationship with another man he had met at a swimming pool. He insisted to both his lover and me that this was not a sexual relationship. I put it to him that he had felt bereft during my break and had sought out a platonic relationship with another man to compensate. He was insistent that there was no connection between meeting this man and my being away on holiday.

For my own part, the homoerotic countertransference was equally vague. I considered J a very handsome and intelligent man who had a particularly nice taste in T-shirts. Once when I was out shopping, I saw some T-shirts similar to his. I tried one on to see if it would suit me, too. It did! I was aware that this was both suggestive of some extra-analytic acting out whilst expressing some erotic identifications with him.

In the four years I had seen him, we had done much to relieve not only his depression, his mental blocks and his chronic underachieving, but we had also brought a more ambivalent attitude to both parents. Mother was still the preferred parent but, now seen as having let him down, was therefore not so idealized. Father had died while J was in analysis. This had stirred considerable grief and brought forth memories and affects previously unacknowledged; he particularly understood his father's caring attitude, which had been obscured by the latter's lack of skill in demonstrating such care, and he valued, given his father's white settler background, his acceptance of his son's homosexuality.

It was not until we had fixed a date for termination that anything more erotically explicit emerged. In all likelihood, setting a date to finish both impelled him to complete unfinished work, as well as making it safe to bring material from which he could then run.

He arrived fifteen minutes early. When I pointed this out he was shocked at his mistake. When the session began he asked to use my toilet, something he had never done before. When he came out he said he was concerned that he 'didn't want to bugger up your timetable, keeping patients separate so they don't meet'. He sat down and spoke for a few more minutes before realizing he had not done up the flies on his trousers. I had not noticed this until he drew my attention to the fact. With much embarrassment he then did them up. I commented on the various events so far that day, arriving early, 'buggering up' my timetable, using my toilet and leaving his flies undone. Over the next few sessions a number of meanings emerged. The earliness *was* intended to 'bugger up' my timetable, and this was related to the termination as an expression of contempt for the therapy he felt he no longer needed; also a spoiling of the therapy to make the leaving easier. 'Buggering up' was also an expression of his homoerotic love: arriving early to see more of me and wanting me to know about his penis. There is probably a whole article to be written about the meaning of patients going to the toilet (before, during or after the session) while in the analyst's house. Amongst the meanings that emerged with J was exposing his penis inside my house – metaphorically buggering me, either as a sadistic or loving homosexual act; going to the toilet is to draw attention to the organ of urination, which with men is also their sexual equipment, with women it is close to the vagina and is thus informing the analyst that the patient wishes to make sure the analyst knows he or she has a sexual organ. Significantly, he was also demonstrating that he now knew how to use his flies properly, the way his mother had taught him grown men go to the toilet.

This sudden flurry of homoerotic imagery at the end of his analysis was not so much a significant departure, but more of a consequence of the subliminal homoerotic experience during the preceding years of analytic work, always there but in the background like wallpaper.

Making contact with a man seemed to be his main goal in life. This was not only reflected in his overt homosexual behaviour, particularly in his need for a much older man which had been the basis of a long-standing, loving relationship. It was also there in his need to maintain eye contact with me from the chair rather than using the couch, and the development of a platonic relationship with another man during one of my breaks. I considered that all these instances were variations on the photo of his christening where he is seeking the contact of his father.

From this I am inclined to consider that his reaching out for his father was an attempt to seek his help to get away from a lifeless, and I suspect depressed, mother. As I said earlier, he preserved a memory of a good mother who seemed all but absent; in contrast, he had a memory of father as shadowy and bad, but in fact he seemed very present. This discrepancy between recalled memory and accompanying affect seemed at the heart of his difficulty. Mother was experienced as a terrible void, full of emptiness, dull, lifeless; to escape this he sought his father. Unfortunately, his father was not able to provide a safe escape to help him pull away from his mother. However, despite father's violence and intolerance, he at least offered a semblance of a relationship, albeit an antagonistic one, which at its worst still felt more alive than the annihilating deadness with his mother. He was seeking his father to escape mother at his christening and he continued to seek the father in his adult years. The homoerotic in this man can therefore be understood as an active search for an erotically charged father.

I now wish to approach the subject of the positive homoerotic in a different way. One of the assumptions made when talking about the erotic transference–countertransference is to equate erotic desire with being attracted to somebody. In fact, though there is much overlap, they are not the same. We may desire the unattractive precisely because it is disgusting. For example, in the Indian tantric philosophic tradition this was integrated into a form of elevated sexual disgust leading to enlightenment: there are particular pleasures and knowledge apparently to be gained from having sexual intercourse with the partially charred remains of corpses after they have been cremated.

This is quite different from, say, the embalmers of ancient Egypt who were reputed to sexually violate female corpses before mummifying them: relatives would usually keep the body of the deceased until decay had begun to prevent such abuse. In Egypt, necrophilia was socially reviled; in the tantric tradition, it had found a way into an advanced philosophical and religious system. To an extent, disgust is relative.

Disgust as an attribute in the erotic transference is more likely to occur where the desire is experienced as ego-alien. In heterosexual therapists this is very likely to be linked with the homoerotic desire. To the best of my knowledge, Searles (1959) is the only writer who has described such an erotic countertransference. He describes wanting to marry a number of his more unpleasant patients. The reader is entitled to assume that 'marry' is a euphemism for more than just standing at the altar.

The following case is from my own practice.

Mr K was in his fifties, from peasant stock in southern Ireland. He was married with a teenage son. He had come to analysis because he was being disturbed by memories of sexual abuse by two priests at the ages of eleven and fifteen. Though he considered himself heterosexual as an adult, he had had a number of sexual experiences with men; also, before meeting his wife, he regularly attended mixed sex orgies.

As a child his home life had been dominated by violence from both his father and older brothers. This had also been institutionalized in that all the family were engaged in amateur boxing. He reported that the punishment for losing a fight would be that he would be beaten by his brothers to make sure he won next time. There were also frequent beatings from his father. He reported an early memory from the age of three when he had seen and touched his father's erect penis. Father then whipped him for his 'disgusting behaviour'. A reverse scenario occurred at fifteen when father had seen him coming out of the toilet with an erect penis. Father had hit it with a wire saying, 'Put that disgusting thing away'.

Particularly vivid was his father's reaction when Mr K first reported the abusing priest. Father denied that a priest could do such a thing and soundly whipped him. Mr K said he felt father's disbelief 'hurt more than the buggery'. One long-term effect of this abuse was his guilt about sexual desires to his son, leading him to withdraw from all fatherly physical contact in case it was misconstrued as sexual abuse. His father's reaction had been a defining moment in Mr K's life. He felt a tremendous betrayal at not being believed, which changed his relationship with his father for the worse from that date. Ten years later, when father died, Mr K caused a great deal of commotion in his family when he refused to kiss his father in his coffin at the wake: despite the family's entreaties he felt that, in all honesty, he could not kiss the man he had come to hate.

For the first couple of months of our work, I dreaded Mr K's physical presence. He was ugly and sometimes liked to joke about this fact. He would always begin our sessions with a mental joust that I found irritating in its predictability. After this he would lapse into a tearful grief. His speech would become high and whispery, making audibility very difficult. Shortly after the tears flowed, the mucus would follow. First, a 'dew drop' on the end of his nose; this would gradually descend like a spider on a long silvery thread. I found myself involuntarily calculating the length: was it eight or ten inches long? I was also worried by it soiling my carpet. Miraculously, Mr K always seemed to wipe his nose (with his hand, of course) just at the point when I thought it was going to bomb the floor.

It was easy to notice my disgust. I began to reflect on my own reaction. I realized I was quite excited by him doing what I would find very hard to do, just letting my mucus flow, especially in the company of others. Further, I realized that I was envious that he had been to an orgy and I had not. Having made this erotic fantasy bond, I further realized I could imagine us both at an orgy having sex with each other. An orgy seemed to represent for me a totally disinhibited sexual pleasure principle, minus the superego inhibitions. I realized that part of me at least considered Mr K very sexually experienced and therefore admirable. In that context, I had the further realization that I had been equating his mucus with semen – the length of his nasal discharge with 'virile' penis size.

Once the content of this self-analysis had sunk in, I considered that the previous absence of homoerotic fantasies had been a form of resistance on my part. Though I was initially surprised by my fantasies, I noted I felt more calm and interpreted more freely, but for a while I did not know how to utilize my fantasies for an interpretation I could put to him. Even without saying any of this, it became apparent that, slowly, Mr K was also less distressed. His blabbering reduced, and then ceased. I could hear what he said and felt we established a more meaningful dialogue.

It was about the time when I was beginning to think differently about Mr K that he then began a new healing relationship outside the analysis. While at a sauna, he had struck up a good rapport with another man. As they dressed in the changing room the other man put on a dog collar, revealing he was a priest. Mr K was shocked and apologetic as he had been freely swearing until then. The priest disapproved of this change, saying people stopped being their natural self once they realized he was a priest. The two of them had struck up a friendship. To preserve the disinhibited relationship from their first encounter in the sauna, both men would strip down to their underpants before they held their discussions. This friendship, despite (or because of) the homoerotic undertones, was purely platonic. Unlike Mr K's earlier experience with the sexually abusing priests, this felt like a partnership of equals.

Mr K also made it quite plain he would like us to strip down to our underpants during the analysis, for the same purpose. I declined, but suggested we look at the issues. I was then able to use my earlier fantasies to formulate an interpretation. He was looking for a loving relationship with a man whose worldly expertise he could admire, and with whom he could feel at ease – different but equal. The platonic homoerotic encounter was to provide the relationship he lacked with his father. In that sense, it was the repetition of the past seeking a more healing rerun in the present. The timing of his encounter at the sauna shortly after my self-analysis and change of opinion towards him seemed a highly suggestive coincidence. It was my impression, though it would be difficult to prove, that Mr K was able to begin his friendship outside the analysis only after I had made a psychic shift that could see this otherwise repulsive man as admirable and desirable. In other words, we could become closer through the conduit of the homoerotic, which allowed a more loving possibility, a different end game to the usual rerun of his homoerotic scenarios – beginning with the abusive father, the priests, and the various casual encounters with men after that. It could be said that he was searching for a more loving penis than that of his father which he was beaten for touching; he was also searching for a fatherly appreciation and love of his own penis which, at fifteen, father had symbolically castrated when hitting it with wire.

DISCUSSION

There is a surprising scarcity of reporting of homoerotic countertransference by colleagues in either formal or informal discussions, written reports, supervision or my workshops on 'Working with the erotic transference and countertransference'. When we do not encounter what we expect to find then either we are wrong and our expectations are incorrect, or some defensive processes are at work leading to resistance and repression. With the erotic transferences, and the homoerotic transferences and countertransferences in particular, I would consider it usually safer to suspect the latter rather than the former. Except with overt homosexuals, the emergence of homoerotic desire in patients or therapists tends to evoke strong superego injunctions, where both sides worry about dangerous enactments. When therapy consists of a mixed sex dyad (male patient with female therapist or female patient with male therapist), the patient may be concerned about the emergence of homoerotic desire towards individuals outside the therapy session. The therapist, who may consider this marks a set-back in the therapy, may also feel apprehension about homoerotic desires developing in the patient.

The transference–countertransference matrix takes on a more anxious and sometimes paranoid quality in same sex analytic dyads: male therapist and patient or female therapist and patient. Here the fear of enactments are greater, with either or both parties suspecting the motives of the other, each fearing a homosexual seduction. My view is that where there is a fear of something happening, this is often a clue to the presence of unacceptable desires. Many patients, and I believe therapists too, beat a hasty retreat from the emergence of homoerotic desire. It does seem to me that a full analysis is dependent on the therapist having the courage to grapple as much with the homoerotic as the heteroerotic: if the therapist cannot deal with this issue in the countertransference what chance is there for the patient working through it in the transference? In this respect, the homoerotic presents one of the greatest temptations for evasion in analysis for both parties in the analytic dyad.

Breen (1993) notes that psychobisexuality is increasingly understood to be fundamental, not just for sexuality, but for psychic integration and structuring more generally. The similar point is made by Cunningham (1991) that psychic bisexuality is important (though she believes, rarely achieved by psychoanalysts) in order to allow the therapist to identify not only with the desire of each sex for the other, but also for each sex for the same. Thus, a well-integrated homoerotic desire is essential for same sex empathy. In my view, although this may be a highly commendable idea, it seems to be another idealization of the therapist's abilities as defined by living up to the ego ideal. I very much doubt whether many people have such a well-integrated sexual identity. I would suggest that a frequent readiness to question our basic assumptions would be a more realistic goal, especially regarding ego-alien qualities. Morgenthaler (1988: 29) makes the point that, however tolerant analysts might be, they are still part of the society they live in and can only maintain tolerance to a certain degree: 'In the psychoanalytic treatment of manifest homosexuals analysts are easily seduced into wanting to decide the manner in which their analysands will finally live and love.' This is in conflict with an espoused purpose of analysis being to investigate, comprehend and explain the background of homosexuality without prejudice. Indeed, it has often been difficult for homosexuals to be considered for training by some psychoanalytic organizations. In my view, this has a bearing on how the homoerotic transference and countertransference will unfold. If the homoerotic desire is deemed an unsuitable quality in a therapist and can stand as an obstacle to training and qualification, the trainee may have good reasons for concealment. Similarly, if the qualified therapist has not dealt with the homoerotic in his or her personal analysis, he or she will hardly have an easy time of it in dealing with the transference or countertransference. I would also add that prohibition on homoerotic desire will also make objective discussion with colleagues less than easy. My concern with the ban on homosexuals doing an analytic training is – quite apart from any issues concerning equal opportunities or even the loss to psychoanalysis of a group commonly associated with high creativity – the fact that such a ban gives the wrong message about homoerotic desire. It is a very well-analysed and secure therapist who can feel confident with either his or her patient's, or his or her own, homoerotic desire while working in a milieu ascribing negative associations and prohibitions to the homoerotic.

Be that as it may, in my view, taboos do not always prohibit the illicit activity; they merely stop it coming to light and being discussed. I believe that, just as the erotic transference and countertransference is a more frequent occurrence in analysis than the infrequent discussion amongst colleagues and the literature would suggest, this is even more true of the homoerotic transference and countertransference, which, I consider, occurs or is defensively resisted with much more regularity than analysts have been prepared to report openly.

The prevalence of the homoerotic in infancy is not doubted. Some authors have proposed the idea of 'primary homosexuality' referring to a primary identification of the son to the father, presupposing a distinction between maternal and paternal objects and proceeding from a narcissistic object choice (Kestemberg 1984). Frejaville (1984) suggests primary homosexuality rests on a shared phantasy between parent and child of the same sex in the context of the primal scene and is important in the foundations of sexual identity. Denis (1982) proposes a form of primary homosexuality in the boy relating to the mother in the stage before sexual differentiation. In this instance, mother is conceived of as like the self; from this, tenderness will develop. Gibeault (1988) considers that, for the girl, it is precisely not having to disidentify herself from the maternal body (unlike the boy) which promotes the primary homosexual movement for her and its destiny in the Oedipus complex: mother can be replaced in Oedipal rivalry without fear of losing love because, by possessing identical bodies, she loves her. In my article on *Castration desire* (Mann 1994a), I proposed that the boy may desire castration precisely to be a girl like mother, and that such a 'homoerotic' identification served to maintain the illusion of similarity and the denial of difference as it is represented by the penis.

Other authors have emphasized the importance of the homoerotic in dealing with the opposite sex parent. Chasseguet-Smirgel (1976) states the important point that the wish to break away from the primal mother drives children of both sexes to project her power on to the father and his penis. In a different manner, Glasser (1985) describes how homoerotic fantasies refer to the need to have the father offering support to avert annihilation from the possessive dominance of the mother. This has transference equivalents in seeking the analyst–father's support against the dominating analyst–mother. Glassner goes on to say that the boy will turn to the father as an alternative object: this internalization step is to stop the danger of the internal world being taken over by the mother. The father serves as a walled fortress (a frequent image encountered in patient's dreams and metaphors) to keep the mother out; father must also be an object of libidinal feelings and need for caring. To become permanent, this internalization must proceed to identification. Greenson (1968) describes a similar process as the boy's need to 'disidentify' with his mother and develop a new identification with the father.

We saw something of these various processes in both vignettes. In the case of J, he had the explicit fantasy of being in a walled garden with no exit. By the same image, it also had no entrance, reflecting his need to keep at bay the void that the relationship with his mother offered.

I think it is also significant that, in both the cases discussed, the father used excessive violence against the son. One effect of this could have been to give a sado-masochistic charge to the homoerotic. In fact, this did not happen. In both cases, J and Mr K sought a more loving, caring man to make good the brutality of the experience with the father. I would say that this suggests there are instances in which the transference is not just a repetition, but also a hope that the new transformational object will heal the wounds of the past.

In the two cases I have discussed in this chapter, I have sought to emphasize the positive side of homoerotic desire. I do not doubt that the homoerotic, like the heteroerotic, may also be defensive – for example, representing a defensive avoidance of the opposite sex, or a denial of the procreative primal scene. However, to see it purely as defensive seems to miss the point of the homoerotic in the developmental structure of the psyche. Homoerotic love may be detected within many same sex affinities: for men, for example, in very 'manly' activities such as physical contact sports and the military. There is a desire in the infant and the adult for a homoerotic bond. This does not mean homosexual activity, as I would imagine most men would be shocked and deny such an unconscious desire. I also mean more than just a form of identification with the father. What is of vital importance is for an erotic bond to exist between father and son (or between mother and daughter) in order for the child to feel him or herself secure as an object of the same sex parent's desire. It is not enough to be like the same sex parent, *the child needs to know the same sex parent also desires him or her. This is equally true in the inverse: the parent needs to know he or she is desired by the same sex child.* It goes without saying, that this remains at the level of desire and is not acted out.

We could suppose, therefore, that since the homoerotic plays such a crucial role in the maturational processes, it would, by analogy, have a similar significance within the analytic transaction. If the homoerotic is conceded to play a useful part within the family context, it will concomitantly have a developmental function for the positive homoerotic transference and countertransference matrix within analysis which reproduces the family transferences. The analyst's ability to draw on homoerotic, as well as heteroerotic, desires will have a deep influence on his or her ability to help patients integrate maternal and paternal erotic identifications within the transference.

6

TRANSFERENCE AS SYMBOLIC SEXUAL INTERCOURSE

INTRODUCTION

There are two aspects to the patient treating the psychoanalytic situation as an expression of sexual intercourse. First, in recent years clinical observation has led me to the view that the patient's way of relating in a psychotherapy session frequently mirrors how they relate during sexual intercourse, and this in turn is related to the patient's image of the primal scene. Second, the process of psychic change, birth and growth follows a similar process to physical birth and growth – that is to say, following a creative psychic coupling between the patient and the analyst, change in a therapeutic encounter follows the same path of conception, gestation and labour as does the body. These two aspects of the transference as symbolic sexual intercourse are related.

In some respects it might be objected that a suitable comparison cannot be made between sexual intercourse and the analytic process. This line of argument would point out that sexual intercourse is essentially a physical process while therapy prohibits any physical contact and is primarily a psychological process. My rebuttal of such objections are to say: first, I do not consider sexual intercourse to be essentially physical, but deeply enmeshed in the psychological and fantasy processes (conscious and unconscious) of the lovers. Second, while I accept that therapy avoids physical touching, the degree of intimacy and the activation of unconscious phantasies is so pertinent between lovers and the patient–analyst dyad that it merits comparison. This chapter will endeavour to elaborate this second point.

The relevance of childhood experience to adult sexuality has long been known to psychoanalysis. In 1905 Freud was writing: 'There are thus good reasons why a child sucking at his mother's breast has become the prototype of every relation of love. The finding of an object is in fact a refinding of it' (1905c). More recent infant observations show that the mother–infant relationship is much richer than even that described so clearly by Freud. It has also been known for a considerable period that the mutual interaction between mother and infant is the precursor of the adult erotic experience.

For example, Lichtenstein (1961) writes: 'In the primitive sensory exchanges taking place between mother and infant one could see the precursor of adult sexuality'.

This chapter will focus on the implications of this for the transference. Sexual intercourse is one of the human experiences that encapsulate the essential features of an individual's psychic life: it represents in microcosm the major components of the total psychic experience. The sexual encounter, particularly where there is sexual dysfunction, is often the leading edge of chronic difficulties in all of the individual's life problems. Because of this it is likely to be encountered as transference phenomenon in the analytic setting. Freud wrote in his *Three essays on sexuality* (1905c): 'the symptoms constitute the sexual activity of the patient'. We may say, therefore, that by the same token, the transference also constitutes the sexual activity of the patient. I would further propose that, like dreams, the individual's sexual experience or phantasy presents a 'royal road' into the unconscious and psychic world.

What I am suggesting is that the patient relates to the therapist as he or she relates to his or her sexual partners, or as an expression of masturbation fantasies. These in turn are related to the patient's image of the primal scene. I will deal with this latter point in the next chapter.

Within psychoanalysis there are a number of models of the mind and psychic growth. Probably the dominant model of the British Object Relations School is the equating of the mind with the digestive processes. Meltzer (1984), for instance, describes the mind as operating like the intestines: some material is wholly absorbed and digested; some things only partially digested and utilized; other products cannot be digested and assimilated. It is quite common to hear psychotherapists or their patients describe good sessions or interpretations as a 'good feed', meaning that something had been said that led to psychic nourishment and growth. Part and parcel of this model is the view that the therapy is symbolic of the mother and baby relationship.

I am in no way disagreeing with this model of the mind and find it is extremely useful in my daily clinical practice. However, its limitations are obvious: the body needs more than food to grow and develop. In the discussion section, I will introduce some of the findings from recent infant observations. For now, I would like to emphasize my point with reference to two classic studies. Spitz (1945) showed that infants raised in orphanages do poorly because of the absence of a single committed parent, while those raised in equally poor conditions, but with their own mothers, do nearly as well as advantaged children. The children in the orphanages failed to thrive in every respect, showing slow physical and emotional development with high incidence of illness and death. The problems were not around feeding and nutrition but about the absence of stable TLC – tender loving care.

The other famous study is Harlow's (1958) experiments with rhesus monkeys. In his experiments, these monkeys were separated from their mothers at birth. They were placed in a cage with two pseudo-mothers – one a wire frame with a teat attached to give milk, the other a frame covered in a soft fabric. The baby monkeys invariably spent their time clinging to the soft mother and only reached across to the wire frame with milk when they needed food. This 'contact comfort' seemed more important than the satisfaction of feeding needs. Relevant to the subject of this chapter is that, as adults, these rhesus monkeys raised without real mothers could not perform sexually. Males could not perform at all even though they had been given the chance to learn from observation; females would collapse and succumb to rape-like sex with competent monkeys. Those females that did become pregnant were unable to nurse their young, often abusing them. A generational cycle of deprivation was thus set in motion. Some of these mother monkeys improved substantially in their ability to nurse with the birth of their second infant. Harlow's experiments indicate that a failure of 'good enough' mothering in infancy, especially in the erotic bonding between the nursing couple (which, as I shall shortly illustrate, are aspects of comfort and responsiveness), leads later to sexual disorganization when the infant becomes an adult. A more vivid example of the importance of sensual experience to the infant is hard to imagine. Of course it is not possible simply to generalize from monkeys to humans, but I highlight these examples because what a baby also needs for psychic and physical growth is sensual contact.

Sensual experience is essential to the infant for its survival and well-being. As Stern (1993) has shown, the early sensual experience is the precursor of the later adult sexual experience. This sexual component of the mother and baby unit is often overlooked or ignored. I stress it here as it relates directly to the theme of this chapter: if the therapeutic process is likened to a mother and baby couple there is an inherent sensual–sexual component in this model (distinct from, though related to, feeding) which we would then expect to find in the transference.

This sensual–erotic component of the nursing couple is frequently not stressed in psychoanalytical thought. This is evident, for example in two of the most important proponents of the mother–therapy analogy, Winnicott and Bion. Though psychoanalytic theory places the development of sexuality in infancy, somehow the mother–infant pattern of relating is left out. In Winnicott, the good enough mother provides a holding and containing environment, mirroring, primary maternal preoccupation and gradual frustrations, transitional phenomenon, and so on, but not an erotic experience; when translated into the therapeutic context, the erotic component is similarly lost.

In the work of Bion the same applies: the mother provides through her reverie an alpha function to detoxify the baby's projectively identified beta elements. This same model accounts for transformations in the analytic therapeutic process. Again the erotic disappears from the mother–child relationship. Strange! Let me be clear here: I am not disagreeing with what Winnicott and Bion ascribe to the maternal–therapeutic process. My point is that they do not consider, or at least ignore, the erotic component of the mother–infant couple, and when this model is applied to the analytic process the same oversight occurs.

Wrye and Welles have also remarked on the absence in the analytic literature of discussion concerning the erotic pre-Oedipal mother. They write:

> The early sensual bond between mother and baby, when marked by reciprocity and attunement, makes separateness tolerable and engenders baby's 'love affair with the world' (Mahler et al. 1975). That love affair becomes the basis of loving relations and all eroticism after the separation–individuation phase and into the oedipal and post-oedipal period. When we use the word 'erotic' we are talking about the gamut of feelings – from tender, sensual and romantic to anal erotic, sadistic, aggressive, and masochistic – that stem from the original mother–baby bond. The feelings pertain to bodily contact and arise in the transference. . . . We locate the origins of erotic experience in the preverbal arena, when the mother's and baby contacts are really about dealing with body fluids.
>
> (1994: 34–35)

As I discussed in Chapter 3, the analytical dyad, the number two, is not only the number for the mother–infant relationship, but is also the number for sexual procreation. Much of the analytic encounter can be understood as an equivalent of the incest taboo which places restrictions on both the patient and the therapist and serves to keep sexual desire in the realms of fantasy, rather than expression.

In the context of this chapter, I would like to emphasize that the model for biological procreation – coitus, conception, gestation and birth – applies also to psychological growth and development. Of course, using the metaphors of physical love to described psychical phenomenon is not new. In Christianity, the *Song of Solomon* and many mystical writings speak of the soul, or the Church, as the 'Bride of Christ'. Plato's *Symposium* (1951), written two and a half thousand years ago, is full of erotic metaphor – 'spiritual procreation', 'marriage of noble minds', a man's soul 'pregnant with some creation or discovery'; even the Socratic art of 'midwifery' by which he helps his associates to bring birth to ideas and discoveries with which they are in travail.

Using sexual metaphor to describe the mind is not new to psychoanalysis either. Freud (1913) made the same comparison that analysis represents a child or birth:

> But, on the whole, once begun, it [analysis] goes its own way and does not allow either the direction it takes or the order in which it picks up

its points to be prescribed for it. The analyst's power over the symptoms of the disease may thus be compared to male sexual potency. A man can, it is true, beget a whole child, but even the strongest man cannot create in the female organism a head alone or an arm, or a leg; he cannot even prescribe the child's sex. He, too, only sets in motion a highly complicated process, determined by events in the remote past, which ends with the severance of the child from its mother.

Ferenczi considered analysis a rebirth, as did Balint. Rank's theory of birth trauma is also applied to analysis where the psychoanalytic situation is considered a revival of the initial trauma – analyst equals midwife. Chasseguet-Smirgel (1984a: 175) makes a direct link between sex and analysis:

> All things considered, it seems to me that the analyst's bisexuality must be well integrated to enable the development of the baby, made by the analyst and analysand in their work together, the baby which represents the analysand himself, recreated.

I would add to this view that I believe it is not just the analysand who is transformed: the analyst will also undergo a birth and produce a psychic baby.

In the analytical context, the patient and the analyst will either affect each other or have no effect at all. A similar point has been made by Jung (1946). Here he studies the transference in terms of alchemical imagery and cites ten stages in development: (1) the mercurial fountain, (2) the king and queen, (3) the naked truth, (4) immersion in the bath, (5) the conjunction, (6) death, (7) the ascent of the soul, (8) purification, (9) the return of the soul, and finally, (10) the new birth. Jung obscures his thesis by resorting to alchemy and Latin. To de-mythologize the alchemical symbols, I would propose the following translation of Jung's metaphor to stages in intercourse: (1) the setting (soft lights and a bed/couch – which most therapists have; music and wine – traditionally absent from the analytic encounter!), (2) the lovers, (3) mutual desire, (4) foreplay, (5) sexual intercourse, (6) orgasm (the 'little death'), (7) unification in psycho–soma entwinement, (8) the satisfaction of desire, (9) de-climax, and, (10) birth, either of greater emotional closeness and/or conception of a baby. Converting this into the metaphor for analysis, I would like to state the matter as: the patient and the therapist come together in a psychic intercourse that will either lead to a new conception (gestation and birth) in the psychic development of both, or there will be psychic impotence and sterility.

It should be noted that analytical language prefers the term 'impasse', but this amounts to the same thing. I would add that conception does not automatically lead to birth. In biology this would be due to miscarriage. The same is true of its psychic equivalent; the process of psychic growth and birth is not always a straightforward process, complications and set-backs can occur at any stage. I consider the erotic (in all its symbolic forms) to play a central part in therapeutic efficacy.

As Meltzer (1973b: 59) accurately describes development: 'Emphasis must be placed on the function of the coupling in development for, where sexual intimacy is not stabilized sufficiently for an atmosphere of potential parenthood to enter the relationship, further development of the personality is severely impeded in both members.'

CLINICAL VIGNETTES

I will now illustrate my central point with some clinical examples.

The parallel between how the patient experiences therapy and his or her sexual experience was first brought to my attention by the following case. L was 27 years old when he began psychotherapy. His presenting problem was increasing sexual performance anxiety relating to repeated premature ejaculation; he found it impossible not to stop himself from ejaculating the instant he penetrated his wife.

During his initial assessment, and for the first phase of therapy, the session would follow a set pattern. He would begin each session talking quite volubly about either an aspect of his history or particular events that had happened since our previous meeting. After about five or ten minutes, he would stop speaking and complain he had suddenly run out of things to talk about; several times he referred to this as he had 'dried up'. The rest of the session would vary in difficulty, with him sometimes able to find things to say, or not, as the occasion determined. He found the silences and the difficulty to speak excruciatingly unbearable. This happened for seven or eight sessions until it dawned on me that he was bringing his presenting symptom, premature ejaculation, directly into the analysis. Entering my consulting room was like entering his wife's vagina and, once in, there was a quick burst of activity or speech and then it was all over. His speech was a symbolic representation of semen, his silence and the ensuing difficulties were symbolic representations of premature orgasmic climax followed by anxiety. When I interpreted this to him, it produced a diminution of both his sexual inhibition and his difficulty in talking in sessions.

The following example is of a 27-year-old woman I saw many years ago before thinking about transference as symbolic sexual intercourse. M came for one assessment only. Throughout our meeting, her hair hid one eye. She presented with sexual difficulties having never had full intercourse. She enjoyed cuddles, but would always move her boy-friend's hand away if he became too intimate. She said she was not frigid, but froze and could not have sex even if she wanted to. This had resulted in all her previous relationships breaking up. She reported that she did not want children; she used contraceptives even though she had never been sexually penetrated and would have an abortion if she got pregnant as she did not want the responsibility of somebody else's life. She described her father as a womanizer and drinker who put his wife on a pedestal and would not have sex with her, only other women. We discussed terms for her to begin psychotherapy and she appeared keen to start. However, her parting remark, as she went out of the door, was more revealing. She said she sometimes wondered if she went to a hospital and was strapped down in order to have sex, they could then say, 'See. Look. You haven't died.' Before her next session she wrote to cancel her appointment saying she felt there was more she could do to help herself. Had I been more alert to the transference I might have interpreted her presenting problem and closing remarks as an inability to let the therapy penetrate her. In other words, she felt all right with an assessment akin to cuddles, but froze at the prospect of going further and deeper into therapy.

It is possible that the transference as symbolic sexual intercourse is most apparent where there are sexual dysfunctions. However, I have also noted that its influence on the transference is recognizable where there are no sexual dysfunctions, as in the following example.

N was married, but thought he was unlikely to have children. He experienced his life as a series of reactions to outside events that caused him to do something or take action. He felt unable to initiate, but recognized this was also pleasurable as it avoided taking responsibility.

In our previous session, he had talked about how he experienced himself as a little boy in a room full of adults. He gave an example of how people seemed to pass him over or remember him as an afterthought. This led to material which I eventually interpreted as his feeling that his penis was too small compared to his father's. Consequently, he had been left wondering how he could compete and satisfy his mother. He then admitted that, in describing the scene previously in which he had felt like a little boy, he had stopped himself describing the other adults as 'big knobs' (slang for 'penis'). He then confessed he had always considered his penis was smaller than his brother's and that this had always left him feeling inadequate.

The following session he reported that our previous work had left him depressed. He did not want to feel like a little boy any more. He wanted to be a 'big knob', but all his achievements were either small, insignificant, superficial or false. It was no accident that he would never have children – how can you prove you are really a man unless you have had children? He wanted to be a big man – he feels good when having sex with his wife, especially if he is on top. I asked him to describe more about his experience during sex. He felt at his most powerful when entering his wife from behind. He liked to think he was the biggest man in the world and imagine himself as a stud, though he acknowledged his wife was his only long-term relationship. He felt different when underneath her, less in control, less powerful, it was less enjoyable, less life-enhancing. When she was on top, he would look at her behind and imagine anal sex, which they had sometimes engaged in.

After describing this, he then considered his plight. How should he proceed? Should he make a clean break with his past and forget it, though he thought (rightly) that I would say that would not work. He really wanted me to tell him what to do. I replied that he felt powerless, that he felt I was the powerful one on top. I added further that I wondered if the act of lying on his back on the couch left him feeling as though he were underneath in a sexual position here, with me and the analysis on top. He agreed, then said he had thought while I was speaking of having sex with me: he imagined he was having anal sex really aggressively, like he wanted to humiliate me, to show me he was powerful after all. At that point he felt all weak, and described all his strength draining from his body and falling through the couch. This was like a sudden bowel release. I recalled that some time earlier he described being excited by images of women defecating, with particular reference to a scene in Philip Roth's *Portnoy's Complaint* where a woman character excretes over a glass table while the man is underneath. What was being enacted in N's life, in the transference and was crystallized around the sexual act was his passive excitement and enjoyment counter-balanced by the fantasy of all-powerful, aggressive sexuality.

O had a hormonal problem that produced extra bodily hair especially on her face, something about which she was acutely sensitive. There was also some suggestion that the hormonal problem would effect her fertility and her ability to have vaginal sex. In early adolescence, her mother had taken her to visit various specialists. This had, amongst other things, entailed vaginal inspections which she had quite understandably found traumatic. As an adult, she found penetrative sex too painful to allow full penetration. There was some suggestion that this was part of the hormonal problem, but she also related it to the doctors' examinations during her teens. She had never had penetrative sex as she found this extremely painful; this made all her relationships with men very problematic. She also reported that penetration would also be painful when masturbating, but because she knew her limits, it did not hurt so much. She felt that her body would expel the penis since it felt so painful; it was also about stopping somebody getting too close to her.

Our work together seemed to progress satisfactorily. She was clearly moved by our sessions and thought a lot in between meetings. However, she began to report that, although psychotherapy was useful to her, she was not able to do anything with what emerged. It depressed her that it left her stuck. I proposed at this point that therapy was experienced rather like a penis or fingers: she wanted it, desperately, yet could not allow it inside her and was only left with the pain and depression of unsatisfied need. She was visibly shaken by this comment and felt confused. At the next session she described how my interpretation had confused her precisely because it had got inside her like nothing else I had previously said.

P was in his mid-thirties. He was a very creative and successful artist, but very schizoid. His relationships were superficial. He had an intense relationship with his girl-friend, but he experienced this as claustrophobic and could not commit himself to her. I found him equally distant in the therapy. I had the impression he was seldom quite in the room; bodily, yes, but that his mind was elsewhere. Something in him held back. I was often bored. He worried about being boring. Sometimes, even while he was talking, I found my mind wandering to such thoughts as 'Shall I decorate my room?' Such thoughts as these were indicative of our lack of contact and that I considered him as blending in with the wallpaper. On another occasion, I had been preoccupied with a problem of my own and found it difficult to focus on him. The following session he reported that he had found our previous session particularly useful! I understood this as he appreciated the fact that I was preoccupied and uninvolved with him and he rather enjoyed the psychological distance. The lack of involvement continued for a considerable period of time and proved resistant to interpretations or mirroring.

At one point he revealed his sexual fantasy. He usually found masturbation more satisfying than sex with a partner. Even when having sex with a partner he used his masturbation fantasy. This fantasy was a variation on the following theme: 'He is with a woman. They sometimes have some kissing and foreplay. Eventually they begin to undress.' Before they had taken off all their clothes or had sex he would have ejaculated. Often, he said, he had no sexual wish at all and would neither have sex nor masturbate for several months on end. I understood his fantasy and the transference as having the same meaning. He would protect himself during intercourse with a woman, or in therapy with me, by a fantasy that would help him keep his distance. He would not be totally naked or exposed; he might even avoid thinking about or considering the presence of genitals. The excitement was in starting to take off the clothes, not the intimacy this might lead to. He kept me at a distance. My talion countertransference in response was of a similar order, avoiding a meeting of minds. The transference was dominated by his active masturbation fantasy of going no further than partially stripping and never participating in intercourse, physical or psychical.

DISCUSSION

Analysis, sex and the symbol of creativity

Analysis is clearly not an exact metaphor for sexual intercourse. The most obvious difference is the absence of physical contact. Only in a few instances, such as when the analyst feels it is therapeutically useful to touch the patient, such as holding his or her hand, or, at the other extreme, turning the analytic encounter into a sexual liaison, is there a crossing of body egos. However, in many other respects the analogy between analysis and coitus holds good. In many ways, the intimacy between the analyst and analysand is often greater than between sexual partners. Frequently patients tell the analyst things they would never tell their parents, spouse, lover or best friend. In this respect, psychotherapists are highly privileged to hear that which cannot be spoken to anyone else.

The parallel between coitus and analysis has been made, usually in passing, by other authors. For example, Rycroft (1979) highlights that usually the only other people to exchange and discuss dreams, apart from therapists, are lovers, who do so for the intimacy induced by sharing dreams. McDougall (1978: 1) also makes a connection between analysis and lovers, drawing the parallel that 'the psychoanalytic adventure, like a love affair, requires two people'. A connection is also made by Meltzer (1973b: viii), who suggests that the psychoanalytic process needs (amongst other things) 'the passion of the coital couple'. Following a similar line of thought, it is interesting to note that Freud's wife, Martha, who was not interested in psychoanalysis, regarded analysis as 'a form of pornography' (quoted in Sayers, 1991: 150). None of these authors explore the full implications of their analogy for the development of an analysis or the transference. In a previous paper of mine (Mann 1988), I make a reference to a patient's work. This woman had begun her therapy by painting a picture she first described as a razor blade cutting skin; the next association was of a vagina. As a metaphor for the therapy this again held true, for this was indeed a tortuous birth. Yet, like the previous writers, I did not fully develop this point at the time.

Jung describes the transference in terms of the *coniunctio*, the royal or divine marriage, the 'higher copulation', or 'psychic pregnancy' (1946: 255) – like a chemical reaction when two substances combine, both are altered. Jung recognizes that the therapist may be influenced by, or often 'take over', the sufferings of his patients. The heart of the therapy relationship is that it is 'founded on mutual unconsciousness' (ibid.: 176). Jung seeks illumination (and to my mind substantially clouds matters) with reference to an important book in the alchemy opus, the illustrations from the *Rosarium Philosophorum*. These ten pictures show a symbolic king and queen in the various stages of courtship, coitus, death and resurrection. Jung's comment on the explicit nature of the pictures is worth quoting:

> As to the frank eroticism of the pictures, I must remind the reader that they were drawn for medieval eyes and that consequently they have symbolic rather than pornographic meaning. . . . Our pictures of the *coniunctio* are to be understood in this sense: union on the biological level is a symbol of the *unio oppositorum* at its highest. This means that the union of opposites in the royal art is just as real as coitus in the common acceptation of the word, so that the *opus* becomes an analogy of the natural process by means of which instinctive energy is transformed, at least in part, into symbolic activity [author's italics].
>
> (Jung 1946: 250)

129

I am totally in agreement with Jung's view of the therapeutic process as two-way traffic between unconscious to unconscious. I am also in total agreement with his proposal that coitus can symbolically represent other activities. It is precisely that phenomenon that is the subject of this book. However, I am struck by how he pulls back from the implications, not only of his own theory, but also of the evidence of the illustrations he is using. Jung shies away from the implications for the erotic transference when using the king and queen as a metaphor for therapy and transference; he is also reluctant to see that, while the instinctual can represent the spiritual, it can also represent itself, namely, something physical and instinctual. Further, the process works the other way, too: the spiritual can be used to represent the instinctual. It is tempting to consider that Jung's experience of having sex with one of his patients, Sabina Spielrein, and the ensuing controversy, left him feeling he needed to steer clear of the erotic transference–countertransference. It is quite remarkable that a series of ten pictures, mostly of a naked couple, can be so de-sexualized by his analysis and converted into the harmless and de-erotized imagery of chemical compounds.

Some post-Jungians have explored this issue more overtly. For example, Samuels (1980) has made an explicit connection between intercourse and transference. He describes a woman patient who at the start of her sexual relationships would try to orgasm before her partner. When the man commented on this she would stop trying to climax and encourage him to give her an orgasm. This led to a decline in sexual satisfaction for both. In the transference this manifested itself by her asking the analyst to repeat or expand upon his interpretations, he then had the feeling he was being encouraged to try harder to bring about an 'interpretative orgasm'. Samuels linked this to the patient's pursuit of omnipotent control, 'her tendency to create internal phantasied men so that a real penis/interpretation had to be defended against, lest it really make an impact on her' ibid.: 42). There was a denial of mutuality. This is linked to the Jungian idea of 'uroboric incest' (the circular snake that bites its own tail), which involves the creation of others out of material belonging wholly to the psychic world of the individual – or put another way, a denial of erotic feelings towards parents and, I would add also, a denial of the primal scene.

Limentani (1983) also makes a much more explicit link between transference and symbolic sexual intercourse and comes close to what I wish to elaborate on in this chapter. He describes several male patients who appeared to respond to him as they did their partner during sexual intercourse. One sexually passive patient, Alan, would force Limentani into the role of the controlling female of his infancy and love life. He would try to be as exciting as possible, and if the analyst responded positively, this was considered similar to a woman's orgasm. The patient was always preoccupied with his partner's sexual experience, so would feel satisfied by these good responses from the analyst. From the transference, it was possible to reconstruct that the patient's mother had used him as her phallus. Limentani's paper is concerned with aspects of the 'vagina man', so he does not draw out the full implications of this for the transference–countertransference similarities with sexual intercourse.

Scharff makes this same point in his interesting book, *The Sexual Relationship*:

> These six structures of self and object [Fairbairn's model of the mind] can be seen to be psychologically active in the sexual life of the individual and couple. This is seen in the sexual situation when people act as though relating to parts of primary figures from their past.
>
> (1982: 6)

Scharff goes on to give a rich source of examples throughout his book illustrating this view. Strangely, though, as is typical of many authors, he does not draw out the implications of this for the transference towards the analyst or the analysis.

I do not wish to imply that either the therapist or the patient *must* talk about sexual experiences. Such a prescriptive approach will be felt burdensome by both. Nor should the issue spring out of nowhere if it is discussed. As with any other interpretation, transference as coitus interpretations must relate to the material. On the other hand, a number of patients have reported having never discussed sexual experiences with previous therapists; I also know from colleagues and others having therapy that they, too, have not often raised the subject in therapy. Given the nature of psychoanalytic enquiry and that it is, in part, an investigation into the unconscious and all that the psyche finds painful and unacceptable, I do not see how an analysis can fully reach the deepest layers of the psyche without throwing light on sexual experience. Strangely, Meltzer, while noting that the analyst seldom hears about a patient's sexual relationships even though the transference draws to itself 'associations related almost exclusively to the infantile and perverse aspects of sexual behaviour and phantasy currently contaminating the patient's sexual life' (1973: 83), still considers reporting of sexual activity as a 'breach of the primary rule involving acting-in' the transference. Meltzer defends this with the argument that a 'tactful preservation' of the privacy of the adult love life of the patient, and thereby the partner, 'relieves the analyst of part of the pressure of certain countertransference anxieties and intrusiveness'. The difficulty of this line of thinking suggested by Meltzer is: first, it reinforces a defensive avoidance countertransference in the therapist and, second, as I am proposing throughout this chapter, the material is present in the transference whether it is interpreted or not. Certainly, to my mind, it is usually preferable to interpret the transference and not to shrink from doing so just because it feels embarrassing.

In all the clinical cases I described earlier an inhibition was present in the experience of sexual intercourse. This inhibition, in turn, was manifest in the transference, not usually in what was said, but more in the pattern of relating to me as the analyst. The analyst was experienced and treated in the same way as the sexual partner. Thus the transference becomes an act of symbolic sexual intercourse. The analyst becomes the unconscious representation of all that another means to the analysand. The analysis is thus treated as an act of sex with all the inhibition and defence manoeuvres that implies for the patient.

I am proposing that the patient experiences the analysis as he or she habitually experiences sexual intercourse and, in this respect, experiences the analyst as they would a sexual partner. The patient is not specifically experiencing either consciously or unconsciously sexual or loving feelings towards the person of the therapist. What is being experienced is the patient's habitual way of dealing with the most intimate forms of human contact. Indeed, as numerous analytic writers have shown, many unconscious sexual phantasies exist precisely to avoid any genuine psychical contact between the couple in intercourse.

In each of the cases described sexual intercourse was not felt by the patient as pleasurable in itself. This led to various problems and solutions, the latter of which normally compounded the difficulties of the former, resulting in impasse. This impasse was repeated in the same manner in the analysis. Psychical development had stagnated, change had ceased. The analysand was not able to engage the analyst in a creative coupling whereby the process of association and interpretation led to psychic growth, not only thereby freeing the patient from inhibition and re-edition but, in my opinion, should ideally also stimulate growth and new ideas in the analyst. In other words, a process of analytic change entails a coming together in symbolic intercourse of the analysand's material and associations and the analyst's interpretations. To paraphrase Winnicott, I suggest that a 'good enough interpretation' should result in a development in the patient's associations; in turn, this should lead to new interpretations, a genuine expansion of the analyst's understanding of psychic processes (not text-book replies). We may say that the confluence of association and interpretation leads to new thoughts (conception) which need to be faced wholeheartedly (carried in gestation) and not repressed by the analytic couple. Psychic change (birth) is the new developments in the self. The analytic process thus becomes a creative intercourse between two individuals who come together and produce something new between them.

In the examples I have cited as illustrations, this process had only partially occurred. An impasse had been reached, sometimes only briefly, on other occasions lasting many months. The creative coupling was not achieved: the patient's sexual inhibition was repeated to create an analytic impasse. Instead of conception, gestation and birth, there was a symbolic *coitus interruptus* or what appeared to be sterility. The patients felt the analysis to be like intercourse thus causing them to be unable to 'give' themselves fully. There was a limit to how they were able to use the analyst's interpretations for psychic transformation and birth. The sexual inhibition had imposed itself on the analysis so that the analysand could make only a partial coupling. Analysis and analyst had become like a sexual partner, something to keep at a distance from in the selfsame way.

If we look further at this inhibition I would postulate that what the patient experiences in a sexual partner is a mixture of the experience with the mother's body and primal scene phantasies. (I will deal in detail with this latter in the next chapter.) According to Scharff (1982) the symbolic functions of sex include:

1 The attempt to hold on to the memory of a loving parent and recollection of mutual care.
2 An attempt to overcome and forgive the withholding parent.
3 Most importantly, an attempt to synthesize and repair these two images, to make whole a sense of feeling and giving love, but in the context of overcoming distance and frustration.

In other words, in the sexual encounter the other lover and his or her copulation is unconsciously seen as an embodiment of parental sexual intercourse and actual knowledge of the mother's body.

How free or comfortable an individual will feel during sexual intercourse as an adult will, in the first instance, be influenced by his or her experiences with the mother's body. Sexual experience is a bridge between the deeper needs of individuals and their everyday life. Sexual intercourse revitalizes the old bonds between physical and symbolic levels of gratification. Freud showed how the infant–mother bond is not only the prototype for the infant's sexual experiences, but also how relating to the infant is part of the sexual experience of the mother:

A child's intercourse with anyone responsible for his care affords him an unending source of sexual excitation and satisfaction from his erotogenic zones. This is especially so since the person in charge of him, who, after all, is as a rule his mother, herself regards him with feelings that are derived from her own sexual life: she strokes him, kisses him, rocks him and quite clearly treats him as a substitute for a complete sexual object. [In a footnote here, he adds:] Anyone who considers this 'sacrilegious' may be recommended to read Havelock Ellis's views (1903) on the relation between mother and child, which agree almost completely with mine. [Freud continues his paragraph:] A mother would probably be horrified if she were made aware that all her marks of affection were rousing her child's sexual instinct and preparing for its later intensity. She regards what she does as asexual, 'pure' love, since, after all, she carefully avoids applying more excitations to the

133

child's genitals than are unavoidable in nursery care . . . [but] . . . She is only fulfilling her task in teaching the child to love.

(1905c: 145–146)

As Scharff (1982: 4) notes:

The urgency of this physical aspect of a couple's intimacy is often so compelling that it can only be readily compared to the physical interaction between child and mother in the first years and months of life, the other time in the life cycle when intense physicality is a major characteristic of the interaction of people who are each others primary love objects.

Stern (1993) has admirably demonstrated how the behaviours and psychic processes of adult lovers find their prototypes in infancy by the age of two. Stern notes that 'expressions of love begin strikingly early. The most basic physical language of affectionate love is both performed and learned by the fourth or fifth month of life' (ibid.: 176). He cites recent infant observations as illustrations. A comparison of infants and aspects of an adult's motor love show striking similarities: the overt behaviour of adult lovers such as gazing into each other's eyes without talking; maintaining very close proximity of faces, with parts of the body always touching; performing special gestures such as kissing, hugging, touching and holding the other's face and hands. These same sets of behaviours are performed in infancy: mother and infant begin mutual gaze around two and a half months for as long as a minute (infants do not do this when looking at other objects); Stern wryly notes that prolonged mutual gaze is rare in adult life: 'If two adults look into each other's eyes without talking for more than five seconds or so, they are likely to fight or make love' (ibid.: 177). The same holds true regarding physical proximity, where only intimate lovers and babies violate cultural norms of distance between two people.

Parents talking to infants, and much of the speech between lovers, violate the norms of speech. The music is emphasized over the lyric. Lovers and parent–infant dyads make parallel alterations, violations and exaggerations of facial and vocal expression with each other. Lovers tend to move in choreographed patterns; parents and infants show the same patterns. 'It is largely these patterns that alert us within seconds of the lover status' (Stern 1993: 177). There are also special gestures shared between lovers that develop early in infancy. Kissing is learned before the second year. Children like to caress the parent's face with their hands. When lying on a parent, children before the age of two frequently make pelvic thrusts as part of a wave of affection. Expressions of coquetry appear before the Oedipal phase.

All these behaviours are not only configurations of affection and love but also entail passion: excitement, crescendo and climax, decrescendo. Stern writes: 'the excitation envelopes that will one day be filled with sensual (sexual) content-contours are being established' (ibid.: 178). Infants appear to be 'falling in love' several times over as they progress developmentally.

The interpsychic experiences of love begin early. By the age of one, the infant has the theory of 'separate minds', that inner worlds are shareable: 'I know that you know that I know', which is the path lovers take in mutual discovery. Towards the end of the second year of life the infant acquires the capacity for shared meanings: code words and concepts, mutually defined, as lovers do. Another interpsychic feature in common between lovers and infants with mothers is the exclusive focus and preoccupation with one person's existence.

Stern concludes that:

> the experience of falling in love and being in love have a rich early developmental history . . . [and that] . . . these 'preconditions' and prototypes are registered in memory as motor memories, as procedural knowledge.
>
> (1993: 180)

How the mother greets the infant's gestures, either by under or over stimulation or good enough responses will obviously affect how the child comes to feel about his or her body and the body of his or her future sexual partners.

I have dwelt at length with the examples Stern cites. The important implications I wish to draw out are these. First, that the mother–baby relationship is the prototype for the adult sexual relationship. Second, that there is an inherent erotic component to the mother–infant bond. Given these two points, third, this has implications for the transference. By this, I mean that the erotic component of the mother–infant relationship will form a part of the patient's transference as much as any other part of his or her infantile experience. The erotic component is normal and healthy and to be expected in most analyses. This is to say that far from being the exception, the erotic transference is part of most, if not all, transference. Fourth: implied in all this, of course, is a challenge to the preferred knowledge in psychoanalytic practice and theory. If, as therapists, we are going to use the mother–infant analogy in our work, and most analytical therapists do, then we can no longer idealize out of existence the erotic nature of being a mother, any more than we can avoid placing the erotic centre stage in the 'therapeutic mothering'.

When the patient treats the analytic situation as though he or she is having sex, what is the internal psychic structure? A number of processes seem to occur simultaneously. Sexual intercourse entails the lowering of ego and body boundaries. That is to say, the other is allowed into the body and mind. Obviously this is an ideal description, as much can go wrong with either aspect.

The individual in a couple having intercourse will therefore be operating at a number of psychic levels. Firstly, he or she is faced with the closest physical contact that has been experienced since infancy. In fact, so long as there has been no history of early sexual abuse, the physical intimacy is greater during sex, with the probing tongues, vaginal or anal penetration, kissing and stroking all parts of the body, especially those areas prohibited to a mother with her infants. In other words, the body boundaries are breached like never before. Provided the couple are consenting and are reasonably neurosis-free, coitus will not only be pleasurable, but will also afford the deepest intimate and trusting contact adults will have with each other. It is no accident that countless generations of poets have described this type of intercourse variously as 'two laid down as one'. Sex that fulfils these kinds of conditions will be experienced as a regeneration of loving for physical and emotional needs in both the here and now with the partner, and also at a symbolic level with the actual and/or phantasized parents. Such is the ideal state of sexual intercourse.

If there is an inhibition or disturbance in the psyche, sexual intercourse becomes more problematic; sexual experience reactivates feelings of trauma and actual or phantasized failures of parenting. The sexual experience recalls the individual's psychological and physical relationship with primary care-givers in infancy. When problems emerge in the adult's sexual life they will also be indicating early anxieties around closeness and loss with mother. Scharff suggests that sexual symptoms embody the failure to mourn early aspects of separation from parental figures. I agree, but would add that various traumas, and failure of insufficient differentiation between parent and infant, will also find themselves embodied in coitus.

At the physical level, intercourse may not be wanted by one or the other partner. At a psychological level, many defences may activate the body in such a way as to make intercourse difficult or impossible, for example, premature ejaculation, erection difficulties, vaginismus, frigidity, impotence, etc. Fetishisms and perversions achieve a similar result in this respect. Various other distancing mechanisms may be employed such as indicated by the 'Lie back and think of England' recommendation. Woody Allen humorously explored this in his film *Husbands and Wives*, where a woman with intimacy problems begins distracting herself during sex by likening her friends to animals. Of course, there is a tragedy here, and it is frequently encountered in our psychoanalytic patients. The mind and body become split, as do sex and love. The psychological reasons are inevitably complex and have received attention from analytical writers. Such distortions in the experience of sexual intercourse include fetishism, sado-masochistic fantasies, bodily inhibition right through to necrophilia fantasies. A word of caution needs to be expressed here. I do not wish to imply that fantasy, or thinking about other things apart from your sexual partner is always necessarily a sign of sexual disturbance. Fantasy may play a large part in normal and totally healthy sexual activity. What I am describing is a habitual distortion in the sexual expression where, for whatever reasons and in whatever manner, the individual employs a psychological defence (which may have physical manifestations) that comes between his or her experience and the experience of his or her partner.

I am not suggesting that transference is nothing but symbolic sexual intercourse as clearly a good many other re-editions are being transferred in an analytic encounter. What I am suggesting is that there are certain pivotal phantasies which organize the individual's unconscious life. Freud (1918) called these 'primal phantasies' which included primal scene, castration and seduction phantasies. These phantasies are responsible for organizing phantasy life regardless of personal life experience. These phantasies, like collective myths, provide a representation of a solution to whatever constitutes a major enigma for the child. Freud was inclined to see primal phantasies as phylogenetically transmitted inheritance. I am doubtful about this last point, however. As Laplanche and Pontalis (1973) point out, there is no reason to reject as equally invalid the idea that structures exist in the phantasy dimension which are irreducible to the contingencies of the individual's lived experience.

The individual in coitus is experiencing a repetition of his or her own experience of personal intimacy as it was experienced first with the mother, and then later with the development of intimate relationships. This applies equally to men and women. In addition, individuals also bring to coitus their internal image of their parents in coitus, the primal scene. It is these elements that find their way into the transference when the patient unconsciously treats the analysis as sexual intercourse. We may therefore propose further that what is re-enacted in the transference, and the patient's actual sexual encounters, may be an expression of the patient's experience of the primal scene. That is, how the sexual coupling creative intercourse is internalized as a child is then played out in the adult's actual sexual encounters with others. These, in turn, will be expressed in the experience of psychoanalysis. This idea will be explored more thoroughly in the next chapter.

7

TRANSFERENCE AS SYMBOLIC PRIMAL SCENE

Did you ever see your father's cock, your mother's cunt? Yes or no, doesn't matter, the point is . . . these are mythical locations, surrounded by taboo, put off thy shoes for it is holy ground.

(Salman Rushdie *The Moor's Last Sigh*)

This chapter will focus on the ambiguous nature of the primal scene and is explored by considering various theorists, mythology, Freud's work with the Wolf-Man and my own clinical experience. The importance of the 'good enough' primal scene and its relation to creativity will be explored in the final section. I will attempt to show how the primal scene has a relevance to the transference and countertransference.

In a letter to Fliess, Freud wrote in 1899: 'I am accustoming myself to regarding every sexual act as a process in which four individuals are involved.' (Masson 1985). Actually, I think Freud got the mathematics wrong. There are not four but six individuals present: the couple in intercourse, plus two pairs of parents, thus totalling two bodies and six psyches. (I would presume that, characteristically, Freud neglected to include the person of the mother in his calculations.) He does not pursue his line of thinking to the logical conclusion here. Analysis has much in common with the symbolic significance of sexual intercourse, coitus consisting of two lovers plus their internal representations of the primal scene; it follows therefore that not only does the transference represent the patient's unconscious representation of the primal scene, also the countertransference will contain the therapist's unconscious representation of the primal scene. To paraphrase Freud, we would then say that *we must accustom ourselves to regarding every analytic session as a process in which six individuals are involved.*

Each partner in sexual intercourse brings with him or herself an unconscious phantasy of the primal scene. The best definition I have come across is in McDougall (1978: 56) who describes the primal scene as follows:

This term being taken to connote the child's total store of unconscious knowledge and personal mythology concerning human sexual relations, particularly that of his parents.

The primal scene is held as a frame of reference not only for all sexual states of mind, but also as a central structure in the unconscious of infants and adults. An individual brings to sexual encounters his or her personal phantasy of what coitus is. The foundation for this personal phantasy is the primal scene. To an extent, this is modified by his or her own experience of sexual intercourse. However, in as far as the primal scene exerts a disproportionate and rigid influence in the unconscious, each lover will not be able significantly to modify and change his or her sexual experience or learn from subsequent sexual experiences.

The primal scene phantasy contains all the unconscious knowledge and phantasies about two people in sexual intercourse. This, in turn, is brought by each lover into a sexual encounter. In this way, sexual intercourse may then become a symbolic re-enactment of the primal scene. For example, the sexual partner may be experienced as a combined parent. More often, the sexual partners will divide the roles in their unconscious phantasies. One of my psychotherapy patients, who was heavily identified with his father, had married a woman with the appearance and personality of his mother.

Freud (1905c) in his *Three essays on sexuality* was fully aware of how an adult may seek to marry the desired parent of childhood. He writes:

> It often happens that a young man falls in love seriously for the first time with a mature woman, or a girl with an elderly man in a position of authority; this is clearly an echo of the phases of development that we have been discussing, since these figures are able to re-animate pictures of their mother or father. There can be no doubt that every object-choice whatever is based, though less closely, on these prototypes. A man, especially, looks for someone who can represent his picture of his mother, as it has dominated his mind from his earliest childhood; and accordingly, if his mother is still alive, she may well resent this new version of herself and meet her with hostility. In view of the importance of a child's relations to his parents in determining his later choice of a sexual object, it can easily be understood that any disturbance of those relations will produce the gravest effects upon his adult sexual life.

I would add here that this transference is not dependent upon the respective ages of the lovers, older man with a younger woman, or vice versa, though the transference is perhaps more transparent in these situations. What I would wish to highlight are the primal scene implications of this. When an individual forms a sexual relationship with someone like the parent, a variety of psychic mechanisms are at work. In the first instance, there will be an attempt to recapture the lost relationship with the parent: the wife becomes a mother substitute or the husband a father substitute. Armstrong-Perlman (1991: 351) has described how obsessive love for an exciting object is a refinding of the bad object. This is particularly the case with men who had experienced mothers as both exciting and rejecting. In seeking a different type of woman they are blind to the similarities and 'like Oedipus, married their mothers in ignorance'.

In addition, the identifications with the remaining parent are also re-enacted: if a man is unconsciously (or even consciously) equating his wife with his mother he is thereby also equating himself with his father. The same is equally true for the woman who sees her father in her husband; by association she becomes as mother in the parental intercourse. In this situation, the sexual life of the parents is transposed on to the current sexual encounter, thereby representing the parents in coitus. Nor is the situation fundamentally different with those individuals who have deliberately attempted to choose a partner who is the opposite of their mother or father. Experience shows that, frequently, the partner often still has the qualities of the avoided parent. In a later paper, Freud (1915c) describes just such a process in the case of a woman patient whom he saw for two consultations. She was a sexually inhibited woman who had formed a brief, non-genital relationship with a man. She quickly became paranoid and accused him of taking photos while they embraced on a couch and of discussing her with her boss. Freud deduced that this was determined by her phantasy of watching sexual intercourse between her parents and the woman's unconscious identifications with her mother:

> The patient's lover was still her father, but she herself had taken her mother's place . . . instead of choosing her mother as a love-object, she identified herself with her – she herself *became* her mother' [Freud's italics].

It is worth mentioning that, though Freud states several times that this woman was quite reluctant to see him (she was there on her lawyer's advice), he does not draw out the transference implications: that he was being experienced as the lover–father and the consultations were a re-enactment of the patient's view of the primal scene.

In my view, transference as symbolic sexual intercourse and primal scene are aspects of the erotic transference and countertransference matrix. This matrix is expressed and mediated through the erotic bond that forms in the analytic dyad.

IN THE PARENT'S BEDROOM:

Observations and theories on the primal scene

Discussion of the primal scene falls broadly into two groups in the literature. The first of these includes writers who explore the significance of the actual experience of hearing or seeing parental intercourse: Freud (1918), Abraham (1913), Peto (1975) and Silber (1981). Typically, this experience is described as over-stimulating for the developing ego and one which places unremitting instinctual pressure on the psyche. It is of note that there is some anthropological evidence to suggest that in those societies where parents and children sleep in the same room, exposure to the primal scene is not enough by itself to cause psychic disturbance: Devereux (1961), Boyer (1964), Boyer and Boyer (1972) and Jackson (1989); the same point is also made by Esman (1973).

The second group consists of writers who focus on its symbolic significance irrespective of actual experience. These two distinctions are not absolute: those who emphasize actual experience also recognize that this has symbolic effects.

Since Freud, primal scene trauma has been evoked to explain many diverse symptoms.

McDougall (1978) explores the primal scene from its symbolic position. Her emphasis is to discuss primal scene in relation to perversion. The primal scene is reinvented. The genital organs of the parents are not intended to complete one another and mutual desire is non-existent.

Klein considers the parental couple become internal objects. In her paper of 1925, Klein connects a child's curiosity with the primal scene for which a one-and-a-half-year-old child can find no explanation.

In her later work, Klein (1955) describes how the infant is both enticed and repulsed by the image of watching and listening to the primal scene. The child comes to feel excluded by the parental intercourse (Klein 1952) where the parents enjoy the objects (penis and breast) which the child wants. The infant may have the fantasy of the parents in a state of constant mutual gratification. This may lead to the image of the combined parent: mother contains penis or whole of father; father contains breast or whole of mother. In this phantasy the parents are fused inseparably in coitus.[2]

The primal scene has become a major focus with several of Klein's followers. Racker (1968) describes how the Oedipus complex is repeated in the transference and that one of the most painful and anxiety-provoking Oedipal experiences is of the parents' sexual relations. While acknowledging that the patient relives these fantasies and impulses with the analyst, Racker's emphasis is on viewing the analyst as the unified couple which represents everything desirable and pleasurable and is therefore the object of envy, rivalry and hatred. Both the patient and the therapist may have to overcome resistances to making these fantasies conscious.

Money-Kyrle (1968, 1971) saw the aim of analysis as helping the patient to discover what he or she already knows by overcoming the emotional impediments that inhibit insight. He considers that there are a few fundamental *facts of life* which can be distorted in adult thinking: (1) recognition of the breast as a supremely good object; (2) recognition of the primal scene as a supremely creative act; (3) recognition of the inevitability of time and death. All produce powerful defences against recognition.

I shall focus on only the second of these 'facts of life'. Steiner (1993) elaborates Money-Kyrle's points further. The primal scene is associated with the Oedipus complex. The intrusion of the third object, the father, provokes jealousy. The issue of creativity is symbolized by the child's curiosity about where babies come from. If the primal scene is successfully negotiated, the child recognizes the creativity of the parental couple and, by identifying with them both, can embark on his or her own creative life. The disavowal of the primal scene takes various forms, for example, the fantasy of participating in parental intercourse via identification with one of them; a homosexual coupling may be made via sex identification: a boy taking his father's place, a symbolic murder as Oedipus killing his father.

The maintenance of such phantasies requires that the facts of life, which ensure fertile creativity, must be disavowed. Correct perception requires the infant to see that he or she is excluded by virtue of size and immaturity. A similar point is made by Britton (1989) where an 'Oedipal illusion' denies the significance of the parents' relationship to each other.

Steiner goes further to suggest that these issues might also be evaded when splitting is more total. The original split between the good and the bad breast is further complicated by the father, who is split into the good and the bad penis. Two versions of the primal scene then exist: a loving one between a good mother and father and a hostile, violent one between the bad couple. Out of this latter the terrifying combined object emerges. Only as these splits lessen can the parents be seen as coming together in a supremely creative act.

I would develop some of these ideas further. The infant's anxiety is not simply that the parents are making more babies. Equal to this, if not more terrifying, is the recognition of the parent's desire for each other, a desire that does not include and cannot be satisfied by the infant or any feared babies.

Winnicott (1958) suggests that the capacity to be alone depends on the individual's ability to deal with the feelings aroused by the primal scene. The primal scene is an exciting relationship between the parents which is perceived or imagined, and if the child is healthy he or she can master the hate and gather it into the service of masturbation. This is essentially a healthy process whereby the child accepts responsibility for being the third person in a triangular relationship.

The child cannot act on his or her desires; this is partly because the parents are unlikely either to be killed or marry the child, but also due to the child's developmental immaturity. Arlow (1980) and Ikonen and Rechardt (1984) suggest this leads to humanity's universal trauma: fragile self-esteem and a propensity to shame, uncertainty and compensatory stirrings: 'Because I'm not included there, I am outside everything.' Primal scene phantasies contain a narcissistic element, reflecting a sense of self that is incomplete

The last two authors I will outline are Samuels (1989) and Arlow (1980).

142

Following on from Jung, who saw the value of primal scene in containing seeds of psychic integration and conscious discrimination, Samuels sees the symbolic nature of primal scene as an individual's emotional attempt to function pluralistically: coupling together various psychic elements and agencies without losing their individual tone and functioning. Primal scene comes to represent an attempt to develop one's own ideas within a tradition. It is about origins and mystery and, therefore, has a powerful fascination as a symbol for life as it develops: 'Bringing things together is a precis of creativity' (Samuels 1989: 124). Arlow (1980) also sees primal scene as representing a type of memory schema around which material relating to an individual's crucial conflicts are organized. As such, primal scene symbolically represents the coming together or integration of opposites. A fertile image of the primal scene is something divided and unstuck. The ability to sustain an unstuck, vital and imaginable image of the parents in bed determines a person's capacity to sustain conflict constructively. A stuck primal scene imagery is intolerant, with an inflated superiority; difficulty in imagining the primal scene is related to fear of conflict.

Freud believed that the primal scene is not recollected as such, but has to be reconstructed. Lukacher (1986) discusses in detail the problematic status of the primal scene in the psyche. He proposes that it is located between historical memory and imaginative construction, between archival verification and imaginative free play. The primal scene points to the reality in the very act of establishing its inaccessibility. It represents the question of origin that must be remembered but memory fails utterly. Lukacher writes:

> The remembrance of that forgotten history and of that forgotten scene does not occur within the mode of subjective or personal recollection; it occurs as an act of interpretation, as a construction, as reading.
>
> (1986: 43)

If nothing else, what these various theories about the primal scene demonstrates is the continual fascination that it holds on the human imagination. The primal scene is both thought about and denied and its significance is difficult to comprehend. In the next section I will demonstrate this as a universal preoccupation.

PRIMAL SCENE REPRESENTATION IN MYTH

The difficulty in imagining the primal scene finds expression in a number of myths. The mythic representations of the primal scene indicate that a preoccupation with it is, throughout history, a fundamental issue and is probably universal. The primal scene is significant, not just in pathology, since it also represents ubiquitous potential for fantasy formation. As I have stated elsewhere (Mann 1992), I do not use the term myth in its pejorative sense. Rather, I see the value in myths as embodying deep underlying psychic

143

reality and human preoccupations. The prevalence of myths dealing with similar themes is an indication of psychological issues that seek some form of expression and resolution and which need to be worked through by succeeding generations.

The gods and goddesses are given the attributes and projections of their maker, the human psyche. Consequently, they represent either idealized or split-off aspects of significant objects, parents, siblings, etc., in the unconscious. We would expect, therefore, frequently to encounter primal scene imagery in myth and this is indeed the case. We find that the sexual behaviour of the gods reflects the unthinkable nature of the primal scene. I will cite just a few examples to illustrate the point.

There are two principal images of the primal scene in Christianity: the conception of Jesus and the creation of Adam and Eve. I will deal with the former first. Mary is a virgin, Joseph has not sexually consummated the marriage, the father is God, conception is immaculate. This raised anatomical difficulties of considerable proportions for early Christians. Medieval art typically represents the conception as a shaft of light entering Mary's stomach: thus conception is achieved without either penis or vagina. Psychoanalytically speaking, we might say here that the primal scene, the coming together of the penis and vagina, has been denied. The moment of conception is magically displaced, thereby avoiding the recognition of parental coitus. The same holds true in various other myths. In Egyptian mythology, the creator of all things, Ra the sun god, is self-created (having sexual union with himself), as is Mother Earth in the Greek Olympian creation myth and the Judao–Christian god of *Genesis*. We may speculate on the denial of the primal scene and of the procreative couple which gains further evidence as subsequent children of these creator gods are also parthenogenically reproduced. What is disavowed is the role of the two parents jointly coupled in a creative procreation. In a similar vein, we might also wonder about mythic accounts of the origins of the first people. In Egyptian mythology there are two gods credited with creating humanity: the ram-headed god, Eleplantine Khnemu, who formed people upon his potter's wheel and Ptah, the god of artifice. In Greek myth, Prometheus is credited with forming mortal men from clay and water. In the Judao–Christian *Genesis*, man is also made from clay. We could ask two questions here: first, why is there an absence, or denial of a procreative couple as the originators of humanity; second, could this also be, perhaps, an expression of cloacal fantasies of anal birth similar to those found in children (Freud 1908)? Other mythic accounts seek to undo the primal scene. For example, Zeus' wife Hera would regularly bathe in the springs of Canathus near Argos and thus renew her virginity; Aphrodite used the same procedure, bathing in the sea at Paphos, where she renewed her virginity after cuckolding Hephaestus. Regaining virginity, as though there had been no penetration by a penis, is a manoeuvre that turns the primal scene into nothing, as though it had never happened.

144

Another method of distorting the primal scene is also well illustrated in Greek myth: the sexual relations between gods and mortals are disguised. Zeus turned into a quail and begat Apollo and Artemis; on another occasion he metamorphasized into a serpent when he coupled with Persephone; on yet another occasion he was a swan when he coupled with Leda; at other times he became a bull and a shower of gold. Apollo, likewise, turned first into a tortoise then a serpent when seducing the nymph Dryope. I would suggest that these myths are dealing with a psychic mechanism whereby the primal scene is distorted rather than viewed directly: the coupling parents cannot be viewed as two people enjoying each other in a creative intercourse. Another myth tells of how Semele, mother of Dionysus, was consumed by thunder and lightning after demanding to see Zeus in his true aspect, without disguise; Actaeon is torn to pieces by the hounds of Artemis after seeing the goddess bathe naked in a stream. Both myths imply that witnessing even the nakedness of the parent is both dangerous yet also exciting.

The act of coitus is denied mostly by denial of the father's penis. In a more explicit primal scene image, Noah's son is cursed for seeing his father's genitals. In other words, these myths suggest that the primal scene cannot be looked at directly (rather like death and the sun) but only through a veil of illusion. To see the parents copulating is to court disaster. One might add further that Jesus appears to have no sexual desire nor does he procreate. In that sense his penis is ascribed no sexual functions. Christianity, a bastion of paternity, actually denies the penis and its paternal role. It is little wonder, then, that most people cannot picture their parents having sex unless with disguised symbolism.

This brings me to my second point about mythic images of the primal scene, namely, the frequency with which it is imbued with a sado-masochistic phantasy. The other significant primal scene in Christianity is that of Adam and Eve, the grandparents of humanity. Their intercourse was acceptable so long as they were neither aware nor conscious of their genitals. Eating the apple gave them shame and the need to hide their sexual organs. This act of hubris was severely punished with the permanent loss of paradise. In other words, the primal scene is unthinkable because to imagine the parents having sex is punishable. There are superego injunctions against the primal scene.

I would also like to cite a literary, but not mythological, example at this point. The recognition of the punitive nature of primal scene thoughts brings me to what is perhaps the most famous literary example in English, from Shakespeare's *Hamlet*. After the 'play scene', Hamlet harangues his mother in her bedroom for all his problems, which include his primal scene fantasy:

> Nay, but to live
> In the rank sweat of an enseamed bed,

> Stew'd in corruption, honeying and making love
> Over the nasty sty . . .
>
> *(Hamlet* III: iv)

Hamlet has no image of a creative intercourse between his mother and step-father. With staggering insight, Shakespeare has Hamlet's thoughts of the primal scene interrupted at the height of passion. As Hamlet launches into the shortcomings of Claudius' masculinity (he is a 'slave . . . A cut purse . . . A king of shreds and patches') either the ghost of Hamlet's father enters the room or his presence is hallucinated in what his mother firmly believes is Hamlet's madness. The effect is to tear the latter's thoughts away from the primal scene for which he is rebuked by his father's ghost. Shakespeare has intuitively grasped the unthinkable nature of the primal scene and that it is subject to severe punishment from the superego.

Edelheit (1974) cites other myths as primal scene representations, principally the crucifixion (the cross being an ancient symbol of sexual union and fertility) and the Gilgamesh motif. In Sumerian myth, Gilgamesh separates and kills two lions, then identifies with them by wearing their skins. This finds representation in decorative designs such as heraldic images: two beasts (parents) separated by a warrior (child).

The last myth I will discuss is that of Hermes, which is cited by Samuels (1989). On the first day he is born, Hermes sings to both his parents, Zeus and the nymph Maia, a song on 'all the glorious tale of his own begetting', and acknowledges the participation of both parents. His qualities include: he is a soul guide, agent of transformation and connection, but also a trickster, liar and thief. Samuels sees Hermes as representing a synthesis of opposites. What I find interesting about the Hermes myth is precisely its difference from the majority of primal scene myths. Conception is neither parthenogenic nor disguised, and as such is an apparent recognition of both parents in creative intercourse. However, even in the Hermes myth, parental intercourse is acknowledged only within limits: Zeus and Maia come together in order to produce Hermes. In other words, the Hermes myth embodies the infantile omnipotent fantasy of parents existing for the child's benefit. What is still denied is the parental desire for each other.

Collectively, what these various myths imply is that the primal scene is a source of fascination that is repeatedly reworked by successive generations of human beings. It stands as a continual focal point demanding expression across widely geographical and temporal zones. In addition, the myths indicate the extensive use of distortion that ensures the primal scene is almost incomprehensible or even unthinkable. It stands as a fact of life that can never be known, only to be imagined or navigated by a circuitous route.

Before giving some examples from my own work, I will consider the primal scene transference implications with Freud's most famous case, the Wolf-Man.

146

FREUD AND THE WOLF-MAN

Freud (1900) first draws attention to parental coitus as a source of anxiety in his book on dreams. From then on, he gives increasing value and importance in analytic work to the primal scene phantasies which are seldom absent in human beings. The term, primal scene, is first introduced in his study on the Wolf-Man, *From the History of an Infantile Neurosis* (1918). In this he suggests a complete analysis must reveal the primal scene, which he pieces together in minute detail from the material. His conclusion in this study is that the primal scene is understood by the child as an act of aggression by the father in a sado-masochistic relationship, and that infantile sexual theories lead the child to imagine that what is taking place is anal sex. Furthermore, the scene is exciting, but also provides the basis for castration anxiety. As Laplanche and Pontalis (1973) state, Jung criticized Freud's thesis, saying that such scenes are merely phantasies constructed retrospectively by the adult. Freud's reply is that perception furnishes the child with clues. The primal scene comes to represent a solution to whatever constitutes a major enigma for the child. My own view here is that both Freud and Jung were correct in their own way: the child will construct his or her theories about the primal scene regardless of clues, but such clues that are available will greatly influence the phantasized view of the primal scene. Moreover, this image will change over time and the adult's reconstructions may or may not be accurate, historically speaking. However, the adult's phantasy of the primal scene will be a truthful or accurate expression of his or her current state of phantasy (reconstruction).

The case history of the Wolf-Man is both Freud's most important and complete treatment of the primal scene. Freud's patient had a dream before his fourth birthday (on Christmas day) that six or seven white wolves (he drew only five in his picture) were sitting motionless in a tree outside his window. Deriving from a carefully pieced-together reconstruction, Freud's view was that the dream had arisen from the actual witnessing of parental intercourse at the age of one-and-a-half, leading to the development of a severe neurosis as a young adult. Freud's case demonstrates that he certainly considered the Wolf-Man had actually witnessed the primal scene. However, he does also say: 'It is . . . a matter of indifference . . . whether we choose to regard it as a primal *scene* or a primal *fantasy*' (Freud's italics). I both agree and disagree with this statement. My agreement is that the primal scene will usually be a significant structuring phantasy in the unconscious, and this is regardless of whether it exists only as a phantasy or actuality. My disagreement is that, since in our society the sex life of the parents is usually shrouded in mystery, any actual exposure is frequently detrimental, but is also likely to be compounded by other aspects of the parents' behaviour. I will discuss this further shortly.

In his study of the Wolf-Man, Freud had seen brilliantly clearly how the primal scene fantasy becomes re-enacted in the individual's experience of sexual intercourse. At the age of one-and-a-half, the Wolf-Man had seen his parents having sex, with his father entering mother from behind. As an adult, the Wolf-Man's own sexual preference was for the woman to assume the posture which was ascribed to his mother in the primal scene. He felt the greatest excitement with women with large and conspicuous buttocks, and copulating in any way other than from behind gave him scarcely any enjoyment. This expressed the patient's identification with his father. There were also identifications with his mother. The Wolf-Man always complained that the world was hidden from him by a veil which could be torn away in only one situation. This took the form of anal erotization in the use of enemas. The Wolf-Man preferred these to be administered by a male servant until necessity forced him to do it himself. The effect of the enema was that, as he passed a motion, he was able for a short while to see the world clearly. The veil related to his birth as he was told he had been born with a caul. Tearing the caul–veil away and passing the stool was his phantasy of rebirth, but his preference to have the enema–penis delivered by a man indicated that the Wolf-Man had identified himself with his mother, and the servant was acting as his father; the enema was a repetition of the primal scene. Freud concludes that the phantasy for the Wolf-Man's recovery took the following form:

> Only on condition that he took the woman's place and substituted himself for his mother and thus let himself be sexually satisfied by his father and bore him a child – only on that condition would his illness leave him. Here, therefore, the phantasy of re-birth was simply a mutilated and censored version of the homosexual wishful phantasy.
>
> (Freud 1918)

I would not want to take issue with Freud's analysis thus far, as essentially I am in agreement, and the case of the Wolf-Man nicely illustrates the connection between the primal scene phantasy and the adult's experience of sexual intercourse. What I would wish to explore further are the transference implications.

In his study on the Wolf-Man, Freud makes only three references to the transference. Doubtless, more than three were made during the course of treatment, but the three that Freud cites give us a flavour of how he used the transference. Two of the references concern the influence of the respective nationalities of the patient and analyst: Russian and Austrian. One of these related to the positive transference. The Wolf-Man had a positive figure in his past, a German tutor, which led to a preference for things German, 'for instance, physicians, sanatoria, women'. Freud comments on how useful this had been during the treatment. The second concerned a negative transference relating to the outbreak and effects of the First World War. The Wolf-Man had terminated shortly before hostilities and later told Freud that, after a few months, he was seized by a desire to tear himself free from Freud's influence.

The third transference reference related to the Wolf-Man's manner of dealing with difficulties during the analysis: at these points he would threaten Freud with 'eating me up and later with all kinds of other ill-treatments – all of which was merely an expression of affection'. This related to the patient's identification with his father, who would play wolf or dog games with his son and threaten jokingly to gobble him up.

We may note that, despite the importance he lays on the primal scene in the development of the Wolf-Man's neurosis, Freud seems not to have drawn out the implications of the primal scene for the transference, or even the quite apparent erotic transference, or, more accurately, the homoerotic transference. And yet the primal scene is clearly significantly influencing the transference. We may note Freud being cast in the mother role, the Wolf-Man's preference for things German, in one breath mentioning physicians and women; in addition, the Wolf-Man's taunts to eat Freud up, thereby defining the Wolf-Man–father in coitus with Freud–mother.

Perhaps the most significant part of the primal scene transference is the Freud–father, Wolf-Man–mother relationship. In *Analysis terminable and interminable* Freud (1937) tells us more about the analysis of this man. He spells out that progress in the analysis had been made, but had stagnated in that the Wolf-Man found his treatment comfortable. Freud's response was to fix a time-limit. This caused the patient's resistances to shrink and, in the last months of work, produced all the memories and allowed connections to be made. My interpretation of this process is as follows: setting the time-limit was the equivalent of the enema that tore the veil away from the world; the time-limit–enema allowed for the free passage of associations–stool which brought insight and clarity. Further, we should connect this to both the witnessing of the primal scene at eighteen months and the dream of a four-year-old. The Wolf-Man awoke to see his parents copulating. The dream at four begins with the doors of the room slowly opening, later associations indicating this was symbolic of the infant waking and opening his eyes. In other words, seeing the parental sex, the doors opening, was like the enema: the tearing away of a veil, allowing clarity and things to be seen. This, of course, is also the function of analytic insight. The primal scene transference thus becomes apparent: setting a time-limit was like an enema, which was like the doors opening, which was like the infant waking up. The time-limit–enema–parental intercourse forced its way into the Wolf-Man's psyche, where things could be seen as they really were, without veils or illusions. When Freud set the time-limit he was symbolically re-enacting the primal scene with the Wolf-Man as mother. Setting the termination date was like the child awakening: both situations ensuring the Wolf-Man would see (have analytic insight) into what would otherwise not be seen.

There are a number of other elements that need to be elucidated from

Freud's use of the Wolf-Man's material that is relevant to the subject of primal scene transference.

Lukacher (1986) brings together a number of interesting ideas concerning Freud, the Wolf-Man and the primal scene. The Wolf-Man is unquestionably Freud's most important case study and he returned to it with further reflections for the rest of his publishing career. The Wolf-Man, as Freud knew, pushed him to the limits of his theoretical understanding and clinical practice. Apart from these professional considerations, Freud's gratitude to the Wolf-Man also took a more personal form. For many years after the Russian had been dispossessed of his wealth by the Bolsheviks, Freud organized collections of money to support him in exile. Lukacher cites the work of the French analyst Granoff (1976), who points out that the Wolf-Man came from Odessa, the one Russian city with which Freud's own mother and father were associated. Freud approved of the Wolf-Man's marriage to a woman called Therese who looked like a czarina (in his autobiography, the Wolf-Man tells us he kept going to Freud only because he was the sole physician who did not disapprove of this woman). The Wolf-Man was particularly keen on her 'blue black hair' which was parted in the middle and is mentioned twice in his autobiography. Granoff suggests that Freud saw in her his own first love, a Gisela Fluss, or even his mother. Ernest Jones tells us Freud attributed his infatuation with Gisela to her black hair and eyes. Granoff points out that in an 1876 family portrait, the only woman with a centre parting is Freud's mother. After the First World War, Therese's hair turned white. When returning to Vienna in 1918, the couple probably reminded Freud of his own parents and past.

Now, if the Wolf-Man and his wife represent Freud's parents, we may then make some justifiable speculations about the implications of this for the transference. Lukacher, in his chapter on the Wolf-Man, has a section entitled, 'Analysis *a Tergo*', a play on 'coitus *a tergo*', the term Freud uses to describe the scene of the Wolf-Man's father entering his mother from the rear. 'Analysis *a tergo*' refers to the therapist sitting behind the patient on the couch. Freud had adopted this procedure in order to diminish the erotic acting out during clinical work, originally sitting where his patients could see him. In his autobiography, the Wolf-Man recalled Freud explaining to him that one woman patient had tried to exploit being able to see him. Freud later gave an account of the same incident in his *Autobiographical Study* (1925), where he describes the woman throwing her arms around him and mutual embarrassment being averted only by the unexpected entry of the maid. After this, Freud sat behind the couch. Now, it is inconceivable to imagine that such a genius as Freud could not see that simply moving a chair is not going to influence the existence of affects or fantasies or in anyway diminish desire. At best, moving the chair merely places a slight obstacle to the expression of desire; it is not so easy for the patient to throw his or her arms around the therapist, but it is not impossible, and certainly does not do away with erotic wishes. Lukacher puts it nicely: Freud sitting behind the couch is 'more than a little reminiscent of the primal scene' (1986: 145). We might wonder, then, that the Wolf-Man's case was significant to Freud since the former's experience of the primal scene plays out the primal scene of Freud and psychoanalysis itself: where, in effect, the interrupting maid had been placed in the position of the child as spectator to the parents' primal scene, whilst Freud, now sitting behind the couch, becomes the spectator, seeing but unseen. We might push this point further. Until the end of his life, the Wolf-Man asserted he had no recollection of the primal scene that Freud had constructed from his material. Freud had always insisted that the memory would come. It never did. The primal scene was always more Freud's reconstruction than the Wolf-Man's. This is not simply a conundrum for Freud and the Wolf-Man, but is at the heart of all analytic encounters. In the subtle interplay of transference and countertransference in psychoanalysis we might wonder about 'coitus *a tergo*', and who is in front and who is behind.

CLINICAL VIGNETTES

Having detailed how the primal scene phantasy affected Freud's work with the Wolf-Man, I will now explore the idea of transference as symbolic primal scene with some material from my own practice.

Q is married with no children. I had seen her for two years with considerable success and improvement in both her presenting problems and the underlying causes. There was one area, though, that seemed intractable: she and her husband refrained from sexual intercourse, largely because Q did not like to be touched in a sexual way. We had discussed this on numerous occasions and, though we achieved new understandings each time, the problem remained.

Whilst coming for analysis, Q had changed careers and had begun training as a doctor. Part of this involved doing a placement on a maternity ward. This development was a catalyst for us to explore her sexual difficulties further. In one session, she reported that she still had not seen anybody giving birth on the ward. Then there was a long silence. She considered she had nothing more to say on the subject; she had said all there was to say the week before when she wondered whether going on the maternity ward would make her broody; she thought not. She continued to speak in single sentences, and eventually said it was like wading through mud that day. She was sure there was nothing else to say. I agreed it was like mud, but suggested it felt as if she had come up against a brick wall, and that if there was nothing else to say it would be easy to move on, but she had ground to a halt. She said that when any of her friends asked her when she and her husband were going to have children, her 'stock' reply was 'Oh, I suppose we'll get round to it some day'. I replied that a 'stock reply' required no new thoughts;

perhaps it felt worrying to think about the problem. Q then said she thought the difficulty in getting her mind around the subject of children was related to the sexual problem with her husband. Things still had not changed. I said my impression was they both made detours around the subject of sex. She agreed and added that, though they had a lot of affection, touching and cuddles, it did not go further than that. I then felt I had a better understanding of the impasse over this subject. My interpretation at this point was that I thought the difficulty she had in talking about the problem in analysis was replicating the problem with her husband: she and I could go so far in dealing with her problems, and not without success, but there was a turn-off point where she would not let us go deeper or achieve a symbolic intercourse – something always remained untouchable. Just as she could go so far and no further with her husband with sex, she could similarly go only so far in her therapy with me. She was a little embarrassed by my interpretation, which related to her resistance to conscious awareness of the erotic transference. She became very upset at this point and, not by coincidence, it was the end of the session, so we could not explore this further, another repetition of the sexual avoidance with her husband.

The next session she still felt stuck. She believed my interpretation from the previous session had been right, but she did not know where to go from there. She talked a little more about her experience of sex. After intercourse, she always felt she wanted to die. She would begin to feel suffocated and choke during intercourse. Afterwards, she would feel extremely lonely, unsafe and exposed. This, too, repeated itself in the transference with her feeling that, though my interpretation had been right, it had left her exposed and with nowhere to hide.

This led us to a discussion of her early sexual abuse from her grandfather, which we had talked about before. The most striking memory she had of this experience was remembering the weight of his heavy body on hers, and the ensuing feeling of suffocation. At this point, I reminded her of two other things she had told me, neither of which she was sure were memory or a figment of her imagination. The first was that her mother, grandmother and she had all slept in the same room; grandfather slept in a room by himself; father had left home when she was much younger. Q recalls that her mother would sometimes get up in the night and leave the bedroom for several hours. All this Q clearly recalled. What she was unsure was a memory or not was a recollection of following mother one night after she left the room. Mother went into grandfather's room and Q saw her mother and maternal grandfather having sex through a slightly ajar door. Q does not know if she made this memory up. I do not know either, but I am aware that incest does often travel down families into later generations; if Q was abused, the chances were her mother had also been abused.

The other memory, the authenticity of which Q also doubted, was from a time after her grandfather had become terminally sick. He was ill at home lying in his room. One night Q believes she followed her mother out of the bedroom and again spied into her grandfather's bedroom, this time to witness her mother placing a pillow over grandfather's face. He was dead the following morning, and the doctor registered the death as of natural causes.

There is no way a therapist can know whether such material is fact or fantasy; Q herself was not sure, though she came to believe it was probably true. By and large I assume that, unless I am dealing with a patient who I know tells lies, most analysands have little to gain from either lying or even unconsciously fabricating bad memories (this is distinct from screen memories). What is a fact, and is of importance, is the symbolic meaning these 'memories' had on Q's psychic structure. I now understood and interpreted her sexual difficulties and the analytic impasse as an expression of these key memories. For psychic purposes, the image of her mother and grandfather having sex was for Q a primal scene experience–fantasy. Her own experience during sex was to feel suffocated, which was a combined memory of the weight of her grandfather's body on hers, plus her mother's patricide by suffocating grandfather. In other words, regardless of their actuality, the image of her mother having sex with the maternal grandfather, and the later one of mother killing him, were memories which served as major primal phantasies that structured the foundations in Q's unconscious life. Around such primal phantasies are gathered and crystallized fragments of experience or other phantasies which gather their shape from the foundation ones. That is to say, primal scene phantasies are pivotal unconscious phantasies which influence the coherence (or its lack) of other phantasies. Q's unconscious sexual phantasy was an amalgam of incestuous primal scene memory plus an erotic murder, which led her to experience sexual intercourse with her husband, and symbolically in the transference with me, as though he and I were her grandfather in a suffocating, murderous sexual intercourse with her mother. Her sexual inhibition and the impasse in the therapy thus had the same origins.

I would like to say some more about N, whom I described in the previous chapter. His exposure to the primal scene was not as glaring as with Q. In his case, he would lie in bed listening to his parents arguing or having sex. N described a picture he had brought as looking like his father. The picture was of a figure spitting fire. He had never seen his father angry, though there was a family story about his father's rage. Mother once locked herself in N's bedroom and father smashed the door down. Mother still taunts him with the memory of the event. As N described this, he recalled another memory. He would lie awake at night listening to sounds coming from his parents' bedroom. He recalled mother screaming, 'Don't hit me' or 'Don't do those things'. If he inquired about the noise his parents would tell him it was all right. He realized now that some of the sounds he listened to must have been sexual, but that he must have forgotten the content. He imagined that his father would force his mother to do sexual things she did not want to do. This conflicted with another image of his parents in which he imagined that it was his mother who was more interested in sex than father. All this material had immediate transference relevance. N had arrived for our session in a defiant mood: he did not want to use the couch that day but had sat close to me with the picture between his legs representing his aggressive ejaculation on to me. He wanted to be in charge, but felt embarrassed about which of us had the (sexual) power, as he was equally confused about which of his parents had the stronger sexual desire. In other words, he reproduced in the transference his confused version of the primal scene which was essentially sado-masochistic, but unclear who the victim or aggressor might be.

My final example is a patient who appeared to have no direct experience of her parents in intercourse, but, as I will relate, had built up a picture based on piecing clues together. R is in her early thirties. I had seen her for nearly two years when she began talking about an evening with a man with whom she was infatuated. It had taken them some time to begin to have sex. The more she knows somebody the harder it becomes to tell them what she needs sexually. With men she hardly knows, it is no problem. She had wanted to talk to me about this for quite awhile as it was a considerable problem. When she was first with her boy-friend, B, they exchanged sexual fantasies and she told him everything. This time she felt too embarrassed. This was a typical pattern; it had happened with her husband, too. She then began to describe how much she and this man had in common, how well they got on, how much she was attracted to him and how he complimented her on her appearance. I remarked that she had changed the subject and was unable to tell me what her need was. She was doing here in the session what she had said had happened in bed, not telling me what she wanted. This focused her for a while. She reported fearing to appear like a fool if she told a man what she wanted, yet was perfectly aware about not worrying about this with men she hardly knew. She felt suddenly embarrassed about discussing this; she blushed, and conceded that she was now feeling what she had felt with the boy-friend. She thought I was asking her to tell me the exact details of her sexual needs. She became very flirtatious, saying it was not as if she had wanted to go to bed with me, or that she was asking me to come over to the couch, or 'even to provide a rubberman during the sessions'. We discussed the obvious connection between her difficulty with intimacy and her not voicing her needs to the people to whom she was close as a way of keeping her distance. She again shifted the focus, saying how incredibly handsome the boy-friend was; he was the most attractive man she had had sex with. She felt really lucky with him. She wanted him to feel really lucky that he was with her. She would get so excited by him she 'could get wet knickers just talking to him on the phone'. It was the end of the session. As she gathered her belongings she said the room felt warmer that day. I replied I thought it was because we had been discussing hot issues and perhaps she would prefer the relative anonymity afforded from the telephone. She looked embarrassed again, then agreed.

I was left feeling dissatisfied and deflated after this session. Initially, I had taken R's comments rather personally, and saw myself as no longer attractive to younger women. I recalled reading something Freud had said to one of his training patients about how she did not feel it worth while falling in love with him because he was such an old man in his seventies. I had just turned forty and thought to myself, 'So this is what it will be like for the rest of my life!'

Having got this piece of self-indulgent misery out of the way, I found myself thinking about R the following day. I thought about her parading her sexuality in an 'I've got this and you can't have it' fashion. I recalled her saying that, as an adolescent, she had taken boy-friends home after her parents had gone to bed. She would then have sex with them on the sofa in the living room, which was directly under the parents' bedroom. She had thought at the time that if her father had caught her 'he would have gone mad'. I realized that what had happened in the analysis the day before was a repetition of the sofa experience. I also wondered if my sense of sexual unattractiveness was in any way similar to what her father, the only man in a household of wife and five adolescent daughters, might have felt as he saw his children leaving the nest for younger men, his once little girls no longer held to his home by paternal authority or appeal.

In the subsequent sessions we discussed this further. She recognized her sexual teasing. I suggested that she was feeling sexually more confident, that she was dressing in more flimsy garments in therapy, too, and that she wanted to excite me and deflate me as she had done her father. She was embarrassed by this, but conceded it was true. She hastily added that she had not wanted to have sex with her father, though. She used to focus only on his faults; she now considers him a ' bit of a wanker' but can see his good qualities. I replied that a 'bit of a wanker' implied she wanted to be a subject of masturbation fantasy for him and perhaps for me, too. This illuminated her unconscious compromise solution to the Oedipal struggle. She would concede that father had her mother's body, but imagined that in sexual intercourse he would be thinking of her. This led to material about her being his favourite daughter, and about how she wanted to be attractive for him. This produced a climate in which she could discuss her sexual fantasies, which took several forms. With a partner, she preferred to have her hands tied behind her back with a silk scarf or have her arms held above her head. Her masturbation fantasies followed one of two scenarios. If she were in a good relationship she often thought of the man; at other times she would think of two women having sex with a man, she as a spectator, but might also be having sex.

The transference thus became abundantly clear. Watching the couple in intercourse is a primal scene fantasy; the observer is excited, rather as she

155

wished to excite me in the analytic dyad. Her sexual preference for bondage had come to represent an inescapable yet passive arousal in intercourse. In the transference, this meant that, rather like the parents (especially the father), who are in the bedroom while R had sex in the room underneath ('underneath' was also her phantasy that underneath the parental coitus was the deeper fantasy of coitus with her), the parents or myself are made unwilling witnesses to R's sexual activities. In effect, R was symbolically tying my hands in the analytic transference, the symbolic intercourse. This also represented a reversal in phantasy: she was in actuality the unwilling witness to her parents' relationship together; she wished to come between them by becoming the object of her father's desire.

Later material confirmed this:

R   I prefer to wear red and black underwear as these are my father's favourite colours; I know he is 'a tit-man not a bum-man' from remarks he has made. I don't like big breasts, I think they are whorish. My breasts are the best part about me.

DM   (*I found myself involuntarily looking at her breasts, a process I considered both pleasurable and voyeuristic. I wondered out loud:*) Well, you were saying you were your father's favourite, you seem to be saying he would like your breasts.

R   Put like that I would have to agree. I just had two thoughts. All my sisters have big breasts, I must be saying I think they are whores. I hadn't considered how rivalrous I am. I just had a shocking thought: perhaps I haven't had a baby because I don't want to spoil my breasts for my dad.

This session went on to reveal her secret masturbation activities as an adolescent. She would go through the drawers in her parents' bedroom. It was this way she found out her father's preference in female underwear. In addition, she found the soft pornography on her father's side of the bed. She would use this to lie on the floor and masturbate. If her parents were in the house she would take the magazines into her room for the same purpose. This was the precursor of having sex underneath the parents' bedroom. This led to further discussion about wanting to push mother out and marry her father, when she eventually proclaimed that she 'would have made a better wife for her father than her mother did'. Further material related to her being transfixed by the primal scene image of what she could not have: she might have made a better wife, but mother had father anyway. The frustration of this stopped her from looking around for creative alternatives in her own life. This session had visibly affected R.

The next session after the weekend she reported two dreams. The first was on the night of our previous session. She had dreamed she was on a flimsy raft that was entering a whirlpool. The session had clearly sent her unconscious into a spin. The second dream, the following night, seemed to suggest movement to a resolution. It took a dream within a dream format: 'I am at college. Somebody asks "What is written on the board?" I reply, "Wasps." The rest of the class ridicule me. I begin to wring my hands and as I do they turn into putty. In the dream I wake up having experienced this as a nightmare. I then go to my parent's bedroom. I am upset and go to my mum for comfort which she doesn't offer. Instead my parents begin to make love, with my mum still looking at me. The look wasn't critical but more of a "this is how things are" kind of expression.'

R's associations were that she felt some disgust and embarrassment in the dream, watching her parents having sex. But there was also an acceptance that she could not have her father. Hands turning to putty would mean she could not do creative things with her hands. She became upset as she described a relationship with another unavailable man. She felt I was withholding useful information that would help her. I related this transference to the dream and a sense of being excluded, as I had come to represent both parents who had something together she could not have. This dream marked the beginning of a more creative process of integration of primal scene imagery, moving from an Oedipal denial, the belief that she was secretly participating because father was thinking of her not her mother, to an Oedipal anger, her feeling excluded but definitely on the outside of the primal scene, acknowledging that her parents had a relationship together in which she had no part. Gradually, she was moving to a less paranoid and more mature acceptance of her parents' relationship.

PRIMAL SCENE: TRANSFERENCE AND COUNTERTRANSFERENCE

I would now like to make further considerations regarding the implications of the primal scene for the transference. While the significance of the primal scene has received considerable attention in analytic writing, it is striking that rarely do authors emphasize the implications for the transference.

The primal scene is nearly always present in the transference and is often represented in disguised form in dreams and symptoms (see also Silber (1981) for the relationship between tics, dreams and the primal scene). I have found that merely asking patients about what sort of ideas they have about their parents' sexual relationships usually brings forth large amounts of material. It is not of importance whether or not this material is a factually correct account of the erotic life of the parents. What is more important is that what the patient says about his or her parents' sexual relationship represents a store of their knowledge, and shows how the patient has made intrapsychic attempts to understand the primal scene.

Edelheit (1974) illustrates how the primal scene schema is projected on to the analytic situations in the form of double identifications: male–female, mother–child, and other polarities such as active–passive, victim–aggressor, viewer–exhibitor, and so on. The primal scene schema acts as a framework for the representations of the polymorphous sexual organization of childhood.

Some authors have noted how the primal scene influences the transference directly. Di Ceglie has made a direct link between primal scene phantasies and their implications for the transference. She describes one patient, Mrs A, in whose mind the parents did not feature as a couple. Her own marriage was almost asexual, her husband being treated like a child. In her mind, the parental couple was replaced by the mother–child couple, and this was reproduced in her marriage. In her therapy, she was co-operative and the transference felt like a 'good mother–child couple'. However, part of her remained 'out of reach': she wanted interpretations, but without making a contribution; she wanted to be understood, 'but not as a result of the work done by two people together' (1995: 54). Di Ceglie emphasizes that the internal couple was experienced both as a 'wish for the parental couple to exist and the wish for it to be destroyed' (ibid.: 58).

In Chapter 6, I showed how the transference becomes a symbolic re-enactment of sexual intercourse: the patient experiences the analysis as he or she experiences a partner during coitus. In this chapter, I have developed this thought further to say that one way of understanding the transference is that the analytic dyad comes to represent a symbolic representation of the patient's unconscious and pre-conscious sexual phantasies. Sexual experience is unconsciously informed by the individual's phantasy of his or her parent's sexual relationship. This, too, is played out in the transference.

The primal scene gives form not only to the individual's experience of sexual intercourse, but also to his or her sexuality. As such, primal scene phantasies are not only barometers of sexual problems, they also relate to the individual's capacity for creativity and/or destructiveness; in addition, they indicate how the individual has negotiated the Oedipal phase and, finally, how all these are played out in the transference. As I demonstrated earlier in this chapter, the uninterpreted primal scene transference dominated Freud's analysis of the Wolf-Man. This was also the case in the three examples I cited from my own practice. With all three patients, the image of the primal scene was underneath particular difficulties in the analytic impasse. Interpreting the material as such enabled the work to move forward and, in all three instances, enabled deep restructuring of the unconscious.

Clearly the primal scene comes to mean many things. However, one of the most central in importance is how the individual deals with transgression, how he or she walks a line between rigidity and an adherence to strict boundaries, on the one hand, and anarchy, disorder, perversion and abuse on the other. Primal scene is the measure of taboo that can be creatively transgressed. Therefore, it is an image of risk; not just a fear of conflict, but of risk, chance and discovery. Conflict, after all, can be highly destructive, not only in external war, but also in the mind; caution against conflict *per se* is probably a realistic stance. The unimaginable primal scene is closer to the conservation of thought: the desire not to explore, to maintain the *status quo*; this is the opposite of risk, at least a calculated risk, which can allow for something new to transpire. Its relation to intimacy is illustrated in how an individual can still feel close and not cast out by parents who are preoccupied with each other.

Thus the unconscious foundation of a mature person includes the establishment of internal parents available for creative coupling and an identification with both masculine and feminine roles. Money-Kyrle (1971) aptly calls this a 'supremely creative act'. By this he means the firm establishment of the first good object (the mother) allows for easier recognition of the parents' relations to each other. Failure here may lead to a 'misconception of intercourse', which forms the basis for perversion and insanity. Money-Kyrle recognizes that most people have a mixture of these two extremes.

In that sense, I would suggest we think in terms of an image of a good enough primal scene. The good enough image of a primal scene is not what the parents *actually* did during sexual intercourse, but how the individual later constructs their phantasy of the parents' sexual relationship. The good enough image of the primal scene would be in between an idealized magical intercourse that 'makes the ground move', or a more denigrated image which perceives the parents' intercourse as, in the words Shakespeare:

> . . . within a dull, stale, tired bed,
> Go to the creating a whole tribe of fops,
> Got 'tween asleep and wake?
>
> (*King Lear* I: ii)

I would add that the good enough image of the primal scene is pivotal to creativity in that it relates to the notion of a good enough self. In that sense, if parental intercourse can be seen as good enough, the individual can internalize a view that he or she was conceived from a parental relationship that was creative. To create, it is necessary to believe in a fertile penis and a fertile womb, especially of the internalized parents in sexual intercourse.

Further, there is another consideration. I suggested elsewhere (Mann 1990) that creativity does not spring from nowhere, like an immaculate conception. Rather, it is the bringing together of disparate elements in a new way. In the infant's mind, the greatest disparity is represented by the differences between his or her mother and father. The parental coupling in intercourse, therefore, provides a psychological resolution of how these disparate elements may be creatively reconciled.

As demonstrated in the previous chapter, if sexual intercourse is a crystallization of the individual's experience of the dyadic relationship with mother, the primal scene represents the experience of triangular relationships, the Oedipal scenario, and the resolution that is constellated in the unconscious. In other words, the primal scene phantasy can be considered as a primal structuring of how each individual deals with the various exclusions and inclusions of the Oedipal triangle. Primal scene phantasies also point in the direction of growth and Oedipal development: why else grow up, if not to be included in the life of the parents? Ikonen and Rechardt put the matter more succinctly: 'What else could be the doorway to adulthood than the bedroom door of the parents in the mind of the child?' (1984: 65). When at last the individual grows up and matures into the 'mature dependency' (Fairbairn 1941) of adult relationships, then he or she has progressed sufficiently; the Oedipal situation has lost its libidinal and narcissistic components.

Primal scene phantasies can be considered as attempts to create structure out of otherwise formless experiences. The primal scene gives sense, order and meaning to an individual's inner world.

Unconscious sexual phantasy becomes crystallized around primal scene phantasies. It follows, then, that if we accept that the primal scene is a major structuring dynamic in unconscious sexual phantasy, and if we accept that the transference can be understood as, and come to represent, a symbolic representation of sexual intercourse, it follows that the analysand's primal scene phantasies will also find expression in the transference. In this sense, we can say that the transference can then be understood as a symbolic representation of the parents in sexual intercourse.

In the transference, the primal scene represents the patient's internal image of what it means for two people to be by themselves in an intimate relationship. As such, it is a primal phantasy of what two people do to and with each other. In this regard, it comes to represent either creative, neurotic or perverse possibilities. This has a direct relationship to the transference in which the analysis or the analyst will be experienced in terms of primal scene phantasy.

Very few writers on the primal scene have commented on its relevance for the countertransference. As mentioned earlier, Racker (1968) describes how both the patient and the therapist will encounter resistance to dealing with the pain of recognition. However, at the risk of stating the utterly obvious, since we all have parents we would expect, therefore, to find the primal scene also having significance in the countertransference.

I would like to propose the following schema: we can more or less assume that the patients presenting themselves for psychotherapy have a difficulty with their internal representations of the primal scene. That is, creative coupling in all or some of its forms is problematic or non-existent. In a sense, when a patient comes for therapy, he or she is seeking to find a good enough image of the primal scene. The patient presents the difficulty with creative coupling in the therapy by way of the transference which becomes symbolic of both sexual intercourse in general and the parental coitus in particular.

The scene will be true of the countertransference, too. The therapist's internal representation of the parental coitus will also have significance. In other words, the countertransference will also be influenced by the therapist's ability to have a creative intercourse. In this schema we could say that, if there are six participants in the copulating couple, there are also six participants in the psychoanalytic dyad. A successful analysis, or I would prefer a less idealized expression such as a good enough analysis, will be determined by how well both the patient and the therapist can manage a creative intercourse. An impasse reached in an analysis may be due to factors located either in the patient or the therapist, or both: that is to say, an impotent, destructive or perverse primal scene can be located wherever there is a place for coitus. Implied in this schema is the idea that the internalized parents of both the patient and the therapist may also have symbolic coitus, either as a foursome, or in various combinations of heterosexual and homosexual couples.

It is probably worth stating outright what is also implied by this description: namely, that there is a connection between the quality of the therapist's relationships in his or her personal life and the kind of creative coupling possible in the professional work. A therapist who has difficulty with creative intercourse in his or her personal life will almost definitely transfer this into the analytic encounter. Racker is quite right to underline the resistance in the therapist to the primal scene material, since it reaches to the very depths of the psyche's anxieties in the therapist, as it does in everybody else.

CONCLUDING REMARKS

In this chapter, I have attempted to demonstrate both the difficulty of imaging the primal scene and its indispensability in the psyche. A good enough image of the primal scene is a prerequisite for creativity. As a primal structuring phantasy, the primal scene thus becomes a focal point in the transference as an image of what it means for two people to be in a creative, intimate relationship together. This was illustrated with clinical material from Freud's work with the Wolf-Man and examples from my own practice.

8

TRANSFERENCE PERVERSIONS

In this chapter I will be exploring some of the dynamics of working with perversions. In keeping with Etchegoyen (1978) and Baker (1994), I am making a distinction between perverse transferences, which may appear with patients with no evident perverse sexuality, and transference perversion, which is specific to patients with frank sexual perversions. Transference perversions do not simply engage a form of resistance in either the analyst or analysand, whereby a diligent and persistent process of interpretation (silently made inside the analyst or spoken directly to the patient) liberates the potential growth characteristics that attach themselves to defences. Rather they employ something much more potentially destructive to the whole analytic process and are probably more likely to suck the life out of the therapeutic engagement.

There is an extensive body of psychoanalytical literature on perversion. It is outside the scope of this book to review the literature as a whole. My interest in this chapter is to focus on how perversion affects the transference and countertransference.

My thinking about perversion has been particularly influenced by three writers: McDougall (1978), Chasseguet-Smirgel (1984b) and Stoller (1975). Though they each have distinct and unique things to say about perversion, they are united by at least one central idea: perversion should be defined as a state of mind rather than as specific sexual activities. These authors note that sometimes the sexual activities of individuals we call perverse also find expression in 'normal' loving relationships. These authors would all define a perverse state of mind as one in which the perpetrator attempts to reduce the partner from the status of another human being to that of simply an object; the partner becomes a thing, devoid of individual characteristics. (Along with Stoller, I object to the term 'pervert', which cannot be used without pejorative connotations. Unfortunately, a number of the writers I quote seem to have no such objection to the word.)

In my view, transference perversions, therefore, attempt to reduce the therapist into a thing, devoid of individual qualities. I will suggest in this chapter that it is almost always the case that the perverse patient will distort

162

the transference in perverse ways. In as far as the transference is an embodiment of the patient's sexual experience, the transference thus takes on the forms and psychic processes of the perversion. This has ramifications for the countertransference. I will demonstrate that the patient's attempt to bring the therapist into his or her perversion will almost inevitably result in a countertransference perversion. Perversions are *not* substitutes for relating to people: *perversions are a way of relating to people*. As such, both the patient and the therapist struggle to find individual and creative thoughts.

If follows from this that the erotic transference is perverted. The transformational qualities of the erotic are reduced, since there is no underlying love that can be utilized. Instead, the latent hostility of perversions turns the love into hate, the good into bad. As I will demonstrate, the effect of the perversion on the analytic dyad is to create a transference and countertransference perversion: the analysand and analyst become a perverse couple. The transformational qualities of the erotic are reduced to excrement.

PAST TRAUMA AND PERVERSION

Stoller writes that the heart of perversion is a fantasized act of hostile revenge: 'A perversion is the result of an essential interplay between hostility and sexual desire' (1975: xi). There has usually been a passive experience of trauma connected with either sexuality or gender identity – that is, one's sense of masculinity or femininity. Perversion is a product of anxiety, and perverse sexual behaviour is sprinkled with the remains, ruins and indicators of the past history of sexual development, especially in the dynamics of one's family. The adult, now no longer a helpless child, reverses the childhood trauma, controlling and triumphing in fantasy over those who once humiliated him:

> Perversion is a *fantasy* put into action – a defensive structure raised gradually over the years in order to preserve erotic pleasure [author's italics].

> (ibid.: xiv)

Beneath the hostility of each act of perversion is a dread of emotional surrender. Perversion is, therefore, the erotic form of hatred. It is habitual, necessary for one's full satisfaction and motivated by hostility – the hostility is expressed as revenge. For the greatest excitement, a perversion must also appear risk-taking. A perverse act is not defined by the anatomy used, object chosen or society's stated morality: 'All we need know is what it means to the person doing it' (ibid.: 4). Namely, the desire to harm the chosen object. The need to repeat the same perversion 'unendingly, eternally again in the same manner, comes from one's inability to get completely rid of the danger, the trauma' (ibid.: 6). The result of the perverse fantasy is that one's sex objects are dehumanized. Partners are treated as if they were not real people, but rather as puppets to be manipulated on the stage where perversion is played. In Stoller's view, mystery also has a significant role in perversions as our society obscures the discovery of anatomical differences between the sexes.

THE PRIMAL SCENE AND PERVERSION

McDougall (1978) also talks about 'perverse structures' in the psyche rather than particular sexual behaviour. Perverse structures display a singularly impoverished fantasy life with little erotic freedom in act or fantasy. In people with perverse structures, their sexuality displays little choice and is compulsive.

Typically, mother is idealized and the father plays a negative role in the inner object world of perverse structures. Mother becomes an unattainable phallic ideal and father a denied or denigrated object. The father's penis thus has no role in the mother's sexual life, therefore his penis loses its symbolic value and an important piece of knowledge is effaced.

From this, the primal scene is reinvented. Important links concerning sexual truth are distorted or destroyed. In the perverse structure, the castrator is the mother: she seduces and awakens desire but also places a barrier to its fulfilment. To her child, she is the portrait of perversity. The significance of sexual differences is denied. Sexual desire is then furnished with new objects, zones and aims. In the perverse structure, the primal scene is the drama of castration and the mastery of associated anxiety: castration does not hurt and, in fact, is the very condition of erotic arousal and pleasure.

There is always a spectator present, this part often being played by the individual himself. Roles are reversed: the child, once victim of castration anxiety, is now the agent of it.

McDougall takes fetishism as the paradigm of all perverse solutions. It demonstrates the way a gap is left by disavowal of sexual truth and is then compensated for. She writes:

> Faced first with the fact of separate identity and then with sexual differences and its Oedipal implications, the future pervert finds no veils thick enough to blur the outlines of insupportable reality as the neurotic is able to do. He can only obliterate the problem and find new answers to sexual desires.
>
> (1978: 78)

McDougall implies the role of the mother is crucial here. She cites Hellman (1954), who describes children with intellectual inhibition denying them knowledge of things their mothers could not tolerate their knowing. The mothers may themselves have denied sexual reality and denigrated the fathers' phallic function.

McDougall gives a clinical example of a homosexual man who would collect different partners for fellatio purposes, hoping to find someone he could love. This patient then reported that he had met an older man and was becoming more interested in him as a person than in his penis. This produced a panic attack and the patient made an excuse to get away. He was distraught to discover that his companions existed as only penises. McDougall interpreted that it had been necessary to avoid being interested in his partners in order not to know that the one penis he was seeking to possess was that of his father, and though he wanted to be strengthened by his father's penis, he did not wish his father to suffer the castration this implied. McDougall then tells us that, following this session, her patient ceased his homosexual activity and became involved with an older woman, but experienced feelings of pseudo-pregnancy and hallucinated ghosts in his bedroom. McDougall reflects that the removal of the patient's disavowal of his parents' relations together brought an intolerable flooding with painful affect and he merged with the mother figure by swallowing her up. The re-invented primal scene is preferable to madness.

In some respects, McDougall's example is unsatisfactory. While I am ready to agree that perversions include fetishism, sado-masochism and transvestism, I do not agree – as I suggested in an earlier chapter – that homosexuality finds itself in the same category. We might also wonder why McDougall does not make more of the overt erotic transference implications of this patient suddenly seeking out an older woman. However, these criticisms aside, she rightly points to the pivotal place of the primal scene and how this is denied or recast in the patient's fantasy.

THE ANAL UNIVERSE OF PERVERSION

Chasseguet-Smirgel considers that perversion is an aspect of people's relentless quest to push beyond the narrow limits of the human condition. Perversion is 'a dimension of the human psyche in general, a temptation in the mind common to us all' (1984b: 1).

Like McDougall, she sees that the bedrock of reality is created by the differences of the sexes, adding also the differences between generations. When a male child realizes that he will be an inadequate sexual partner for his mother, and that he cannot rival the potent adult sexual organ of the father, he is reduced to feeling his own smallness and inadequacy. Erosion of these differences between the sexes and generations is the perverse solution. Smirgel also believes mothers play a crucial role here, exhibiting a seductive attitude to the child and rejection of the father, which fosters the illusion that the former does not need to grow up and reach maturity (with father as a model) to be her satisfactory partner.

The principal mechanism here is regression to the anal-sadistic phase which erodes awareness of differences. An 'anal universe' is established whereby all differences between man and woman, child and adult, erotogenic zones are destroyed. The digestive tract becomes an enormous 'grinding machine' where differences are disintegrated and reduced to excrement: all particles are equal and interchangeable. She writes: 'Perversion represents a reconstruction of Chaos, out of which arises a new kind of reality, that of the anal universe' (Chasseguet-Smirgel 1984b: 11). The universal law of difference is reversed by the perverse state of mind into a universe of no difference. In this respect, the perverse individual is trying to free himself from the paternal universe and the constraints of the law, and attempts to de-throne the father and create a new kind of reality. Smirgel points out that Freud's (1917) equation – penis = child = faeces – is taken literally in perversion. Faeces replace the father's penis as the procreative genital. In reality, in order to procreate, it is necessary to grow up, to mature, to wait, whereas faeces are a production common to adult and child, man and woman. Differences between the sexes and generations are abolished at the anal level.

In a another publication (Mann 1997), I described my work with a psychotic patient with anal-sadistic perversions. In this instance, women in his life, fellow patients, the therapy and his art work were reduced to a faecal mess in which individual differences disappeared.

CLINICAL VIGNETTES

I will begin by giving two brief examples of the destructive influence of perversion on the transference–countertransference matrix. The first example was related to me by a woman colleague. She had been seeing her patient for brief time-limited psychotherapy. He had been referred because he felt he masturbated excessively. His dominant masturbation fantasy was to strong, dominant, queenly-like women. The first couple of sessions were uneventful. The patient then gave the therapist a piece of paper upon which he had written down some of his thoughts. One of the things he had written was that he wondered how she would react if he told her about a fantasy he had been having recently. The therapist asked what he meant by this, to which he replied by telling her the fantasy which was about putting a knife in her vagina. The therapist was stunned by this idea, which she reasonably found threatening. Despite feeling therapeutically paralysed, her initial response was to ask how he thought she might react – to which he replied that he imagined she would leave the room. Her reaction afterwards was to discuss the session with colleagues, and to buy a personal safety alarm before the next session in case he tried to attack her. After the initial shock, and some discussion with colleagues, the therapist continued with the remaining few sessions contracted with the patient. In this time she reaffirmed the boundary required by the therapeutic contract that he did not harm her. At the final session, he rang to say he could not attend but wished to speak over the phone. The therapist had the impression he was masturbating while they spoke.

I wish to highlight only certain aspects of this material. The creative possibilities of the therapeutic encounter had been overtly attacked by the patient's sadistic fantasy of violent assault, the primal scene becoming one of sadistic rape rather than love-making. The effect on the therapist was to destroy the capacity to think. She felt he had succeeded in getting inside her in such a way that she was not able to think therapeutically. The perverse sadistic transference had set up perverse countertransference, whereby both participants were mesmerized by the patient's fantasy which precluded any further creative thinking. The patient had expected the therapist to leave the room. In fact, he achieved this metaphorically as she subsequently found it difficult to be with him and keep her mind focused on the material. The therapist's counter-fantasy was to imagine him being taken by the 'scruff of the neck' and driven away by the police. Thus, in her fantasy he is taken outside the therapeutic setting, whilst she introduces the law, the symbolic third party, to avoid catastrophe.

The following is an example from my own practice. I had been seeing Mr S for some months. He spoke of himself as entirely unable to form intimate relationships with either sex, having just one rather distant male friend. He had no sexual experience and was preoccupied about how to talk to women, how to recognize the clues of sexual interest, and how to participate in courtship games. To my mind, he sounded naive and clumsy in these matters.

He had developed a negative transference from the first session. He considered that I never spoke at all. In his view, if I did speak, what I said was so blatantly stupid and useless it was not worth listening to, therapy was useless, and I was not helping him.

From the start I was aware of a curious dynamic. Mr S would lie completely motionless with his arms across his chest and his eyes closed for the entire session, with only his jaw moving as he spat out his criticisms of all those men, women and myself who did not help him. If it were not for the act of speaking, his posture, lack of movement and closed eyes gave the impression of a laid out corpse.

This impression of mine gained some flesh when he reported a piece of written work he had done in his creative writing class. In his story, the leading character performs necrophilia with a corpse. Interestingly, the feedback he got from the class was that he had alluded to events in the story so tentatively that they had not realized what it was about till he explained afterwards. I emphasize this, as Mr S said he usually felt dead inside, devoid of any feelings at all. I also experienced him as dead. Likewise, Mr S experienced me as dead, one of his fondest criticisms being that I just sat in my chair, dead and absent, lifeless. For my own part, nothing was further from the truth. I experienced intense passion with this man: I was furious with him. I was aware of feeling devalued and rendered therapeutically ineffective, castrated. His constant criticisms were getting under my skin. I was finding it increasingly difficult to think or interpret clearly, and I was aware that sometimes I retreated behind a resentful silence.

It was in just this state that, after some months, I then had a brief passing day-dream fantasy. I realized that if I grabbed the jar on my desk that contained my pens, I could rush over to the couch and smash him in the testicles with it before he even knew I was on him! I was rather taken aback by this thought as I ordinarily do not experience such sadistic thoughts about my patients; I must also admit that, in his particular case, the idea was rather appealing. I subsequently came to understand this fantasy in the following way. The obvious meaning was that the patient was castrating the therapy so, by the law of talion ('an eye for an eye'), I wished to castrate him. But I also think something far more destructive was at work. A perverse transference had been created. In this, the patient had woven his necrophiliac desires into the analysis, rendering the treatment sterile and lifeless, incapable of giving and receiving, completely dead. This, in turn, produced a perverse countertransference, a perverse reaction in the therapist to a perverse situation. This took the form of a perverse fantasy of castrating the patient in a sadistic manner.

I give this as an example of how subtly the patient's perverse structures came to dominate not only the transference, but also the countertransference. Rather like the members of the patient's writing class, I was unaware of the plot until it was made explicit – in this instance, by my perverse fantasy. As with my woman colleague described above, my capacity to think had been subverted. The perverse transference had initiated a perverse countertransference. This consisted not only of perverse sadistic thinking, but also the destruction of any other kinds of thoughts. It is in the nature of perversions to obliterate the capacity to have creative thoughts. The perverse structure of a patient's psyche pervades the countertransference through the transference. The patient's stuck anal world of no differences eventually attacks the therapist's mind as this, too, represents differences which must be denied and reduced to a faecal mass, more shitty thoughts indistinguishable from those of the patient.

THE ANAL–SADISTIC TRANSFERENCE AND COUNTERTRANSFERENCE

The following example explores in more depth the development of a transference perversion, and demonstrates how it subtly works its way into the analytic process. I intend to show how difficult it is sometimes to avoid the anal universe of perverse structures of the patient's psyche in the therapy.

I had originally seen Mrs T for brief psychoanalytic psychotherapy. She was in the later stages of another pregnancy. She had come from a large family and desired to create a large one of her own. She had become extremely depressed in the later stages of this pregnancy. I will not describe all the issues we covered as they are not relevant here, but I will limit my account to what is pertinent to the subject of this chapter. Of her history, she reported that her mother had been extremely violent to some of her children, including Mrs T. Father had not known about this at the time as the violence apparently occurred only when he was not in the house. In turn, Mrs T was worried by her own capacity for violence towards her own children. She felt she was a very impatient person.

She spoke of her husband. He was unsupportive with the children and unsympathetic to her, calling her mad and saying she should pull herself together. She thought she loved him, but sometimes was not sure. Perhaps she should leave him; he would not leave her. They would have furious rows. She wondered how much he was deliberately trying to annoy her. He would not speak or talk about things with her and this made her very angry.

It was in this context that, almost in passing, she described some of their sexual practices. Her sexual appetite had always been greater than his and he was critical of her desire for more frequent sex. She did not know how best to describe her husband's sexual demands, perhaps 'strange' was the word. He would like her to bind, then beat, him. She alluded to certain preferences without giving details, which she found embarrassing to discuss. On one occasion, for her birthday, he had bought her a set of hand-cuffs and a horse-riding whip. She admitted to doing what he wanted if she was feeling good about herself. Mostly, she felt it was wrong. She was cagey about how much she participated and complied with her husband's wishes. She said perhaps just two or three times. The hesitancy of her account made me think that there were considerably more than just two or three occasions.

She described one particular instance when they had been arguing in the kitchen. After they had screamed at each other, her husband come meekly to her side and suggested that she punish him. Mrs T was still furious and readily agreed. They went to the bedroom and she just grabbed the riding whip and lashed out at him, chasing her husband around the room while he screamed, 'No, not like this'. Evidently his desire was for a controlled, ritualized, sado-masochistic relationship; what Mrs T delivered on this occasion was pure, uncontrolled and unritualized aggression. This hurt more and did not feel safe.

I saw Mrs T for several months until after her baby was born. Her immediate depression had been lifted by our work, and she had avoided a post-natal depression, which she and her GP had feared. She was enjoying being a mother again. However, the marriage relationship had deteriorated, and she requested that she and her husband be seen together for some couple work. This is a facility provided at the GP practice where I do some of my work. I see couples with a woman co-therapist. I informed my co-therapist about some of the issues discussed in the individual psychotherapy, including the couple's sexual practices.

Our first sessions with Mr and Mrs T seemed to go quite well. Both seemed to appreciate coming and found our interventions useful. As they talked about each other, it seemed that each thought she or he knew what the other was thinking, though the other denied this when given the opportunity. As we progressed, we found more of their sado-masochistic side coming to the fore. As a couple, they were clearly explosive. She was very vocal and sought responses from both her husband and the therapists. He was more quiet, more inclined to bottle up feelings, especially if criticized by Mrs T. This would infuriate Mrs T further and she would redouble her efforts to get a response from him, though he would respond by withdrawing further. This cycle would continue until eventually Mr T would lose his temper and verbally lash out at Mrs T. Obviously, I could not break the confidential nature of the individual work with Mrs T, but I eventually interpreted that they seemed to have developed a sado-masochistic relationship together where it was not always clear who was the sadist and who was the masochist, though they both felt they were victims to the other's aggression.

The penultimate session was an argument between them and us. They both expressed disappointment that we were not able to do more to help their marriage. They were quite specific in their desires. Mr T had no previous experience of therapy, and had originally said he did not know what to expect, he just hoped we would not be critical. Now, at the end of our sessions, he had swung to the other pole. He wished that the therapists had been more interventionist. In particular, he would have liked us to be like the therapists and psychologists on the *Oprah Winfrey Show* who would tear a couple to bits. This would have been more useful to them, he thought, especially if we had taken his side against his wife's anger. Mrs T agreed that she, too, would have preferred just such a critical intervention, with the difference that she would have liked the therapists to have criticized her husband's passivity more. With the end of this session came the realization that they felt we had not been rigorous enough with them.

The next session, the last, reached a destructive climax. Mrs T arrived by herself fifteen minutes late, saying that she had told her husband she was leaving him that day, and asking if we could recommend a place where she might go and stay. It transpired that she had told him straight after our previous session that she had no intention of coming for the last appointment. They had had a blazing argument that morning, after which she had stormed out of the house saying that she would not be coming to therapy. In our session she remained agitated for some more minutes. Eventually, she said she thought that Mr T might be here. I said that it seemed she was hoping to meet him here, despite telling him she would not be coming. Mrs T gave me a deadly look. She gathered up her belongings and, pronouncing that she saw no further point to the session, she walked out. When my co-therapist and I later went to the reception desk, one of the receptionists told us that Mr T had phoned up when the session was due to start. He rang to cancel the session as neither he nor his wife would be attending.

What to make of this sequence of events? I offer the following under-standing. Mr and Mrs T had developed a perverse relationship in their mar-riage. Sado-masochism was the root of this. We knew nothing of Mr T's childhood but Mrs T had told me of the frequent beatings she had received as a child. As an adult, she had identified with her mother's aggression to form the complementary sadistic partner to her masochistic husband. The study of perversions in women has recently been given serious attention, after decades in which psychoanalysis denied that perversions could exist in women. Weldon (1988) and Kaplan (1989) have drawn attention to the inci-dence of perverse structures in women. McDougall (1995) and Maguire (1995) have highlighted that the study of female perversion needs to focus more on the actual sexual activities and sexual fantasies of women. I agree with this. In the particular context of the couple I am describing, a fruitful area of research would appear to be those women who, for their own uncon-scious reasons, mostly perverse, participate with their partner's perversions. There would seem to be an unconscious matching when these individuals find partners: each seeking the complementary opposite of the perversion to find full expression. McDougall has noted that, though many of her female patients had complained about fulfilling their husband's sexual demands, it was her observation that the women had unconsciously chosen their mate and were gaining secret satisfaction from the sexual rituals directly linked to pre-genital excitement in their own lives.

With Mr and Mrs T, the sado-masochistic bond took two forms. First, was the clearly identifiable sexual practices centred around punishment rit-ual and the retribution of the whip. Second, this sado-masochistic solution had developed beyond the bedroom to enter all areas of the couple's life. This was more problematic as it was not ritualized to make it safe. Both partners felt themselves to be the victim of the other's passive aggression. Our observations confirmed that they were each living out both victim and aggressor roles. Each denied the difference of the other by assuming each knew what the other was thinking: there was no difference between their minds. Both had a sado-masochistic image of the primal scene where the passive father is overwhelmed by the powerful, phallic mother. This perverse sado-masochistic structure eventually took hold in the transference. There was the expressed desire that the therapists should be actively more aggres-sive, sadistically attacking the other partner, tearing him or her to bits. As the therapists, we were actively struggling to find a space in which to think clearly so that we might maintain an interpretative stance. That is to say, rather than being sucked into the perverse structure, we were trying to avoid making sadistic attacks in order to preserve our thinking function, our abil-ity to think separate and distinct thoughts. Mrs T had left the final session precisely at the point when she had been invited to think about what she was doing rather than just acting on impulse. In other words, Mrs T left the ther-apy when she was invited to stand back and reflect upon her desire to encounter her husband at the session she had said she was not going to attend. At the point of being asked to think, rather than act, Mrs T left the room, thereby opting for action rather than symbolic thinking functions.

It occurred to the therapists only after the therapy ended that perhaps our attempts to remain outside the perverse structures had been ineffective. I would suggest that in this light the therapists' wish to maintain a thinking space, rather than the sadistic alliance such as the couple described on the *Oprah Winfrey Show*, was in itself a perverse countertransference. In this respect, I would say that the wish to maintain difference and not get lost in the patients' anal universe was experienced by Mr and Mrs T as a sadistic attack in itself. The experience of difference was felt as destructively aggressive. I would draw a parallel here with the account that Mrs T gave of her chasing her husband with the whip around the room while he screamed 'No not like this'. The sado-masochistic desire was centred around ritual, which made the expression of aggression safe. Kernberg (1992) draws attention to the fact that perverse structures may serve to protect the patient from uncontrolled expressions of aggression. In this scenario, the perverse structures of the couple were felt to be mirrored by the talk show rituals of controlled expression of aggression. As the therapists, we stood outside the rituals, attempting to maintain a different thinking space, and this was experienced by the sado-masochistic couple in the same way as the uncontained, non-ritualized attack in the bedroom when Mrs T chased her husband. The therapists were not behaving in the desired roles and their expressed differences were experienced as uncontrolled sadism attacking the existence of the anal universe. In other words, though we thought we were staying outside the perverse structures of the couple, this was a perverse countertransference illusion, and we had been entrapped despite our best precautions. We had ended up playing the role of the threatening uncontrolled sadistic aggressor, rather than that of the controlled ritualistic sadist.

What these clinical examples illustrate is how the patient's perverse thinking contaminates not only the transference, but also the countertransference. Initially, the therapist cannot protect him or herself from this development as the analytic process is itself perverted. The capacity to think separate thoughts, and thereby maintain an analytic stance and space, is precisely what is perverted, so there is no difference between the minds of the patient and analyst. Both the woman therapist and myself found ourselves caught in the patients' fantasy in this way.

DISCUSSION

My clinical examples here are similar in findings to those made by other psychoanalytic researchers. Patients with perverse states of mind create transference perversions which reflect their own particular perversity. This, in turn, will have an effect on the countertransference. I would suggest that a countertransference perversion is, initially at least, the most likely outcome. This will remain the case until the analyst can gradually claw back the capacity for analytic thinking, in this case characterized by separate and distinct thoughts to those of the patient.

A number of writers have experienced similar processes to those I have described. One of the writers who most openly describes this is Chasseguet-Smirgel. She describes how the initial sympathy the analyst feels may, over time, be turned into a feeling of humiliation at the hands of a patient consistently treating the analyst as a contemptible faecal object. Her patient, Rose Selavy, reduced the whole digestive process (literal and metaphorical) to 'all that is ingested is expelled' (1984b: 135) as though there were no processes in between. Smirgel began to imagine her patient as a concentration camp guard. In fact, the later material revealed that the patient and her lover would pretend to be 'playing at Auschwitz'. The analyst's fantasies were an echo of the patient's.

Other writers have been less revealing about the countertransference with this patient group but similar transferences have been reported. Bach (1994) describes how a patient who used bondage with his sexual partners would also try to tie him up in the transference by maintaining a 'technical rather than a personal relationship', keeping himself at a distance. No single interpretation untied the problem and Bach struggled to keep in mind the therapeutic task that, with perverse patients, we are attempting to help them separate, maintain object consistency, and achieve whole object love.

There is a general consensus amongst analytic writers that the development of transference perversion is insidious and almost seems to creep up on the analyst unawares; for example, Gillespie (1952), Meltzer (1973b), Khan (1979), Bach (1994), Wrye and Welles (1994) all describe how difficult it might be for the therapist to notice what is happening as the transference becomes perverse.

Patients with perverse or addictive pathologies will attempt to dislodge the analyst from his or her accustomed role and convert the entire analytic procedure into one which has the structure of their perverse or addictive characteristics. This process is so subtle that the transformation of the transference and the resultant countertransference may escape the analyst's notice until it is too late. Meltzer (1973b: 138) considers that by this time the analysis may be so subverted as to be irretrievable or irreversible. Indeed, he goes so far as to suggest that male analysts are more susceptible to the 'father's vulnerability to infantile sexual excitement, particularly of a masochistic nature'. Women analysts may be more prone to mutual idealization in the maternal countertransference. This leads to generosity and endless optimism that the analysis will soon turn a corner. Therapists of both sexes may experience the transference perversion as a contempt for psychoanalysis (the breast) and awe for the analyst (nipple, penis, or faecal penis confused). In these cases, interpretations become fetishistic whips to be played with. There may also be a case to say that male and female therapists have a more active or passive response respectively. The example of my woman colleague was to fantasize that the law would intervene between the patient and her, as is indicated by her purchase of a personal safety alarm and the wish to see him taken away. Wheeley (1994) describes a similar reaction with her perversely psychotic patient. A more overtly aggressive–sadistic fantasy, such as my own with the necrophiliac patient, may be more common amongst male therapists. This does seem the case in a straw poll I made with colleagues of both sexes.

Wrye and Welles (1994) also report the 'insidious deadening of the relationship' that was difficult to spot. This stops an erotic resonance from forming. Behind this is the patient's fear of dependence. For the therapist, there is the fear that full aliveness and participation in the process will produce perverse impulses, which indeed it does, and these can prove very disturbing. The counter-fantasies experienced by the woman therapist with the knife patient, and my own fantasies with the necrophiliac patient, are examples of this. In both instances, the therapists were shocked by their own reactions and fantasies in response to the perverse fantasies of the patient. It is not just the erotic which is defended against, but the perversely erotic. For the patient, the defence is working the other way: the perversely erotic defends against the creatively intimate erotic, ultimately against the primal scene. What ensues is a 'deadlock', a paralysing unconscious object situation.

Bach also talks about sadistic or masochistic reactions in the transference that are difficult to discern, understand or control. This can lead the parties into a sado-masochistic relationship that exhausts both. Confrontative interpretations can fulfil the patient's beating fantasies. It seems to me, that incidents like these are inevitable and will be re-created in the analytic dyad before they can be understood. The aim would be not to repeat the perverse scenario for eternity. Bach calls this 'mutual enactment in the transference'. I would elaborate this further by saying that perverse structures of the patient make the analysis into a *perverse couple*. However, the onus is on the therapist first to realize that he or she has been drawn into this perverse world, and then to find a way out for them both. This is not easy, as the perverse world attacks the very processes that make this possible – thinking difference. Indeed, enactments may be the nearest we have to genuine early communication with these patients.

The difficulty is that analysis may seek to interpret difference and the thinking behind actions in a world in which differences cannot be tolerated. Perverse structures are at such a primitive level of the mind that symbolic thinking is underdeveloped.

The analytic literature on this subject seems to be divided about how resistible or irresistible the countertransference perversion may be. Khan (1979) urges that therapists need to deal with their distaste and hate in order to avoid fulfilling the patient's masochistic longings. Baker (1994) stresses the need for the therapist to avoid acting out, particularly by rejecting the patient. I find these entreaties laudable and consider that they represent the therapist's goal of seeking to maintain the appropriate analytic attitude. However, given the creeping nature of transference perversion, I am doubtful that it will fail to have any corrosive effect on the therapist's unconscious (or consciousness, for that matter) for some of the time at least. It would seem almost inevitable that this would lead to what Bach calls 'mutual enactment in the transference'. Wrye and Welles describe this as therapists getting caught in a 'perverse misalliance': countertransference responses may be a disavowal of the patient's wishes and a distancing from the patient. My own reaction to the patient with the necrophiliac fantasy is not so simple. Here my fantasy was indeed one of reducing him to an object, but perverse fantasies may be the only form of relating due to the underlying schizoid qualities of the psyche. 'Perverse misalliances' contain a refusal to participate, a lack of interest and deadness.

I think of the analytic dyad becoming a *perverse couple*. At root, the patient is resisting passive dependency. The dread of being penetrated leads to attempts to control the analytic situation with efforts specifically directed at the analyst's interpretation and his or her capacity to think. I consider, however, that the situation is even more complicated than this. It is not simply the interpretation that is attacked, but the analyst's capacity to have different, let alone creative, thoughts. The perverse structure cannot tolerate differing points of view, thinking is split into black and white, ambiguity is felt as threatening. I also doubt whether the analyst can totally avoid the perverse countertransference. To avoid it would in itself be a perverse response in that this would signify a lack of true involvement with the patient. Such schizoid distancing would thus be replicating the patient's perverse problem of not being able to maintain human relationships. It needs to be remembered that the perverse structure is the only way of relating to the other.

In my view, the establishment of a perverse couple is almost inevitable when undertaking psychoanalytic work with patients with perverse states of mind. The establishment of the perverse couple is clearly problematic for any analysis. However, the principal danger to the clinical work is not that the therapist has a countertransference perversion evoked, but that he or she does not try to escape because of failing to realize that he or she is trapped inside a perverse transference and countertransference matrix.

The erotic transference in both its manifestations as either a positive development or as a resistance is converted into something perverted. The positive aspects of the erotic transference are transformed and lost in a perverse scenario. The primal scene becomes anal sadistic. Copulation is at an anal level, faeces to faeces, faecal-penis into an anal-vagina which results in either sterility or a faecal baby. Instead of heading for a symbolic birth, the perverse analytic couple are at best reduced to an anal birth, at worst stuck in a kind of pseudo-analytic rectum where both parties are gradually ground down in eternal faeces.

Perverse patients attack the spirit of inquiry at the heart of analysis: It becomes hard to think creative ideas, or any ideas at all. The vitality is drained as the therapist distances him or herself. Perverse structures transform something good into something bad, love into hate, sense into senselessness, good food into shit. Perverse sexuality may also attack the analytic process because a perverse state of mind can result in acts which may shock. Transference interpretations should avoid oblique moral judgements aimed at causing guilt.

In *Analysis terminable and interminable* Freud (1937) states that the psychoanalytical situation is based on the love of truth. I believe Freud is quite right. Now, the problem with perverse structures is their disavowal and denial of the truth; the difference between truth and lies is lost – in Smirgel's terms, is reduced to a faecal mass where there is no distinction. Perverse structures contaminate the transference.

Smirgel summarizes the essential problem that perversion poses for the transference:

> If I had to summarize what I have just described in overt perverts or in patients displaying perverse organizations within the analysis as hindering the establishment of an actual alliance, I would say that it is the hatred of life, the non-acceptance of the primal scene as liable to give birth to a child, and, consequently the impossibility of forming a couple with the analyst so as to give birth to a child that would be themselves, re-created.
>
> (Chasseguet-Smirgel 1984b: 116)

A little later she writes, 'Thinking: that is the enemy . . . thinking is to be understood as the ability to think differences, that is reality itself' (ibid.: 120).

Perversions pose severe problems for the analysis because the analytic process itself is subject to attack. Analytical work is forced to remain fruitless. Smirgel again would say: 'The baby resulting from the parental intercourse, which is unconsciously acted out in the analytical relationship, is destined to remain in limbo or to be aborted' (ibid.: 127). I think there is another alternative. The 'analytic baby' is equally likely to originate from an anal birth, a faecal baby of expelled waste products where the original goodness and nutrience have been rendered void. The principal mode of operation is the anal–sadistic regression. The primal scene is reduced to a bowel movement. The analysis is engulfed by the 'gigantic grinding machine' (Smirgel's term for the digestive tract) and everything is reduced to homogeneous excrement.

It is because the perverse couple is established at an unconscious level that I doubt whether the analyst's countertransference can be totally free from being caught in the development of this anal universe. The therapist may become aware of what is happening only after his or her unconscious has been drawn into the patient's faecal world. Conscious monitoring of the unconscious does not stop the analyst's unconscious from first becoming caught in a countertransference perversion. The monitoring through self-analysis can bring to light only what has already happened, rather than what might happen, thereby preventing the perversion to take hold. Diligent monitoring, which I advocate, may act as an early warning system that something is going wrong, and thus alert the therapist to the countertransference danger.

At a clinical level, it is probably important that the therapist is affected and, to an extent, caught in the perverse couple. Kernberg notes:

> The analyst's freedom to experience his or her own polymorphous perverse sexual tendencies in the emotional reactions to the patient's material, to identify with the patient's sexual excitement as well as with that of the patient's objects as part of the ebb and flow of counter-transference, may help bring to the surface the patient's primitive fantasies linked to the preoedipal determinants of polymorphous perverse sexuality that will otherwise remain dissociated, repressed, or even consciously suppressed.
>
> (1992: 291)

Such patients bring a pseudo-incorporation of interpretations as a subtle devaluation of the Oedipal father projected on to the analyst. The therapist is left with a 'vague uneasiness' about whether authentic work is being carried out. The patient's chaotic sexual fantasies characterize all his or her relationships and serve as a defence against object relating in depth.

I would add an amendment to this last remark by Kernberg. I agree the patient's chaotic sexual fantasies are a defence against genuine intimate relationships. However, it is also the case that these *perverse fantasies are the only form of object relating that is available to the patient*. Part of the great tragedy of the perverse scenario is that the patient's attempts to love are turned to shit. The perverse relationship is both a defence against genuine intimacy and also the only form of companionship or relationship that is available to the patient. The perverse solution is the closest these individuals come to a genuine relationship. That the only relationships of meaning can be perverse is the great sadness for both the patient and those lovers and partners incorporated into the anal universe. This is the analytic challenge, as it is only through the perverse scenario that the patient may be able to have any type of relationship: a sado-masochistic relationship is better than no relationship at all.

I am doubtful, therefore, when writers like Baker (1994) urge that it is essential that the countertransference acting out does not occur with a transference perversion. The perversion of his patient was to masturbate into his mother's knickers. This abruptly stopped after an interpretation. In its place, the patient developed chronic flatulence in his analysis and, on one occasion, attempted to masturbate while on the couch. Baker (1991) limited his transference interpretations to those only concerned with how the patient relegated the analyst to the 'role of a helpless observer of his humiliating attacks on *himself*' (authors italics). The chronic flatulence continued five sessions a week for six years. Now, I do not doubt that this was a difficult analysis but we might re-interpret this material. We might wonder if Baker's reluctance to allow any acting out was a form of schizoid distancing in response to perverse material as described by Wrye and Welles. Thus, the wish to avoid acting out was, in fact, a form of acting out in the services of schizoid distancing processes. We might then assume that the patient, desperate to have a relationship with the analyst (albeit a perverse one), used a variety of methods, all perverse (flatulence and masturbation), to effect a relationship of some kind with his analyst. The analyst, meanwhile, was busy trying to avoid being caught in the patient's anal world. This is successful, up to a point, in as far as it avoids the particular perverse world the patient intended. However, the perversion is not so easily escaped, and inevitably leads the therapist into a different perverse solution. I find it hard to imagine a therapist would not have any perverse thoughts while a patient continuously farted on the couch, five sessions a week for six years. One wonders that, if the therapist had allowed himself first to get more actively engaged, and then to extricate himself, the patient might not have needed to keep such a bombardment of flatulence for so many years before having a relationship with the analyst.

Part of the extreme difficulty of working with actively perverse individuals is that almost any response of the therapist becomes perverse, including those when the therapist thinks he or she is interpreting his or her way out of the perverse solution. Even then the creative thinking is quickly absorbed into what I would call the analytic rectum, making any differentiation difficult. This was very much the situation in the case I describe of Mr and Mrs T. It was precisely the therapists' attempts to avoid being sadistic that were experienced as uncontrollable and non-ritualized violence by this couple. The point I am stressing here is that patients with perverse states of mind create transference perversions, which in turn create countertransference perversions.

The underlying erotic nature of the analytic process is turned into a perverse faecal mess. From this, the therapist is faced with having to re-establish the analytic process. This is not an easy task. Khan seems quite pessimistic:

> This confronts us with the pervert's inaccessibility to influence and change through his object relations. No human being can do very

much in ordinary life for a pervert because he can be as Lewis Carroll's Tweedledee would say 'only a sort of thing in his dream'.

(1979: 30)

Kernberg (1992), on the other hand, has some optimism. He demonstrates that it is not possible to think of perverse pathology as presenting a unified group that can be included within a single frame or category; for example, organized perversion in neurotics presents a better prognosis than structured perversion in borderline and narcissistic pathologies. What seems to determine whether perverse structures are amenable to normal analysis or not is the degree of superego integration and the stage of developmental progression.

My own experience has been closer to Khan than to Kernberg in this respect. However, I am reluctant to give a decisive opinion on the amenability of perversions to psychoanalysis. I maintain a belief that, if the therapist can maintain or re-establish an analytic attitude, there is hope that he or she will begin to extricate him or herself from the patient's anal universe, thus leading the latter into a new form of object relating. These patients may gradually relinquish their perverse states of mind when the transference is experienced as genuinely intimate rather than as sado-masochistic. The paradox that perverse states of mind pose for the analytic therapy is the dilemma and challenge to enter into a dynamic of perverse thinking along with the patient, but without losing one's capacity to move on and progress and develop.

9

THE TEMPTATION OF
TRANSGRESSION

CURIOUSER AND CURIOUSER!

This chapter will propose that transgression is integral to curiosity and questioning in creative development. By transgression, I mean the necessary act of going somewhere that previously seemed off limits. Transgression, in the way I use it here, means to denote a pushing beyond the accepted norms, a stepping outside the expected – going past known boundaries. In the therapeutic context, I will suggest that the therapist and the analysand need to find themselves in a different place. From this, I will suggest that psychotherapy should be considered as a mutually transforming process: the analytic couple are thought of in terms of the transformational couple. This classification also applies, of course, to the mother and child and between lovers. The significance of this for the erotic transference–countertransference matrix is that the erotic, by its very nature, will produce the greatest possibilities for transgression.

First, I will illustrate my point with the full quote from Lewis Carroll's *Alice's Adventures in Wonderland* that forms this sub-heading:

> 'Curiouser and curiouser!' cried Alice (she was so much surprised, that for that moment she quite forgot how to speak good English).

Alice might not have been speaking *good* English, but she was using English and language *creatively*. She may have transgressed against grammar, but the result is a saying that has become anecdotal in the English tongue.

A distinction needs to be made between healthy and destructive transgression. Clearly the breaking of some taboos, such as that of actual incest, are destructive. The erotic in psychotherapy is certainly destructive, if the therapist is tempted to stop treating the material as symbolic, and decides instead to act on his or her feelings by trying to develop a fully-fledged sexual relationship with the patient.

It must be said, though, that some kinds of inquiry can certainly lead to trouble. Perhaps some inquiry can come close to hubris. Pandora's curiosity led her to open a box that let all the evils enter the world. In Sophocles' *King*

180

Oedipus, Oedipus defies the warnings of the seer, Tiresias, that some knowledge is best left unknown. The pursuit of this knowledge led to Oedipus' downfall. Bion (1965) also draws our attention to the myth of eating the apple in Eden which led to harsh punishment from a god opposed to people tasting the knowledge of good and evil. The building of the Tower of Babel where humanity sought to know the realm of God also led to punishment that confounded language. In the Oedipus myth, the Sphinx commits suicide when her secret is found out.

Away from mythology we find equally graphic accounts: Bruno was burnt at the stake and Galileo forced to recant because the Church did not like the proposal that the earth was not at the centre of the universe. On a lesser scale, at the beginning of his career Freud was ostracized, and later his books were burnt by the Nazis, because of his views on childhood sexual experience. The pursuit of knowledge can be a dangerous thing.

The pursuit of knowledge is also part of healthy psychological development. Hamilton (1982), summarizing infant research, demonstrates that knowledge and the thirst for knowledge are inextricably linked to the relationship to the mother. Our knowledge of the world is first our knowledge of the mother's body. If this secure base is established, the infant will have the confidence to explore the world from the safety of the mother's lap. Bowlby (1969) would thus state that the infant's exploration develops in the presence of the mother. This is similar to Winnicott's (1958) description of the development of the capacity to be alone. Both Bowlby and Winnicott noted that curiosity is inhibited when the mother's presence, the secure base, is absent. Anxiety then swamps the infant in the absence of the link with the mother, and curtails further exploration. Eventually, the infant will explore with the mother out of sight, but only if the child leaves and not vice versa. When a child is secure about the mother's whereabouts, he or she is free to turn attention away from her. Such acquisition of knowledge is linked to play and security. I do consider that the knowledge of the facts of life (see Chapter 7) also has a role. Here the curtailment of curiosity is the child's knowledge that the parent cannot bear the child to know.

Hamilton is critical of the Freudian theory of knowledge, in which it is linked to the primal scene and the discovery of forbidden secrets. She is also critical of the Kleinian model where feeding at the breast is the prototype for an incorporative theory of knowledge. Hamilton calls this the 'tragic vision of knowledge' which sees curiosity and pain as inseparable. Knowledge is seen as all or nothing, thereby omitting the other side of curiosity, the 'mystery' of reality, which one may describe in the words of Einstein as the ability to 'comprehend a little each day'. She writes:

In my view, sexuality is one aspect of exploratory activity rather than its cause. If babies find that the problem solving is motivating in itself

181

we don't have to search for ways to make babies learn to acquire knowledge.

(1982: 264)

She goes on to elaborate the importance of play in the development of curiosity and the individuation process. Thus, play stands as an intermediate area in which primary and secondary processes, action and reason, combine.

My own view is somewhere between this 'tragic vision' and the function of play. It seems to me that there is ample reason to consider that both have a role to play in the acquisition of knowledge. Knowledge is a paradox: it can be both pleasurable and painful; exploratory and transgressive.

By going beyond conventional and charted territory, we can find ourselves in a new place. This can be both a source of anxiety and creativity. So long as we are in known territory, that which is familiar, there is little that is new to be discovered. A psychic place needs to be entered where we have not previously been in order for something different to occur. I would like to add that I am only using a geographical metaphor for descriptive purposes.

The history of mythology tells us that the human psyche is often tempted to transgress. Only with this risk is a creative leap possible. The process of progression and individuation makes transgression a temptation.

I agree with the above quotation from Hamilton that sexuality is only one of a number of reasons to be found for exploratory activity. However, it is of such central importance in the psyche that there is no reason to suspect it to be on equal terms with other forms of motivation. Knowledge begins with what the baby knows about his or her body and that of the mother. Bodily experience cannot be understood without reference to the sexual, or, as I would prefer to say, without reference to the erotic.

All that I have just written has significance for working with the erotic transference and countertransference. The erotic leads the individual into the interrelated areas of the sacred and the profane. The erotic transference–countertransference matrix is historically seen as posing the greatest dangers to analytic work. Through those same risks we might suppose that the greatest therapeutic opportunities lie.

COMMON KNOWLEDGE INTERPRETATIONS AND TRANSFORMATIONAL INTERPRETATIONS

There is no denying that the psychoanalytic process is complicated and cannot be reduced to a single thread that runs throughout its whole course. I do think, though, that it is sometimes useful to consider the models with which we work. To my mind, the therapeutic passage is a very physical process. Often what is most essential is experienced first in the body; I think of this as a visceral process, rooted in emotional experience, with thinking and intellectual activity only secondary.

This is not true of all everyday analytic experience. In the discussion of our theory, I would like to make a distinction that is not possible in clinical practice. This distinction relates to two kinds of knowledge: what I call common knowledge and transformational knowledge.

Most therapeutic practice is involved with common knowledge. By this I mean the things the therapist (or patient) knows, which are drawn from conscious and preconscious formulations. For the therapist, this includes ideas derived from our understanding of theory, our use of empathy, our general knowledge about what makes people 'tick'. Most analytic interpretations fall into this category. Their usefulness to the patient is to engender a spirit of analytic inquiry and to demonstrate that the therapist is endeavouring to understand. They show the therapist's love and concern. These interpretations and other non-interpretative actions (such as reliability, the frame, tolerance, empathy, holding, the survival of the therapist, and so on) lubricate the flow of the everyday work of therapy. They build trust and understanding, and without them major psychic work is not possible.

I see transformational knowledge as different. This arises from the unconscious and/or its bodily manifestations. As such, it is outside what the therapist (or patient) has previously known. Such interpretations arise first from the 'guts' of the therapist and are felt as physical sensations, affects and fantasies about the patient. These sensations live first in a preverbal form. Ideally, over a period of time, the therapist will come gradually to understand these sensations. The resolution of these sensations is only reached when something which is experienced is utilized for verbal understanding. This will take the form of an interpretation that is spoken or unspoken. Such interpretations are the result of major internal work inside the therapist. The interpretation marks the culmination of this process, which can then be put into words. Such interpretations are the therapist's intellectual understanding of his or her emotions, or, put in terms of classical psychoanalysis, the sense made by the secondary processes of the primary process experience. I think of this process as resulting in transformational interpretations. Transformational in that they signify a transformation in the therapist, since the power of these interpretations broadens the depth and range of his or her knowledge. In so doing, they also offer a greater transformational opportunity to the patient. This transformational interpretation does not always need to be uttered to the patient, but does need to be thought. This is because the transformational interpretation is a consequence of internal change in the analyst. As I believe the unconscious of both analyst and analysand to be porous, the patient's unconscious will register a change in the therapist's unconscious, regardless of any spoken words. I do not think these transformational interpretations are part of the everyday work, and are less frequent than the common knowledge interpretation.

This sort of distinction between types of interpretations is not new. I think various writers have described different aspects of a similar process.

Meltzer (1973a) makes a distinction between 'routine' and 'inspired' interpretations which arise from joint investigation; Young (1994: 53) talks of didactic and evocative knowledge: 'didactic knowledge is imparted, while evocative knowledge is elicited or brought forth'.

With common knowledge, I refer to the phenomenon where both patient and therapist are on more or less familiar ground. The territory under discussion has at least been partially mapped and both participants know roughly where they are, that is to say, consider (rightly or wrongly) they have some understanding of the situation. However, in my view, though the map is important there is not much to be gained by exploring what is already known. There is an area outside the mapped territory, a hinterland, where neither the patient nor the therapist know the territory, it is uncharted. In my view, it is here where the greatest therapeutic change is possible, precisely because the land is unknown and something new can therefore be discovered. This is the territory from which transformational knowledge and interpretations originate.

Again, I would say that phenomenon has been described in different ways by other writers and has been termed 'negative capability'. In a letter of 1817 to his family, the poet John Keats describes a mental process important to creativity:

> *Negative Capability*, that is, when a man is capable of being in uncertainties, mysteries, doubts, without irritable reaching after fact and reason [author's italics].
>
> (Forman 1935)

This idea of negative capability, embracing uncertainty and avoiding a premature common knowledge has appealed to analysts as various as Bion (1970), Green (1973), and Rycroft (1979) amongst others.

Symington (1983) gives a good illustration of how the patient and therapist get inside each other. He describes the analyst's act of freedom as an agent of therapeutic change. He talks of a sadistic patient who 'honed in' on areas of his own vulnerability. After a while, she abandoned her normal chair and sat in the seat behind him. Symington felt he had resolutely to stay in his own chair. This pattern continued for eight sessions. He then became uncomfortable with this procedure as he was unable to be spontaneous. The next time it happened he changed chairs. He did not know why, just that it felt he could be more free. The patient was furious, as if he had no right to move, but then she moved back to her original chair. This event enabled the therapy to become unstuck, the patient was more able to listen and communication became easier. Symington understood this as the therapist's act of freedom leading to change with the patient. I mostly agree with him. I would, however, emphasize the partnership. It was the patient's act of freedom, changing chairs in the first place, that enabled the therapist to relocate himself (physically and psychically) with the patient. The difference was that the patient, caught in her own psychotic defences, was unable creatively to utilize her own actions. As such, hers was a limited act of freedom. The therapist needed the patient's potentially creative gesture to enable him to make his own act of freedom. He was thus able to do something creative with an aspect of the patient's pathology which was otherwise circular.

In other words, the therapist brings something new to the patient's previous experience. In Chapter 1, I linked this to Bollas's (1987) idea of the 'transformational object' and Baker's (1993) notion of a 'new object'. I linked these theories and proposed that the patient is seeking a new transformational object which offers a new experience to facilitate psychological growth. I would say that Symington enacted a transformation by being a new transformational object for his patient.

This distinction between common and transformational knowledge is particularly relevant to the erotic transference–countertransference matrix. As discussed in Chapters 1 and 2, it is in the nature of the erotic to be both backward and forward looking, regressive and progressive, repetitious and transformational. The erotic is reliably paradoxical. *Probably more than any other subject, the erotic takes both the patient and the therapist into the unmapped territory, the hinterland, where something new may be discovered or occur.* Neither participant knows what to expect, which is a source of play and anxiety. The mapping of this territory, the discovery of knowledge that transforms the psyche, is both pleasurable and painful. This is not a prescription for sado-masochism. As discussed in Chapter 8 on transference perversions, perverse states of mind are characterized by rigidity, impoverished fantasy formation and an inability to appreciate distinctions. In the hinterland I am describing, the pleasure is in the delight in discovering something new, and the pain is that of relinquishing the old; this is a dynamic not a static model.

The potency of the erotic transference and countertransference matrix resides in the fact that it almost always takes both partners in the analytic dyad into new territory. They find themselves faced with an experience that is new and intense to them both. In the heat of the erotic bond that is established unconscious to unconscious, old links can be broken and new ones forged. With this in mind, it is probably the case that not only is the therapist a new transformational object for the patient, but the patient may also be a new transformational object for the therapist.

The experiences that have emerged out of my workshops on *Working with the erotic transference and countertransference* around Europe seems to suggest that most analytic dyads find it preferable and easier to side-step the erotic. On the other hand, some of the literature seems to suggest that about 10 per cent of therapists seem to find it easier to give way to destructive sexual acting out with the patient than to deal therapeutically with the erotic. Neither of these solutions is satisfactory. I consider it is wiser to work therapeutically with it. Finding words for the unconscious, naming the beast, mapping the erotic hinterland, is the nature of the therapeutic process. If the therapist is anxious with the erotic, the patient will sense this and help the therapist avoid the subject. And if we do not deal with the erotic, which lies at the centre of our unconscious fantasy life, what meaningful deep psychic work can possibly be achieved? Both avoidance and sexual acting out follow paths away from the erotic hinterland. Therapists choosing either of these options may do interesting work, but it will most probably be in a known, mapped territory.

The psychoanalytic process encourages curiosity and inquiry. Preferably nothing is taken for granted or merely accepted on authority. To my mind, the therapeutic process will frequently need to take the patient to a place they have never been before. The therapist is confronted with the same dilemma. That is precisely where the creative experience is located: therapy is a 'curiouser and curiouser' wonderland–hinterland.

CLINICAL EXAMPLE: Y (WHY?)

Y is in his thirties and had sought psychotherapy because he was feeling depressed about his looks. To my eyes, he appeared unremarkable, perhaps above average for good looks. This was not his view. His looks had led him to acquire several painful nicknames at school. In his teens, he had had some cosmetic surgery which he felt was unsuccessful. He was particularly concerned about the size of his head, which he thought was too small for his body. He recalled that, as a child, his father would stick back his ears with tape because they stuck out too much.

He presented with a number of other concerns. He found it hard to get work and was unsuccessful with women. In his dreams, he wanted to be a successful musician with a beautiful girl-friend. In reality, he was not in a regular band and had few sexual relationships.

His sexual encounters had felt traumatic. He had experimented with mutual masturbation with one girl in his teens. With another girl, he had had difficulties keeping his erection so the relationship 'fizzled out'. Cosmetic surgery had been undertaken to improve his looks, in order to make himself more appealing to the woman he loved. She was unavailable – the girl-friend of his best friend. Once when an opportunity for infidelity arose he found himself on top of this girl, but unable to think of what he should do next – nothing happened. Another friend suggested he was unable to perform sexually because he 'fancied the girl too much'. All these experiences had been bad for his confidence. His main defence against possible sexual encounters was to avoid them. He recalled an incident when a friend and he were cycling: two girls made encouraging remarks to them. His friend wanted to go over to them, but at this point Y suddenly noticed he had lost his bicycle-pump and went off to look for it. He was sure he was heterosexual despite these failures, and reported that he was not attracted to men, though he was clearly worried to the contrary.

He reported he had little erotic desire as a consequence of these failures. He masturbated two or three times a week. His fantasies on these occasions were that he was 'kissing and being considerate' and he would think of girls he had known, except 'the one I supposedly loved. That would be pervie-like to think of her face while masturbating' (his neologism for 'perverse'). He thought that he was quite feminine in some respects in that he wanted somebody else (the woman) to make the first move. He always felt uncomfortable with intimacy. He remembered squirming if his mother tried to cuddle him.

Of his family he told me that father was not self-conscious. He was impatient with his son, Y, and did not like to explain things more than once. When having help with his homework, Y would pretend to understand his father's explanations rather than be thought stupid for incomprehension. In this way, knowledge was linked with what father could bear to tell him. Y told me: 'I grew up feeling I didn't want to be in the world.' Another family member told him father did not want him. His dad would get jealous of the attention that Y would get from his mother.

Y felt much closer to his mother who had died fifteen years previously. She, along with his sisters, were described as very attractive and 'fanciable', a fact that several friends had told him. He always spoke of his mother in glowing terms, but just below the surface could be detected criticisms. He had heard that his mother had taken the thalidomide pill when pregnant with him. Though this had not led to any noticeable deformities, it clearly had worked itself into his body image fantasies. He wondered if the thalidomide had made his head smaller than the rest of his body. He also reported being told by a doctor that he had only two, not three layers of skin. He thought this might have been caused by the drug.

He found it hard to regard his parents as a couple. His sexual researches as a child had led him to observe that his parents had separate beds, which he took to mean they had no sex life. Much later, after his mother died, father told him that he had wanted to divorce when Y was four but stayed together for the sake of the family. Y then wondered if his dad did not show mother any love and whether copying this had led to his own difficulties with women.

He found women to be a complete enigma. He could not make sense of any mixed message. He was only attracted to very pretty women. He always put appearance before their personality. In that much, he was like his dad: they both preferred attractive women. His friends had told him he was unrealistic to expect a 'Page Three' type of woman to go out with him. He could see their point. He was sure he knew what his favourite colour was, what music he liked, what his taste was in cars; he did not know why he could not be equally clear about women.

Our work together proceeded very well. We basically liked each other and found one another interesting. However, in every session we would also feel exasperated with each other. Y presented himself as somebody who could not understand things. This took several forms. He filled each session with a barrage of questions (which is why I am calling him 'Y'), some simple, others on complicated issues. At other times, he would be actively seeking paternal guidance, hoping I would advise him what to do. When I gave no direct answers or advice, he would feel at a loss to know how to proceed. He would feel desperately confused, as though I were letting him struggle with his problems alone.

My reaction felt equally difficult. Though he was showing signs of learning from experience, there were some experiences he seemed habitually to repeat with me: asking questions he knew I would not answer and seeking advice I told him I would not give. But what I have written about my response is not strictly true. I felt under tremendous pressure to answer his questions. His questions were asked in such a way that there were times I felt totally unable to stop myself from answering them or proffering him advice in a thin interpretative disguise. I would end up doing what I said I would not do, and giving what he expected I would not give. The problem for us both, as it later emerged, was that he was not asking the questions for which he really wanted answers; consequently, the answers I gave, while relevant to his questions, were not the answers he was looking for. In a way, his questions were a smoke-screen for what he really wanted to know, this defensive procedure thus made these questions compelling and sometimes impossible for me to avoid.

Interpreting this through the paternal transference did not help. I could see a 'role responsiveness' in that I was like his father who got irritated with Y's questions, and that this resulted in Y's compliance and his pretending to understand. Interpreting this did not relieve either of us. It left me feeling I was partly right, but that I had somehow missed the crucial point. In that respect, I felt rather like Y with his father. That did not help either. This aspect of the therapy appeared intractable.

This situation continued for a considerable period. Over time, though, I noticed that his questions related slightly more to matters concerning the body of a woman. For example, during one session he asked my advice: 'Does a woman's vagina get bigger after having a baby so that it takes a bigger penis to fit tighter?' He was concerned about the size of his penis, which he considered to be 'less than normal length'.

Earlier in the analysis, I had interpreted his anxiety about the size of his head spoiling his chances with women to be related to his concern that his penis would not satisfy a woman. At the time he had denied this, saying, 'out of sight, out of mind'. His head was more of a worry because it was conspicuous. Now, either because my earlier comment had put the idea in his mind, or because my comment had watered a dried seed, further material was emerging. I reminded him of our earlier discussions. He had said he thought his small head was due to his mother taking thalidomide. I said, perhaps he was saying he thought his mother was responsible for giving him what he considered a small penis, too. I anticipated he would reject this interpretation but, to my surprise, it resonated with him. I took this as an indication that perhaps something was beginning to move in the unconscious of us both. The end of the session stopped our discussion.

Next session he reported that, unlike his usual practice, he had not been thinking about what we had said. My first comment was to suggest that perhaps what we were talking about, his mother's effect on his sexual development, had been unthinkable. This realization in me set of a chain of new thoughts about Y's material. We discussed the nature of thinkable and unthinkable thoughts further.

I eventually said that it had occurred to me he was asking all these questions because he thought there was some basic knowledge outside his grasp, which he thought I possessed but that, like his parents, kept from him. It was my impression it was something to do with the facts which he thought he did not know. He said he did not know what to make of what I said. And, as I expected, asked if I could repeat it so he could try to understand.

He went on to say that neither parent told him about the 'birds and the bees'. He had gathered more information from his sisters and friends. He recalled a fragment of a memory from about ten: he had climbed into bed with his mother and had had sexual thoughts. Now he could not imagine why she would let him into bed with her at that age. He thought his mother was attractive, but was worried about sexual thoughts towards her. There appeared to be more he wanted to say about this, so I commented on his hesitation about speaking his thoughts. He recalled a recurring dream as a child around about eight-years-old: 'I get into bed with mum, it feels warm and sensual, I can't remember if we had sex.' He also had dreams about sex with his sisters. He had been so horrified at these dreams that: 'I stopped having them because they were abnormal'.

He went on to talk about how attractive his mother and his older sisters were. He asked me if I thought it was a problem that he could not have incestuous thoughts about them. He is not now attracted to older women. He was sure that he would never be attracted to women with the same names as his mother or sisters. I said that would feel like an incestuous experience. He concurred.

This led us to talk about how he splits women: the attractive ones he cannot have sexual thoughts about – his mother, sisters, his friend's girl when she wanted something sexual. On the other hand, any woman he might have sex with, he denigrates as unattractive, saying she did not 'turn him on'. He had linked attractiveness with incestuous desire and was thus unable to have satisfactory relations with women. In fact, his sexual researches as an adolescent had confirmed this view: seeing that his parents had separate beds was construed to mean that they did not have a sexual relationship, further placing in his mind the phantasy that his mother was beyond the sexual, that no one, not even his dad, would have sexual thoughts about her. He had found it unthinkable to allow incestuous thoughts: sexual knowledge towards his mother and sisters could not be tolerated and must be banished from thought. None the less, in my view, he was still curious and this led him to formulate questions which 'beat about the bush'.

A while after this, he reported going out with an older woman. It sounded a reasonable relationship, though not without its difficulties. The therapy had been observably helpful: Y had now been able to get a job that he liked; he was actively improving his relationship with his father and felt less depressed. He felt he wished to terminate at this point. I thought this might be something similar to the time he avoided sexual matters by racing off to look for his bike pump. In that context, I wondered if our recent discussions were causing him to flee. However, he seemed adamant, and clearly he had achieved some of the things to which he aspired.

THE TRANSFORMATIONAL COUPLE

Various other strands of the transference with Y were discussed that I have not described here, such as transference as symbolic sexual intercourse and his strong homoerotic transference. A fuller account of my views on these are found in earlier chapters. I have limited the material here to that concerning the temptation of transgression. Though there were areas of knowledge that could not be openly inquired into, this did not put an end to all curiosity. Instead, Y had developed the art of the tangential question: questioning around the area in the hope of getting enough fragments to form a picture. He could not ask what he really wanted to know, so would ask about other things with the desire it would answer his unspoken, unthought question. In other words, though he could not know what went on in the parents' bedroom, that did not stop him from trying to find out. His line of inquiry, though, did not give him the answers he required.

What this clinical example illustrates is the patient's fear of crossing into the unknown. As far as Y was concerned, this was the knowledge of incestuous desire towards his mother and a denial of the primal scene. However, fearing the knowledge did not kill his curiosity. His enquiries would always bring him to the very brink of what he really wanted to know, but not step beyond the safely acceptable to face that knowledge. He stopped short of transgressing.

Like spaces between words, the erotic bond that links the analytic dialogue binds the unconscious of both participants into a relationship whether they like it or not. This relationship will almost always oblige each participant in the analytic dyad to experience the other in terms of unconscious erotic phantasy. This will take both participants, like lovers, to where they are familiar and also to where they have never been. In my view, this makes the erotic transference and countertransference matrix inescapable. Rather like the primal scene, we can disavow its presence or significance, but we cannot escape its influence. With Y, this reached to the very heart of what is knowable. We both struggled to leave what was known in order to find knowledge from a different place.

I would suggest that the turning point, where we both stepped into the unknown, was when Y reported that he had not been thinking in between sessions after we talked about his mother taking thalidomide tablets. To paraphrase Symington I would say that the patient's act of freedom led Y to break his usual habit by not thinking about our sessions, this led to a creative act of my own which enabled hitherto unthinkable thoughts to be known. Perhaps this could be described more precisely: Y broke his usual habit because our line of inquiry was leading to an area he was anxious about transgressing. By deciding not to think about our work in between sessions, he broke his habit for defensive purposes; we could describe this as an act of inhibited freedom. Y's pathology could not let him make a truly creative leap into the unknown – this is why patients seek a therapist, as they cannot manage this struggle on their own (for that matter, neither can lovers). However, his movement was enough to create a gap where somebody else might creatively step. As in the Symington case I cited earlier, I believe this first step is often taken by the patient, but their neurosis stops them capitalizing on it. The therapist's act of freedom is to complete this first stage and precisely because they are a new transformational object they do not repeat the patient's pathology and so take the process to a more creative place. In this mutual process, both Y and I stepped from familiar territory into a different place where things looked different. This different place gave the opportunities for fresh discoveries.

TRANSFERENCE AND COUNTERTRANSFERENCE: A MUTATIVE PROCESS

In his influential article of 1934, Strachey introduced the concept of the 'mutative interpretation' as the main source of therapeutic action. The mutative interpretation would come from the analyst acting as an 'auxiliary superego' to the patient and by 'small steps to allow the patient's id energy to become conscious, thus able to progress to more normal adult development'.

Carpy (1989: 289) saw that tolerating the countertransference could also be a mutative process. By this he meant the ability to 'experience the patient's projections in their full force, and yet be able to avoid acting them out in a gross way' by not being taken over completely by the experience. By this process, the patient is gradually able to re-introject both previously intolerable aspects of him or herself, and develops the capacity to tolerate them which was observed in the analyst.

Carpy then goes on to say, significantly:

it is the gradual process of introjection as a result of this non-verbal interaction which produces change in the patient's psychic structure, rather than an interpretation whose content is meaningless to the patient. The interpretation can only become meaningful *as a consequence of* the patient's discovery of aspects of himself through this gradual process. It is only then that the patient is able to recognize what he has projected as *his*, and so the 'successful' interpretation, and the sense of mutual understanding produced by it, serves as confirmation of something which has already become available to be more consciously understood [author's italics].

(1989: 293)

I am entirely in agreement with this view. An interpretation, or at least the more potent kind of interpretation that I call transformational, is the end result of an internal working through by the analyst. Something inside the analyst has been transformed to allow this interpretation to emerge. The process of the analyst grappling with his or her own unconscious is conveyed to the patient by an interpretation. Like lovers, the patient and the therapist psychically get inside each other. Often, though, the initial 'nudge' will come from the patient.

Carpy seems to imply this must always be spoken. I am not always convinced of that necessity. He notes earlier that the patient is always looking to see, consciously and unconsciously, how the analyst is being affected and what is done with these strong feelings. In my view, this suggests that the patient will register a change in the therapist whether the latter speaks or not and this change will have a mutative effect on the patient. Both participants have a porous unconscious which conveys and receives information about the other. This is similar to the process described by Searles (1979: 374) as 'therapeutic symbiosis' where 'the analyst participates at a feeling-level', but at a manageable degree and always subject to his or her own scrutiny.

Reik (cited in Lukacher 1986) coined the expression that the analyst needs to 'listen with a third ear'. This is a curious term suggesting deformity and mutation, like a person in a freak show. I do not believe it is an image of being deaf, as Lacan (1981) fatuously described it. If we can play with this image, I would suggest that the third ear is provided by the patient from the area where the unconscious of both participants overlap. Except where we are dealing with psychotic processes, the therapist is not wholly taken over by the patient, nor vice versa. The third ear comes from that part of ourselves which we share with an 'other'. As such, it is a body image denoting psychic overlap between the analytic dyad. This also implies the patient also has a third ear to monitor the analyst.

Psychoanalysis becomes a mutually influencing process whereby both participants are continuously revising their theories about the other.

Unconscious phantasies that both hold are gradually replaced with more realistic perceptions of the other. Therapy, the transference and counter-transference thus becomes a mutual mutative process in which projections are diminished, thereby allowing each to learn from experience. For that reason, it is useful to think in terms of the analytic dyad as *a transformational couple: patient and therapist find a new transformational object in each other. The transference and countertransference become a mutative matrix.*

This applies to the countertransference in general. Given the ubiquitous nature of the erotic and the excitement and anxiety generated in both therapist and patient, this process applies possibly more in this area than anywhere else. As with lovers, and mothers with babies, the erotic takes the analyst and analysand deep inside each other, to both the familiar and unknown. The erotic transference and countertransference is more in need of Negative Capability than many other analytic experiences precisely because both participants will rush to foreclose its influence through fear that Oedipal or pre-Oedipal desires will be acted out.

EROTIC HORROR AND EXCITEMENT

Much of the literature on the erotic transference and countertransference contains a curious feature. Many writers feel the need to say something along the lines of, 'Of course, I would not have sex with my patients or sexually act out.' Why do therapists need to give such reassurance to the reader? When therapists write about, say, aggression they do not see the need to reassure the reader that, 'Of course, I do not hit my patients.' There is something about discussing the erotic that leads to defensiveness. The underlying anxiety seems to be that if you talk about the erotic then other therapists will think you act on your feelings; to think about it is to do it. That is very concrete thinking. Indeed, the nature of the psychotherapy profession is such that we all look for unconscious motives in others and are quick to spot psychic fault lines. Writers, perhaps, have a genuine cause for concern about what assumptions will be made about them. I have sometimes found myself on the receiving end of such objections. But I also think that such anxiety has a phantasitical or paranoid element.

It is not always easy to be courageous. For example, Maroda (1991) presents compelling arguments (though, ultimately, she does not convince me) as to why a therapist should be prepared to disclose his or her own internal processes to the patient. This also includes revealing erotic countertransference. She makes the point, correct in my view, that most erotic transferences are fleeting; those that are intense and long-lasting do not persist without the co-operation of the therapist, for example, his or her unworked through erotic countertransference. She discusses a case cited in Atwood et al. (1989) to illuminate her point. Again, I think she is correct.

What I find more interesting, though, is that Maroda gives no example from her own clinical experience. This is a striking exception in a book otherwise replete with interesting personal material. Of course, if therapists put their work into the public domain through publication we are all entitled to form our own opinions, and it is right that we may wish to reinterpret their work, as Maroda does with Atwood. But I also think it is easier to hide behind another's material to avoid putting ourselves on the line. The erotic seems to conjure up unprecedented anxiety between psychotherapists.

This same dilemma is reflected in the analytic encounter. Usually both participants find the presence of the erotic a source of discomfort in what Kumin (1985) aptly calls 'erotic horror' (cf. Chapter 3). There is a thin line between horror and excitement, the sacred and the profane. The erotic is not neutral and cool, but takes the participants into emotional reactions resonating from deep within the unconscious. The erotic bond is neither cosy nor comfortable, and is one in which neither participants are secure in the known terrain of common knowledge. The erotic takes us from such familiarity and we find ourselves in a different place, without a map. In my opinion, it is no wonder that the erotic in therapy tends to be seen as a form of resistance: both participants resist the unconscious stirring of the erotic bond.

The erotic is at the centre of unconscious phantasy life and therefore touches us deeply. Talking about the struggle to love, Zuckerberg sums up the situation:

> Our task is to work through these feelings creatively and with insight. Among the more powerful feelings engendered are love and intimacy. How do therapists, as people, receive love? How comfortable are we with intimacy? The degree to which we are, the degree to which our self-object boundaries are firm, allowing flexibly both benign symbiosis and benign empathic separateness, will determine in part the extent to which our patients will grow in intimacy.
>
> (1988: 156)

I would amend this only to say that I consider the unconscious porous and that there are not firm boundaries around people. What counts is not to feel that the whole sense of self is lost when there is an erotic bond uniting us with the other.

In my teaching, and when running workshops on working with the erotic transference and countertransference, I stress there are no experts on this subject, including me. I have given the matter a lot of thought and read as much of the relevant literature that I can, but in the clinical work that is not enough. In the day-to-day work of psychotherapy each patient is different and so, too, are the challenges of the erotic bond. The struggle is renewed in each therapy: we return to the beginning with each patient. Each patient and therapist will grapple with the search for a new transformational object. The only thing to fall back on is the memory that having trust in the erotic transference and countertransference erotic bond has been helpful in the past with other patients. This means that I may have some confidence that it may also prove useful in the present and future. It may, after all, be helpful to us all to keep in mind the fact that, with humanity at large, the erotic is the most powerful transformational force of all.

NOTES

NOTES

1 The erotic transference

1 I prefer to use the terms 'he and she', 'him or her', etc. Though I recognize this makes language more long-winded and clumsy, it is distinctly preferable to the general, conventional pronoun 'he' to refer to both sexes – or 'she' to refer to both sexes, as you find in some more recent writing, which seems to me merely to repeat the mistakes of the singular use of the masculine pronoun.

I have an additional preference for the use of both pronouns 'he and she', as this reflects the nature of this book, reminding us of both sexes together for a creative intercourse – in this instance, a creative intercourse of language. I have half a mind to consider the singular designation of 'he' or 'she' to refer to both sexes as another instance of denial of the two sexes in the primal scene.

7 Transference as symbolic primal scene

2 I wish to make a few further comments on Klein and the primal scene. In her 1925 paper 'A contribution to the psychogenesis of tics', Klein cites her clinical work with a child called Felix – who is in fact her own son, Hans (cf. Sayers 1991: 215–216). Klein relates the development of the child's tic to witnessing his parents' sexual intercourse. The tic consisted of three movements: a feeling of depression in the back of his neck, an urge to throw his head backwards and move it sideways and, finally, to press his head down as deep as possible, giving the feeling of drilling into something. The whole movement recalled a time before the age of six when Hans shared his parents' bedroom and clandestinely witnessed their sexual intercourse. The three movements of his tic represented 'the passive role of his mother, the passive role of his own ego, and the active role of his father' (Klein 1925).

Now, what is interesting for our purposes is that this account is, in effect, Klein telling us how her son perceived his parents' sexual activity; or more accurately put, her account of how she understood her son's perception of her sexual intercourse. I would make a few speculative suggestions from this material. Klein had felt trapped in an unhappy marriage that had, amongst other things, put paid to her chance of training as a doctor. Married at twenty-one, she had found the sexual relation with her husband repulsive, describing it thus: 'Does it therefore have to be like this that motherhood begins with disgust?' (quoted in Grosskurth:

1986). We might therefore suppose that what Hans saw, his mother merely passively doing her marital duty, was probably a fairly accurate perception. Now, I am implying no criticism, but simply putting forward a thought for discussion. If we make a huge speculative leap perhaps we can conceive the possibility that, for Klein herself, the primal scene was not imagined as a creative intercourse. Rather it was one-sided, one person (the husband–father) doing something to the other, the wife, who was only passively involved. As this is the usual criticism of Klein's attitude to the mother–baby relationship, let us at least toy with the idea before we discard it, that the active father–baby to the relatively passive wife–mother is an expression of Klein's primal scene phantasy.

REFERENCES

Abelin, E. (1975) 'Some further observations and comments on the earliest role of the father', *International Journal of Psychoanalysis* 56: 293–302.

Abend, S. M. (1989) 'Countertransference and technique', *Psychoanalytic Quarterly* 48: 374–395.

Abraham, K. (1913) 'Mental after-effects produced in a nine-year-old child by the observation of sexual intercourse between its parents', in *Selected Papers on Psychoanalysis*, London: Maresfield Reprints (1979).

—— (1924) 'A short study of the development of the libido, viewed in the light of mental disorders', in *Selected Papers of Karl Abraham*, London: Hogarth Press (1953).

Ainsworth, M. D. S. and Bell, S. M. (1970) 'Some contemporary patterns of mother–infant interaction in the feeding situation', in J. Ambrose (ed.) *The Functions of Stimulation in Early Post-Natal Development*, London: Academic Press.

Alexander, F. (1950) 'Analysis of the therapeutic factors in psychoanalytic treatment', *Psychoanalytic Quarterly* 19: 482–500.

Anzieu, D. (1986) *Freud's Self-Analysis*, in S. C. B. Yorke (ed.) London: Hogarth Press.

Arlow, J. A. (1980) 'The revenge motive in the primal scene', *Journal of the American Psychoanalytic Association* 28: 519–541.

Armstrong-Perlman, E. M. (1991) 'The allure of the bad object', *Free Associations* 2(3): 343–356.

Atwood, G. E., Stolorow, R. O. and Trop, J. L. (1989) 'Impasses in psychoanalytic therapy: a royal road', *Contempory Psychoanalysis* 25: 554–573.

Bach, S. (1994) *The Language of Perversion and the Language of Love*, New York: Aronson.

Bak, R. C. (1973) 'Being in love and object loss', *International Journal of Psychoanalysis* LIV: 1–8.

Baker, R. (1993) 'The patient's discovery of the psychoanalyst as a new object', *International Journal of Psychoanalysis* 74: 1223–1233.

—— (1994) 'Psychoanalysis as a lifeline: a clinical study of a transference perversion', *International Journal of Psychoanalysis* 75: 743–753.

Balint, M. (1939) 'Love for the mother and mother-love', in M. Balint (ed.) *Primary Love and Psychoanalytic Technique*, London: Tavistock (1965).

—— (1956) 'Perversions and genitality', in S. Lorand (ed.) *Perversions, Psychodynamics and Theory*, New York: Gramercy Books.

Barthes, R. (1978) *A Lover's Discourse*, New York: Hill and Wang.

Bataille, G. (1957) *Eroticism*, London: Marion Boyars (1987).

REFERENCES

Bell, R. Q. (1974) 'Contributions of human infants to caregiving and social interaction', in M. Lewis (ed.) *The Effect of the Infant on its Caregiver*, Chichester: John Wiley.

Belotti, E. G. (1976) *Du côte des petites filles*, Paris

Benjamin, J. (1988) *The Bonds of Love*, London: Virago Books.

Bergmann, M. S. (1980) 'On the intrapsychic function of falling in love', *Psychoanalytic Quarterly* XLIX: 56–77.

—— (1982) 'Platonic love, transference love and love in real life', *Journal of the American Psychoanalytic Association* 30: 87–111.

—— (1988) 'Freud's three theories of love in the light of later developments', *Journal of the American Psychoanalytic Association* 36: 653–672.

Bibring, G. (1936) 'A contribution to the subject of transference resistance', *International Journal of Psychoanalysis* 17: 181–189.

Binstock, W. (1973) 'Two forms of intimacy', *Journal of American Psychoanalytic Association* 21: 543–557.

Bion, W. R. (1959) 'Attacks on linking', *International Journal of Psychoanalysis* 40: 308–315.

—— (1962) *Learning From Experience*, Oxford: Heinemann.

—— (1965) *Transformations*, London: Maresfield Reprints (1984).

—— (1970) *Attention and Interpretation*, London: Maresfield Reprints (1988).

Blos, P. (1985) *Son and Father*, New York: New York Free Press.

Blum, H. B. (1973) 'The concept of erotized transference', *Journal of the American Psychoanalytic Association* 21: 61–76.

Boesky, D. (1990) 'The psychoanalytic process and its components', *Psychoanalytic Quarterly* 59: 550–584.

Bokanowski, T. (1995) 'The concept of psychic homosexuality', *International Journal of Psychoanalysis* 76: 793–804.

Bollas, C. (1987) *The Shadow of the Object: Psychoanalysis of the Unthought Known*, New York/Oxford: Columbia University Press.

—— (1992) *Being a Character*, London: Routledge (1994).

Bolognini, S. (1994) 'Transference: erotised, erotic, loving, affectionate', *International Journal of Psychoanalysis* 75: 73–86.

Bowlby, J. (1969) *Attachment and Loss. Vol I: Attachment*, London: Hogarth Press.

Boyer, L. (1964) 'Psychological problems of a group of Apaches: alcoholic hallucinousis and latent homosexuality among typical men', in W. Muensterberger and S. Axelread (eds) *The Psychoanalytic Study of Society* vol. 3, New York: IUP.

Boyer, L. and Boyer, R. M. (1972) 'Effects of acculturation on the vicissitudes of the aggressive drive among the Apaches of the Mescalero Indian Reservation', in W. Muensterberger and A. Esman (eds) *The Psychoanalytic Study of Society* vol. 5, New York: IUP.

Breen, D. (ed.) (1993) *The Gender Conundrum: Contemporary Psychoanalytic Perspectives on Femininity and Masculinity*, London: Routledge.

Brenman Pick, I. (1985) 'Working through in the countertransference', *International Journal of Psychoanalysis* 66: 156–166.

Britton, R. (1989) 'The missing link: parental sexuality in the Oedipus complex', in *The Oedipus Complex Today*, London: Karnac Books.

Brunet, O. and Lezine, I. (1965) *Le Développement Psychologique de la Première Enfance*, Paris.

Burlingham, D. (1973) 'The pre-Oedipal infant–father relationship', *Psychoanalytic Study of the Child* 28: 23–47.

Canestri, J. (1993) 'A cry of fire: some considerations on transference love', in E. S. Person, (ed.) *On Freud's 'Observations on Transference Love'*, New Haven CT: Yale University Press.

REFERENCES

Carpy, D. V. (1989) 'Tolerating the countertransference: a mutative process', *International Journal of Psychoanalysis* 70: 287–294.

Cassel, Z. K. and Sander, L. W. (1975) *Neonatal recognition processes and attachment: the masking experiment*, paper presented to Society for Research in Child Development, Denver CO.

Cesio, F. (1993) 'The Oedipal tragedy in the psychoanalytic process: transference love', in E. S. Person, (ed.) *On Freud's 'Observations on Transference Love'*, New Haven CT: Yale University Press.

Chamberlain, D. B. (1987) 'The cognitive new-born: a scientific update', *British Journal of Psychotherapy* 4(1): 30–71.

Chasseguet-Smirgel, J. (1976) 'Freud and female sexuality: the consideration of some blind spots in the exploration of the "dark continent"', *International Journal of Psychoanalysis* 57: 134–145.

—— (1981) *Female Sexuality: New Psychoanalytic Views*, London: Virago Books.

—— (1984a) 'The femininity of the analyst in professional practice', *International Journal of Psychoanalysis* 65: 169–178.

—— (1984b) *Creativity and Perversion*, London: Free Association Books (1985).

Chodorow, N. (1978) *The Reproduction of Mothering*, Berkeley CA: University of California Press.

Christie, G. and Correia, A. (1987) 'Maternal ambivalence in a group analytic setting', *British Journal of Psychotherapy* 3(3): 205–215.

Chused, J. F. (1991) 'The evocative power of enactments', *Journal of the American Psychoanalytic Association* 39: 615–639.

Colman, W. (1994) 'Love, desire and infatuation', *Journal of Analytical Psychology* 39: 497–514.

Cunningham, R. (1991) 'When is a pervert not a pervert', *British Journal of Psychotherapy* 8(1): 48–70.

Dahlberg, G. (1970) 'Sexual contact between patient and therapist', *Contemporary Psychoanalysis* 6: 107–124.

Denis, P. (1982) 'Homosexualité primaire: base de contradiction', *Revue Française de Psychanalyse* 46(1).

Deutsch, H. (1945) *The Psychology of Women* vols. 1 and 2, New York: Grune and Stratton Research Books (1947).

Devereux, G. (1961) *Mohave Ethnopsychiatry and Suicide: The Psychic Disturbances of an Indian Tribe*, Washington DC: Smithsonian Institution Press.

Di Ceglie, G. R. (1995) 'From the internal couple to the marital relationship', in S. Ruszczynski and J. Fisher (eds) *Intrusiveness and Intimacy in the Couple*, London: Karnac Books.

Dreyfus, P. (1978) 'Panel and open forum on the ego ideal of the psychoanalyst', *International Journal of Psychoanalysis* 59: 391–393.

Druck, A. B. (1988) 'The classical psychoanalytic stance: what's love got to do with it? in J. F. Lasky and H.W. Silverman (eds) *Love: Psychoanalytic Perspectives*, New York: New York University Press.

Eagle, M. (1993) 'Enactments, transference, and symptomatic cure: a case history', *Psychoanalytic Dialogues* 3: 93–110.

Edelheit, H. (1974) 'Crucifixion fantasies and their relation to the primal scene', *International Journal of Psychoanalysis* 55: 193–199.

Eichenbaum, L. and Orbach, S. (1982) *Outside In, Inside Out*, Harmondsworth: Penguin.

Eichoff, F-W. (1993) 'A rereading of Freud's "Observations on transference love"', in E. S. Person, (ed.) *On Freud's "Observations on Transference Love"*, New Haven CT: Yale University Press.

REFERENCES

Ellis, H. (1903) *Studies in the Psychology of Sex: Analysis of the Sexual Impulse; Love and Pain; the Sexual Impulse in Women* vol. 3, Philadelphia: (1913).

Endleman, R. (1988) 'Love: transcultural considerations', in J. F. Lasky and H.W. Silverman (eds) *Love: Psychoanalytic Perspectives*, New York: New York University Press.

Esman, A. H. (1973) 'The primal scene: a review and a reconsideration', *Psychoanalytic Study of the Child* 28: 49–81.

Etchegoyen, R. H. (1978) 'Some thoughts on transference perversion', *International Journal of Psychoanalysis* 59: 45–54.

Fairbairn, W. R. D. (1940) 'Schizoid factors in the personality', in *Psychoanalytic Studies of the Personality*, London: Routledge (1986).

—— (1941) 'A revised psychopathology of the psychoses and psychoneuroses', in *Psychoanalytic Studies of the Personality*, London: Routledge (1986).

Fenichel, O. (1945) *The Psychoanalytic Theory of Neurosis*, New York: Norton.

Ferenczi, S. (1926) *Final Contributions to the Problems and Methods of Psychoanalysis*, New York: Brunner/Mazel (1980).

Fogel, A., Diamond, G., Langhorst, B. and Demos, V. (1981) 'Affective and cognitive aspects of the two-month-old's participation in face-to-face interaction with its mother', in E. Tronick (ed.) *Joint Regulation of Behaviour*, Cambridge: Cambridge University Press.

Forman, M. B. (ed.) (1935) *The Letters of John Keats*, London: Oxford University Press.

Frejaville, A. (1984) 'L'homosexualité primaire', *Les Cahiers du Centre de Psychanalyse et de Psychotherapie* 8.

Freud, S. (1900) 'The interpretation of dreams', in *Standard Edition* vols. 4 and 5, London: Hogarth Press.

—— (1905a) 'Jokes and their relation to the unconscious', in *Standard Edition* vol. 8, London: Hogarth Press.

—— (1905b) 'Fragment of an analysis of a case of hysteria (Dora)', in *Standard Edition* vol. 7, London: Hogarth Press.

—— (1905c) 'Three essays on the theory of sexuality', in *Standard Edition* vol. 7, London: Hogarth Press.

—— (1908) 'The sexual theories of children', in *Standard Edition* vol. 9, London: Hogarth Press.

—— (1913) 'On beginning the treatment (further recommendations on the technique of psychoanalysis)', in *Standard Edition* vol. 12, London: Hogarth Press.

—— (1915a) 'Observations on transference love', in *Standard Edition* vol. 12, London: Hogarth Press.

—— (1915b) 'Instincts and their vicissitudes', in *Standard Edition* vol. 14, London: Hogarth Press.

—— (1915c) 'A case of paranoia running counter to the psychoanalytic theory of the disease, in *Standard Edition* vol. 14, London: Hogarth Press.

—— (1916) 'Some character types met with in psychoanalytic work', in *Standard Edition* vol. 14, London: Hogarth Press.

—— (1917) 'On transformation of instincts as exemplified in anal eroticism', in *Standard Edition* vol. 17, London: Hogarth Press.

—— (1918) 'From the history of an infantile neurosis', in *Standard Edition* vol. 17, London: Hogarth Press.

—— (1921) 'Group psychology and the analysis of the ego', in *Standard Edition* vol. 18, London: Hogarth Press.

—— (1923) 'The ego and the id', in *Standard Edition* vol. 19, London: Hogarth Press.

REFERENCES

—— (1925) 'An autobiographical study', in *Standard Edition* vol. 20, London: Hogarth Press.

—— (1928) 'Dostoevsky and parricide', in *Standard Edition* vol. 21, London: Hogarth Press.

—— (1930) 'Civilisation and its discontents', in *Standard Edition* vol. 21, London: Hogarth Press.

—— (1937) 'Analysis terminable and interminable', in *Standard Edition* vol. 23, London: Hogarth Press.

—— (1940) 'An outline of psychoanalysis', in *Standard Edition* vol. 23, London: Hogarth Press.

Freud, S. and Breuer, J. (1895) 'Studies on Hysteria', in *Standard Edition* vol. 2, London: Hogarth Press.

Friedman, R. C. (1988) *Male Homosexuality: A Contemporary Psychoanalytic Perspective*, New Haven, CT: Yale University Press.

Fromm, E. (1956) *The Art of Loving*, London: Harper and Row.

Gabbard, G. O. (1995) 'Countertransference: the emerging common ground', *International Journal of Psychoanalysis* 76: 475–485.

Gerrard, J. (1992) 'Rescuers and containers: fathers and mothers?', *British Journal of Psychotherapy* 9(1): 15–23.

Gibeault, A (1988) 'On the feminine and the masculine: afterthoughts on Jacqueline Cosnier's book, *Destins de la feminité*', *Les Cahiers du Centre de Psychoanalyse et de Psychotherapie* 16–17.

Gill, M. M. (1991) 'Indirect suggestion: a response to Oremland's 'Interpretation and interaction'" in J. D. Oremland (ed.) *Interpretation and Interaction: Psychoanalysis or Psychotherapy?* Hillsdale NJ: Analytic Press.

—— (1993) 'One-person and two-person perspectives: Freud's "Observations on transference-love"', in E. S. Person, (ed.) *On Freud's "Observations on Transference Love"*, New Haven CT: Yale University Press.

Gillespie, W. H. (1952) 'Notes on the analysis of sexual perversions', *International Journal of Psychoanalysis* 33: 347–402.

Glasser, M. (1985) "The weak spot' – some observations on male sexuality', *International Journal of Psychoanalysis* 50.

Glenn, J. (1986) 'Freud, Dora, and the maid: a study of countertransference', *Journal of the American Psychoanalytic Association* 34:591–606.

Glover, E. (1955) *The Technique of Psychoanalysis*, New York: International University Press.

Gorkin, M. (1985) 'Varieties of sexualised countertransference', *Psychoanalytic Review* 72(3): 421–440.

Granoff, W. (1976) *La Pensée et le feminin* Paris: Minuit.

Green, A. (1973) 'On negative capability. A critical review of Bion's *Attention and Interpretation*', *International Journal of Psychoanalysis* 54: 115–119.

—— (1995) 'Has sexuality anything to do with psychoanalysis?' *International Journal of Psychoanalysis* 76(5): 871–883.

Greenson, R. R. (1967) *The Technique and Practice of Psychoanalysis*, New York: International University Press.

—— (1968) 'Dis-identifying from the mother: its special importance for the boy', *International Journal of Psychoanalysis* 49.

—— (1974) 'Loving, hating and indifference towards the patient', *International Review of Psycho-Analysis* 1: 259–266.

Grosskurth, P. (1986) *Melanie Klein*, Sevenoaks: Hodder and Stoughton.

Hamilton, V. (1982) *Narcissus and Oedipus: The Children of Psychoanalysis*, London: Karnac Books (1993).

Harlow, H. F. (1958) 'The nature of love', *American Psychologist* 13: 673–685.

REFERENCES

Heimann, P. (1950) 'On countertransference', *International Journal of Psychoanalysis* 31: 81–84.

Hellman, I. (1954) 'Some observations on mothers of children with intellectual inhibitions', *The Psychoanalytic Study of the Child* 9: 258–273.

Hen Co-Op, The (1993) *Growing Old Disgracefully: New Ideas for Getting the Most Out of Life*, London: Piatkus Press.

Hirsch, I. (1988) 'Mature love in the countertransference', in J. F. Lasky and H.W. Silverman (eds) *Love: Psychoanalytic Perspectives*, New York: New York University Press.

Hoffer, W. (1991) *The Freud–Klein Controversies, 1941–1945*, London and New York: Routledge.

Hoffman, I. Z. (1992) 'Some practical implications of a social constructivist view of the psychoanalytic situation', *Psychoanalytic Dialogues* 2: 287–304.

Hopcke, R. H. (1988) 'Jung and homosexuality: a clearer vision', *Journal of Analytical Psychology* 33: 65–80.

Ikonen, P. and Rechardt, E. (1984) 'On the universal nature of primal scene fantasies', *International Journal of Psychoanalysis* 65: 63–72.

Isay, R. (1986) 'Homosexuality in homosexual and heterosexual men: some distinctions and implications for treatment', in G. Fogel (ed.) *The Psychology of Men*, New York: Basic Books.

Jackson, D. (1989) *Three in a Bed*, London: Bloomsbury.

Jehu, D. (1994) *Patients as Victims: Sexual Abuse in Psychotherapy and Counselling*, London: John Wiley and Sons.

Jones, E. (1953) *The Life and Work of Sigmund Freud* vol. 1, London: Hogarth Press.

Joseph, B (1989) *Psychic Equilibrium and Psychic Change*, London: Routledge.

—— (1993) 'On transference love: some current observations', in E. S. Person, (ed.) *On Freud's "Observations on Transference Love"*, New Haven CT: Yale University Press.

Joseph, E. D. (1978) 'The ego ideal of the psychoanalyst', *International Journal of Psychoanalysis* 59: 377–385.

Jung, C. G. (1946) 'The psychology of the transference', in *Collected Works* vol. 16, London: Routledge and Kegan Paul.

Kaplan, L. (1989) *Female Perversions*, New York: Aronson.

Karme, E. P. (1979) 'The analysis of a male patient by a female analyst: the problem of the negative oedipal transference', *International Journal of Psychoanalysis* 60: 253–261.

Kernberg, O. (1974) 'Mature love: prerequisites and characteristics', *Journal of the American Psychoanalytic Association* XXII: 743–768.

—— (1975) *Borderline Conditions and Pathological Narcissism*, New York: Aronson.

—— (1992) *Aggression in Personality Disorders and Perversions*, New Haven CT: Yale University Press.

Kestemberg, E. (1984) '"Astrid" ou homosexualité, identité, adolescence: quelques propositions hypothetiques', *Les Cahiers du Centre de Psychanalyse et de Psychotherapie* 8.

Khan, M. M. R. (1979) *Alienation in Perversions*, London: Maresfield Library (1989).

Klein, M. (1925) 'A contribution to the psychogenesis of tics', in *Love, Guilt and Reparation*, London: Virago Press (1988).

—— (1952) 'Some theoretical conclusions regarding the emotional life of the infant', in *Envy and Gratitude and Other Works 1946 to 1963*, London: Virago Press (1988).

—— (1955) 'On identification', in *Envy and Gratitude and Other Works 1946 to 1963*, London: Virago Press (1988).

—— (1957) 'Envy and gratitude', in *Envy and Gratitude and Other Works 1946 to 1963*, London: Virago Press (1988).

Kohut, H. (1971) *The Analysis of the Self*, New York: International Universities Press.

—— (1977) *The Restoration of the Self*, New York: International Universities Press.

Kumin, I. (1985) 'Erotic horror: desire and resistance in the psychoanalytic setting', *International Journal of Psychoanalytic Psychotherapy* 11: 3–20.

Lacan, J. (1981) *Four Fundamental Concepts of Psychoanalysis*, New York: Norton.

Laplanche, J. and Pontalis, J. B. (1973) *The Language of Psychoanalysis*, London: Karnac Books (1988).

Lasky, J. F. and Silverman, H. W. (eds) (1988) *Love: Psychoanalytic Perspectives*, New York: New York University Press.

Lawner, P. (1988) 'Trust and testing in love relationships', in J. F. Lasky and H.W. Silverman (eds) *Love: Psychoanalytic Perspectives*, New York: New York University Press.

Lear, J. (1990) *Love and its Place in Nature: A Philosophical Interpretation of Freudian Psychoanalysis*, New York: Noonday Press.

LeShan, L. (1989) *Cancer as a Turning Point*, Bath: Gateway Books.

Lester, E. (1985) 'The female analyst and the erotized transference', *International Journal of Psychoanalysis* 66: 283–293.

Lichtenstein, H. (1961) 'Identity and sexuality', *Journal of the American Psychoanalytic Association* 9: 207.

Limentani, A. (1977) 'Clinical types of homosexuality', in *Between Freud and Klein*, London: Free Association Books (1989).

—— (1983) 'To the limits of male heterosexuality: the vagina-man', in D. Breen (ed.) *The Gender Conundrum*, London: Routledge (1993).

—— (1994) 'On the treatment of homosexuality', *Psychoanalytic Psychotherapy* 8(1): 49–62.

Loewald, H. (1951) 'Ego and reality', *International Journal of Psychoanalysis* 32: 10–18.

—— (1960) 'On the therapeutic action of psychoanalysis', *International Journal of Psychoanalysis* 41: 16–33.

—— (1988) *Sublimation. Inquiries into Theoretical Psychoanalysis*, New Haven CT: Yale University Press.

Lukacher, N. (1986) *Primal Scenes: Literature, Philosophy, Psychoanalysis*, Ithaca NY: Cornell University Press.

McDougall, J. (1978) *Plea for a Measure of Abnormality*, London: Free Association Books (1990).

—— (1995) *The Many Faces of Eros: A Psychoanalytic Exploration of Human Sexuality*, London: Free Association Books.

MacFarlane, J. (1975) 'Olfaction in the development of social preferences in the human neonate', in M. Hofer (ed.) *Parent-Infant Interaction*, Amsterdam: Elsevier.

McGuire, W. (1974) *The Freud/Jung Letters*, Princeton NJ: Princeton University Press (1994).

Machtlinger, V. (1984) 'The role of the father in aiding the elaboration and consolidation of a differentiated gender identity in the phallic-narcissistic stage', *Bulletin of the Anna Freud Centre* 7: 25–40.

Maguire, M. (1995) *Men, Women, Passion and Power*, London: Routledge.

Mahler, M., Pine, F. and Bergman, A. (1975) *The Psychological Birth of the Human Infant*, New York: Basic Books.

Mann, D. (1988) 'Countertransference: a case of inadvertent holding', *Inscape: Journal of the British Association of Art Therapists* Autumn edition: 9–13.

REFERENCES

Mann, D. (1989a) 'Humour and play', unpublished paper.

—— (1989b) 'Incest: the father and the male therapist', *British Journal of Psychotherapy* 6: 143–153.

—— (1989c) 'The talisman or projective identification? A critique', *Inscape: Journal of the British Association of Art Therapists*, Autumn Edition: 11–15.

—— (1990) 'Art as a defence mechanism against creativity', *British Journal of Psychotherapy* 7(1): 5–14.

—— (1991a) 'Review of Wilfred Bion's "The Brazilian Lectures"' *British Journal of Psychotherapy* 8(1): 117–118.

—— (1991b) 'Some schizoid processes in art psychotherapy', *Inscape: Journal of the British Association of Art Therapists* Summer edition: 12–17.

—— (1991c) 'Humour in psychotherapy', *Psychoanalytic Psychotherapy* 5(2): 161–170.

—— (1992) 'The infantile origins of the creation and apocalyptic myths', *International Review of Psychoanalysis* 19: 471–482.

—— (1993a) 'The shadow over Oedipus: the father's rivalry with his son', *Free Associations* 4(1): 44–62.

—— (1993b) 'The absent father in psychotic phantasy', in *British Journal of Psychotherapy* 9(3): 301–309.

—— (1994a) 'Castration desire', *British Journal of Psychotherapy* 10(4): 511–520.

—— (1994b) 'The psychotherapist's erotic subjectivity', *British Journal of Psychotherapy* 10(3): 344–354.

—— (1995) 'Transference and countertransference issues with sexually abused patients', *Psychodynamic Counselling* 1(4): 542–559.

—— (1997) 'Masturbation and painting', in J. Schaverien and K. Killick (eds) *Art, Psychotherapy and Psychosis*, London: Routledge.

Mann, D., Sumner, J., Dalton, J. and Berry, D. (1990) 'Working with incest survivors', *Psychoanalytic Psychotherapy* 4: 271–281.

Maroda, K. (1991) *The Power of Countertransference: Innovations in Analytic Technique*, Chichester: John Wiley and Sons.

Masson, J. (ed. and trans.) (1985) *Complete Letters of Sigmund Freud to W. Fliess, 1887–1904*, Cambridge: Belknap Press.

May, R. (1986) 'Love in the countertransference: the uses of the therapist's excitement', *Psychoanalytic Psychotherapy* 2(2): 167–181.

Meltzer, D. (1973a) 'On routine and inspired interpretations', in *Sincerity and Other Works: Collected Papers of Donald Meltzer*, Perthshire: Clunie Press (1994).

—— (1973b) *Sexual States of Mind*, Perthshire: Clunie Press (1990).

—— (1984) *Dream-Life: A Re-examination of the Psychoanalytical Theory and Technique*, Perthshire: Clunie Press.

Menninger, K. (1958) *Theory of Psychoanalytic Technique*, New York: Basic Books.

Mitchell, S. A. (1988) *Relational Concepts in Psychoanalysis: An Integration*, Cambridge MA: Harvard University Press.

Moi, T. (1990) 'Representation of patriarchy: sexuality and epistemology in Freud's Dora', in C. Bernheimer (ed.) *In Dora's Case. Freud–Hysteria–Feminism*, New York: Columbia University Press.

Money-Kyrle, R. (1968) 'Cognitive development', in *The Collected Papers of Roger Money-Kyrle*, Perthshire: Clunie Press (1978).

—— (1971) 'The aim of psychoanalysis', *International Journal of Psychoanalysis* 52: 103–6.

Morgenthaler, F. (1988) *Homosexuality, Heterosexuality, Perversion*, Hillsdale NJ: Analytic Press.

Nachmanson, M. (1915) 'Freud's libido theorie verglichen mit der Eroslehre Platos', *International Journal of Psychoanalysis* 3: 65–83.

REFERENCES

Naiman, J. (1992) 'Freud's Jocasta and Sophocles' Jocasta: clinical implications of the difference', *International Journal of Psychoanalysis* 73: 95–101.

Natterson, J. (1991) *Beyond Counter-Transference. The Therapist's Subjectivity in the Therapeutic Process*, New York: Aronson.

Ogden, T. H. (1979) 'On projective identification', *International Journal of Psychoanalysis* 60: 357–373.

—— (1983) 'The concept of internal object relations', *International Journal of Psychoanalysis* 64: 227–241.

—— (1994) *Subjects of Analysis*, New York: Aronson.

Olivier, C. (1980) *Jocasta's Children: The Imprint of the Mother*, London: Routledge (1989).

Orbach, A. (1994) 'Psychotherapy in the third age', *British Journal of Psychotherapy* 11(2): 221–231.

Panel (1992) 'Enactments in psychoanalysis', *Journal of the American Psychoanalytic Association* 40: 827–841.

Papousek, H., Papousek, M. and Harris, B. J. (1986) 'The emergence of play in parent–infant interactions', in D. Gorlitz and J. F. Wohlwill (eds) *Curiosity, Imagination and Play: On the Development of Spontaneous Cognitive and Motivational Processes* New York: Erlbaum Associates.

Person, E. S. (1985) 'The erotic transference in women and men: differences and consequences', *Journal of the American Academy of Psychoanalysis* 13: 159–180.

—— (1988) *Love and Fateful Encounters: The Power of Romantic Passion*, London: Bloomsbury.

—— (ed.) (1993) *On Freud's "Observations on Transference Love"*, New Haven CT: Yale University Press.

Peto, A. (1975) 'The etiological significance of the primal scene in perversions', *Psychoanalytic Quarterly* 44: 177–190.

Plato (1951) *The Symposium*, trans. Walter Hamilton, Harmondsworth: Penguin Books.

Racker, H. (1968) *Transference and Countertransference*, London: Maresfield Library (1988).

Raphael-Leff, J. (1984) 'Myths and modes of motherhood', *British Journal of Psychotherapy* 1(1): 6–30.

Rappaport, E. A. (1956) 'The management of an erotized transference', *Psychoanalytic Quarterly* 25: 515–529.

—— (1959) 'The first dream in an erotized transference', *International Journal of Psychoanalysis* XL: 240–245.

Reich, A. (1951) 'On counter-transference', *International Journal of Psychoanalysis* 32: 25–31.

Renik, O. (1993) 'Analytic interaction: conceptualizing technique in light of the analyst's irreducible subjectivity', *Psychoanalytic Quarterly* 62: 553–571.

Rheingold, H. L. (1983) 'The social and socialising infant', in L. Lipsitt and C. Rovee-Collier (eds) *Advances in Infant Research* vol. 2, Norwood NJ: Ablex.

Ross, J. M. (1982) 'In search of fathering: a review', in A. Cath (ed.) *Father and Child*, Boston: Little, Brown.

Rushdie, S. (1995) *The Moor's Last Sigh*, London: Jonathan Cape.

Rycroft, C. (1979) *The Innocence of Dreams*, Oxford: Oxford University Press (1981).

Samuels, A. (1980) 'Incest and omnipotence in the internal family', *Journal of Analytical Psychology* 25(1): 37–57.

—— (1985) 'Symbolic dimensions of Eros in transference–countertransference: some clinical uses of Jung's alchemical metaphor', *International Review of Psychoanalysis* 12: 199–214.

—— (1985) *The Father*, London: Free Association Books.

REFERENCES

—— (1989) *The Plural Psyche: Personality, Morality and the Father*, London: Routledge.

Sandler, J. (1976) 'Countertransference and role-responsiveness', *International Review of Psychoanalysis* 3: 43–47.

Saul, L. J. (1962) 'The erotic transference', *Psychoanalytic Quarterly* 31: 54–61.

Sayers, J. (1991) *Mothering Psychoanalysis*, Harmondsworth: Penguin.

Schachter, J. (1994) 'Abstinence and neutrality: development and diverse views', *International Journal of Psychoanalysis* 75: 709–720.

Schafer, R. (1977) 'The interpretation of the transference and the conditions of loving', *Journal of the American Psychoanalytic Association* 25: 335–62.

—— (1993) 'Five readings of Freud's "Observations on Transference-love"', in E. S. Person, (ed.) *On Freud's "Observations on Transference Love"*, New Haven CT: Yale University Press.

Scharff, D.E. (1982) *The Sexual Relationship: An Object Relations View of Sex and the Family*, London: Routledge (1992).

Schaverien, J. (1995) *Desire and the Female Therapist: Engendered Gazes in Psychotherapy and Art Therapy*, London: Routledge.

Schopenhauer, A. (1858) *The World as Will and Representation* vols. 1 and 2, New York: Dover (1966).

Searles, H. (1958) 'The schizophrenic's vulnerability to the analyst's unconscious processes', in *Collected Papers on Schizophrenia and Related Subjects*, London: Hogarth Press (1965).

—— (1959) 'Oedipal love in the countertransference', in *Collected Papers on Schizophrenia and Related Subjects*, London: Hogarth Press (1965).

—— (1979) *Countertransference and Related Subjects*, New York: International Universities Press.

Setzman, E. J. (1988) 'Falling in love and being in love: a developmental and object-relations approach', in J. F. Lasky and H. W. Silverman (eds) *Love: Psychoanalytic Perspectives*, New York: New York University Press.

Silber, A. (1981) 'A tic, a dream and the primal scene', *International Journal of Psychoanalysis* 62: 259–269.

Silverman, H.W. (1988) 'Aspects of the erotic transference', in J. F. Lasky and H. W. Silverman (eds) *Love: Psychoanalytic Perspectives*, New York: New York University Press.

Socarides, C. W. (1979) 'The psychoanalytic theory of homosexuality: with special reference to therapy', in I. Rosen (ed.) *Sexual Deviation*, Oxford: Oxford University Press.

Spitz, R. (1945) 'Hospitalism: an inquiry into the genesis of psychiatric conditions in early childhood', *Psychoanalytic Study of the Child* 1: 53–74.

Stallworthy, J. (1973) *Love Poetry*, Harmondsworth: Penguin Books.

Steiner, J. (1993) *Psychic Retreats: Pathological Organizations in Psychotic, Neurotic and Borderline Patients*, London: Routledge.

Stern, D. N. (1985) *The Interpersonal World of the Infant: A View from Psychoanalysis and Developmental Psychology*, New York: Basic Books.

—— (1993) 'Acting versus remembering in transference love and infantile love', in E. S. Person, (ed.) *On Freud's "Observations on Transference Love"*, New Haven CT: Yale University Press.

Stoller, R. J. (1975) *Perversion: The Erotic Form of Hatred*, London: Maresfield Library (1986).

—— (1979) *Sexual Excitement: Dynamics of Erotic Life*, London: Maresfield Library (1986).

—— (1985) *Observing the Erotic Imagination*, New Haven CT: Yale University Press.

REFERENCES

Stone, L. (1961) *The Psychoanalytic Situation*, New York: International University Press.

Strachey, J. (1934) 'The nature of the therapeutic action of psychoanalysis', *International Journal of Psychoanalysis* 15: 127–159.

Swartz, J. (1967) 'The erotized transference and other transference problems', *Psychoanalysis Forum* 3: 307–318, New York: International Universities Press (1972).

Symington, N. (1983) 'The analyst's act of freedom as agent of therapeutic change', *International Review of Psychoanalysis* 10: 283–291.

Tauber, E. S. (1979) 'Countertransference re-examined', in L. Epstein and A. Feiner (eds) *Countertransference*, New York: Aronson.

Tronick, E. Z., Ricks, M. and Cohn, J. F. (1982) 'Maternal and infant affective exchange: patterns of adaptation', in T. M. Field and A. Fogel (eds) *Emotion and Early Interaction*, Hillsdale NJ: Erlbaum.

Tyson, P. (1982) 'The role of the father in gender identity, urethral eroticism and phallic narcissism', in S. Cath and A. Gerwitt (eds) *Father and Child*, Boston: Little, Brown.

Wallerstein, R. S. (1993) 'On transference love: revisiting Freud', in E. S. Person (ed.) *On Freud's "Observations on Transference Love"*, New Haven CT: Yale University Press.

Weinstein, R. S. (1988) 'Should analysts love their patients? The resolution of transference resistance through countertransferential explorations', in J. F. Lasky and H. W. Silverman (eds) *Love: Psychoanalytic Perspectives*, New York: New York University Press.

Weldon, E. S. (1988) *Mother, Madonna, Whore: The Idealization and Denigration of Motherhood*, London: Guildford Press.

Wheeley, S. (1994) 'To be born was the death of him. A clinical study of a self that might have been but never got born', *Journal of Analytical Psychology* 39: 27–53.

Widlocher, D. (1978) 'The ego ideal of the psychoanalyst', *International Journal of Psychoanalysis* 59: 387–390.

Wieland, C. (1991) 'Beauty and the beast: the father's unconscious and the riddle of femininity', *British Journal of Psychotherapy* 8(2): 131–143.

Winarick, K. (1985) 'The "chemistry" of personal attraction', *The American Journal of Psychoanalysis* 45: 380–388.

Winnicott, D. W. (1947) 'Hate in the countertransference', in *Through Paediatrics to Psychoanalysis*, London: Hogarth Press (1987).

—— (1956) 'Primary maternal preoccupation', in *Paediatrics to Psychoanalysis*, London: Hogarth Press (1987).

—— (1958) 'The capacity to be alone', in *The Maturational Processes and the Facilitating Environment*, London: Hogarth Press (1987).

—— (1960) 'Ego distortion in terms of true and false self', in *The Maturational Processes and the Facilitating Environment*, London: Hogarth Press (1987).

—— (1976) *The Maturational Processes and the Facilitating Environment*, London: Hogarth Press.

Wrye, H. K. and Welles J. K. (1994) *The Narration of Desire: Erotic Transferences and Countertransferences*, Hillsdale NJ: Analytic Press.

Young, R. M. (1994) *Mental Space*, London: Free Association Press.

Zuckerberg, J. O. (1988) 'The struggle to love: reflections and permutations', in J. F. Lasky and H. W. Silverman (eds) *Love: Psychoanalytic Perspectives*, New York: New York University Press.

INDEX

Abelin, E. 96
Abend, S. M. 69
Abraham, K. 35, 140
Ainsworth, M. D. S. 85
Alexander, F. 24
Allen, W. 55, 136
ambivalence 68, 71, 78–83, 100, 112
Anzieu, D. 15
Arlow, J. A. 142–3
Armstrong-Perlman, E. M. 139
Atwood, G. E. 193

Bach, S. 11, 173–4
Bak, R. C. 35
Baker, R. 10, 162, 175, 178, 185
Balint, M. 35, 83, 124
Barthes, R. 35
Bataille, G. 5
Bell, R. Q. 79, 85
Belotti, E. G. 84
Benjamin, J. 92, 96, 106
Bergmann, M. S. 34–7
Bibring, G. 103
Binstock, W. 35
Bion, W. R. 18, 57, 69, 83, 122–3, 181, 184
Blos, P. 106
Blum, H. B. 44–5
Boesky, D. 70
Bokanowski, T. 106
Bollas, C. 10, 70, 103, 185
Bolognini, S. 103
Bowlby, J. 181
Boyer, L. 141
Breen, D. 117
Brenman-Pick, I. 75
Breuer, J. 12–13, 16
Britton, R. 142

Burlingham, D. 91

Canestri, J. 30, 50–1
Carpy, D. V. 69, 75, 191–2
Cassel, Z. K. 79
castration desire 118
Cesio, F. 51
Chamberlain, D. B. 78–9, 91
Chasseguet-Smirgel, J. 96, 118, 124, 162, 165–6, 171, 173, 176
Chodorow, N. 89
Christie, G. 80
Chused, J. F. 69–70
Colman, W. 31
common knowledge interpretations 182–6
countertransference 22, 68–71; see also erotic countertransference
creative intercourse 120, 132, 137, 145–6, 157–61
Cunningham, R. 104, 117
curiosity 110, 141–2, 180–2, 186, 190

Dahlberg, G. 56
Denis, P. 118
Deutsch, H. 83
Devereau, G. 141
Di Ceglie, G. R. 158
Donne, J. 4, 8, 25–6
Dora 17, 61–2
Dreyfus, P. 80
Druck, A. B. 24

Eagle, M. 70
Edelheit, H. 146, 157
Eichenbaum, L. 89
Eichoff, F. W. 49
Ellis, H. 133

Endleman, R. 6
erotic bond 10, 18–22, 64, 115, 119, 122,
     140, 185, 190, 194
erotic countertransference 12, 23–6,
     45–7, 56, 58–63, 71–100, 182, 193–5
erotic horror 6, 48, 57–8, 64, 75, 194
erotic Oedipal father 96–100
erotic Oedipal mother 47, 87–91
erotic pre-Oedipal father 91–6
erotic pre-Oedipal mother 47, 74–7, 80,
     83–7, 120–37
erotic subjectivity 17, 46–7, 55–67, 71–2,
     82
erotic transference 28, 41–54, 56, 105,
     135, 163, 176, 182, 185; as passion 4,
     6–7; as resistance 8, 9, 11, 13, 23, 28,
     51, 57, 71, 101; as transformational
     10, 23–6, 30, 163, 185
erotized transference 41, 44, 47, 72–3,
     93, 104
erotic transformation 8, 9, 13, 22–6, 29,
     36; see also erotic transference, as
     transformational
Esman, A. H. 141
Etchegoyen, R. H. 162

Fairbairn, W. R. D. 14, 35, 53, 131, 160
Fenichel, O. 35
Ferenczi, S. 16, 23, 27, 42, 124
Fliess, W. 15, 138
Fogel, A. 79
Frejaville, A. 118
Freud, S. 11–12, 15–17, 27–31, 42, 44,
     50–1, 58, 60–2, 88, 96, 101, 103, 106,
     120–1, 123–4, 129, 133, 137, 138–40,
     147–51, 176, 181
Friedman, R. C. 102
frigidity 125–7, 136
Fromm, E. 6

Gabbard, G. O. 69–71
Gerrard, J. 92
Gibeault, A. 118
Gill, M. M. 50, 70
Gillespie, W. H. 173
Glasser, M. 118
Glenn, J. 15
Glover, E. 101
Gorkin, M. 45–7, 68, 71–4, 76, 89, 93,
     104
Granoff, W. 150
Green, A. 14, 184
Greenson, R. R. 56, 101, 118

Grosskurth, P. 196

Hamilton, V. 85, 181–2
Harlow, H. F. 121–2
Heimann, P. 68
Hirsch, I. 45
Hoffer, W. 14
Hoffman, I. Z. 70
homoerotic 17, 73, 85, 99, 101–19,
     148–9, 190
homosexuality see homoerotic
Hopcke, R. H. 107
hostility 52–4, 99, 109, 142, 163–4
humour 32, 55

Ikonen, P. 142, 160
impotence 21, 136
incest: father–daughter 48, 63–6, 96;
     incestuous desire 30, 43, 60–1, 66, 72,
     78, 94, 103, 119, 190; mother and
     child 7, 48, 87–8, 91, 189; taboo 15,
     48, 56–7, 123, 180
Isay, R. 102

Jackson, D. 141
Jehu, D. 17
Jones, E. 150
Joseph, B. 50, 69, 80
Jung, C. G. 11, 16–17, 27, 124, 129–30,
     143, 147

Kaplan, L. 171
Karme, E. P. 106
Keats, J. 184
Kernberg, O. 35, 73, 172, 177, 179
Kestemberg, E. 118
Khan, M. M. R. 173, 174, 179
Klein, M. 14, 17, 35, 141, 196–7
Kohut, H. 73
Kumin, I. 6, 57–8, 194

Lacan, J. 96, 192
ladder of love 33–4
Laplanche, J. 137, 147
Lawner, P. 24
Lear, J. 10–11, 54
Lester, E. 47–8, 101, 104–6
Lichtenstein, H. 121
Limentani, A. 101–2, 105–6, 130
Loewald, H. 10, 60–1, 96
love 6, 11, 24, 27–40;
     authentic/unauthentic 11, 28–40;
     infantile components 30, 36–7; in

transference 28–40, 113
  (*see also* erotic transference)
Lukacher, N. 143, 150–1, 192

McDougall, J. 8, 129, 138, 141, 162,
  164–5, 171
MacFarlane, J. 77
Machtlinger, V. 91
Maguire, M. 49, 171
Mahler, M. 123
Maroda, K. 69, 72, 105, 193–4
May, R. 17
Meltzer, D. 121, 125, 129, 131, 173, 184
Menninger, K. 24
Mitchell, S. A. 70
Moi, T. 15, 61
Money-Kyrle, R. 141–2, 159
Morgenthaler, F. 117
mythological characters: Adam 144–5;
  androgyne 32–4; Anteros 4;
  Antiphates 83; Aphrodite 4, 33, 144;
  Apollo 145; Artemis 145; Athene 92;
  Calypso 83; Circe 83; Cupid *see* Eros;
  Cyclops 83; Dionysus 92, 145; Eros 4,
  6, 24, 29; Eve 84, 144–5, 181;
  Gilgamesh 146; Hephaestus 144;
  Hera 144; Hermes 146; Jason 87;
  Jesus 144; Jocasta 15, 57, 87–8, 97;
  Karora 93; Laius 57, 96–7; Medea 87;
  Medusa 84; Minotaur 65; Mother
  Earth 144; Noah 145; Odysseus 83,
  96; Oedipus 15, 87, 97, 180; Pandora
  180; parthenogenic birth 16; Perseus
  84; Prometheus 144; Psyche 4; Ptah
  144; Pygmalion 92; Ra 144; Scylla
  and Charybdis 83; Sphinx 181;
  Telemachus 96; Theseus 65; Tiresias
  180; tower of Babel 181; Ymir 92;
  Zeus 92, 144–6

Nachmanson, M. 34
Naiman, J. 15, 88
Natterson, J. 59, 61
negative capability 184, 193
new transformational object 10, 24–6,
  29–31, 54, 119, 185, 191–5

Ogden, T. H. 45, 69–71
Olivier, C. 84, 89
Orbach, A. 43
Orbach, S. 89

Papousek, H. 78

Person, E. S. 25, 35, 37–9, 48–52, 105
perverse countertransference 163,
  168–79, 185
perverse couple 76, 163, 174–9
Peto, A. 140
Plato 32–4, 36, 107, 123
polymorphous perversity 103, 177
Pontalis, J. B. 137, 147
premature ejaculation 125, 136
primal scene 16–17, 20–1, 86, 89, 104,
  111, 118–19, 130, 133, 138–61, 164–5,
  167, 177, 189–90, 196–7
projective identification 45–6, 68, 72,
  76–7, 106, 110, 122
psychic intercourse 120–37

Racker, H. 57, 71–2, 95, 141, 160
Rank, O. 16, 124
Raphael-Leff, J. 83
Rappaport, E. A. 41–2, 44
Reich, A. 56
Renik, O. 70
Rheingold, H. L. 79
Ross, J. M. 106
Rycroft, C. 129, 184

sado-masochism 105, 113, 119, 123, 136,
  145–7, 154, 165–6, 168–72, 178, 185
Samuels, A. 61, 96, 103, 130, 142–3, 146
Sandler, J. 69
Saul, L. J. 42–3
Sayers, J. 129, 196
Schachter, J. 15–16
Schafer, R. 39–40, 50
Scharff, D. E. 131, 133–4, 136
Schaverien, J. 49
Schopenhauer, A. 35
Searles, H. 15, 46, 56, 58, 62–3, 69, 72,
  87, 99, 114, 192
Setzman, E. J. 25
sexual abuse 17–18, 20, 51, 59–60, 114,
  152, 185
sexualized countertransference 45–7
Shakespeare, W. 145–6, 159
Silber, A. 140, 157
Silverman, H. W. 49
Socarides, C. W. 101
Sophocles 88, 180
Spielrein, S. 17, 130
Spitz, R. 121
Stallworthy, J. 7, 36
Steiner, J. 142
Stern, D. N. 50–1, 77, 79, 85, 122, 134–5

Stoller, R. J. 52–4, 107, 162–4
Stone, L. 15
Strachey, J. 10, 191
Swartz, J. 24
Symington, N. 69, 184–5, 191

Tauber, E. S. 31
transference 21, 60, 62, 71, 110, 140, 190;
    as perversion 162–79; as primal scene
    138–61; as sexual intercourse 22,
    66–7, 73, 120–37, 190
transformational couple 180, 185, 190–5
transformational interpretations 182–6,
    192–5
transgression 158, 180, 190–5
Tronick, E. Z. 79
Tyson, P. 91

Wallerstein, R. S. 50
Weinstein, R. S. 45
Weldon, E. S. 171
Welles, J. K. 49, 68, 74–7, 89, 91, 93, 105,
    123, 173–5
Wheeley, S. 174
Widlocher, D. 80
Wieland, C. 83–4, 89, 91, 96
Winarick, K. 38
Winnicott, D. W. 35, 59–60, 70, 81–3,
    122–3, 132, 142, 181
Wolff, T. 17
Wrye, H. K. 49, 68, 74–7, 89, 91, 93, 105,
    123, 173–5

Young, R. M. 183

Zuckerberg, J. O. 194